How to

Think

If You Want to

Change the World

Spiritual Practices For Social Activism

Jean-Robert Bayard, Ph.D.

Contents

Foreword from the Editor

The journey to deliver the wisdom of Dr. Jean-Robert Bayard's life of boundless passion for helping others--regardless of gender, race or species--was in itself a voyage between the Courage and Violence that are at the center of this book.

It began with a promise I made to her during her last days on this Earth.

As her grandson, I only came to know Jean Bayard later in life, in terms of her role in movements for peace: civil rights, being at the march on Washington with Martin Luther King; working to support religious freedom in countries under oppression, and her life-long work for the rights of all animals to live free. She had formed the principles of this tome as early as the 1990's and had them tentatively ready to publish by 2000.

I expected some "woo-woo" fluff from a manuscript with the word "spiritual" in the title. I glanced through one chapter, then another. It came as a surprise to discover one of the best self-help books I have ever encountered. Beyond activism, its powerful principles are of use to the improvement of your very life.

While she suspended publication of these powerful principles, I believed, as I do as of this writing, that getting them into the hands of those selflessly working for the cause they know is right will be the best thing to happen for such cause. I would not allow sixty years' work in psychology for activists to sit in a closet while advocates bang their heads against the same wall they have been for half a century, creating with their own thoughts and feelings the very problems they fight.

Taking over as editor after she passed, I went through every word of each edition dozens of times in a daily regimen regardless of apparent progress – or lack thereof. I had committed to do whatever it takes to fulfill the promise I made to get it out to those who can use it.

I began the Practices myself, adding my own from my experience as a practitioner of N. L. P., whose founder Dr. Richard Bandler referred to Dr. Bayard as a fellow "rebel" of the field.

In doing so, I came to know her at a level like never before, including her recent decades marrying Tibetan Buddhist principles with her own field of clinical psychology.

When I began, I estimated it would all take perhaps six months to complete. I didn't quite grasp what I had committed to. At the time of her passing, the manuscripts of Dr. Bayard's research and writings totaled well over a million words, the result of laboring for fifteen years to write in seclusion, to focus exclusively on her most precious gift to the world which you now hold in your hands.

Having transported these writings from one continental coast to the other, the mammoth daily task of comparing differences in versions until understanding them enough to confidently reflect her most complete treatment of the subject took another six *years*.

In devoting such time to this craft, one could have written at least five books instead. Was it worth it all? The answer to that came by the time the pre-release came off the press, when the stories began flowing in from advocacy leaders, such as one gentleman who cried while reading it as her words spoke right to his post-traumatic stress disorder from all the abuse he'd seen in his line of work in animal rights.

When focusing on a goal, going Wholehearted into what you do can include dedicating time every day without exception. It can mean staying up throughout the night for weeks to get your work to a publisher in time to fill preorders at an event. It's the labor behind the scenes that the screenwriter skips over in the movie about your life before you break past the status quo.

A scorching sunlight beam searing through the mountains of off-the-cuff self-help books, *How to Think if you Want to Change the World* is the result of consecutive decades of sacrifice. Now that it's found its way to your hands, it is up to you to take the torch in the same spirit by *applying it now*.

Stephan Sauerburger, Editor

About the Author

"Jean Bayard was a wonderful, wonderful woman and I wish there were more like her who cared enough to do something."

Ingrid Newkirk, President,
People for the Ethical Treatment of Animals

After earning her Ph.D. in clinical and experimental psychology, Jean-Robert Bayard spent over forty years working as a psychotherapist helping troubled people understand their thoughts and feelings. Her previous works include <u>How to Deal with Your Acting-Up Teenager</u>, a self-help classic for desperate parents with publication in over a dozen countries and several languages.

Throughout her career, Dr. Bayard worked tirelessly as a pioneer of modern activism. With a passionate concern for racial equality, she worked in the civil rights movement throughout the seventies by means of marching, newsletters, negotiating with employers to hire blacks, helping to document discrimination by landlords, and even going to jail for sitting in front of a cement truck to protest the refusal of Pittsburgh's labor union to admit blacks to build the United State Steel building.

Also determined to ease the suffering of animals at the hands of human beings, she and her beloved husband Robert Bayard, Ph.D. founded and ran a two-thousand-member California legislative network that was instrumental in passing a number of animal rights bills. As one of the originals of the modern animal rights movement, she was arrested multiple times and went to jail for protesting cruel and unnecessary animal experiments. She also founded a newsletter for fellow psychologists to garner awareness of and support against unnecessary animal research.

Always a worker for peace, she was active with Beyond War, an organization that seeks to end war, and also supported various organizations including Childreach, Greenpeace, the International Campaign for Tibet, the Peace Division of the American Psychological Association and the Vanguard Society of People for the Ethical Treatment of Animals.

Recognizing no limits in her quest, for over 70 years Dr. Bayard benefited from a variety of spiritual approaches. Having been born into the family of a Dutch Christian Reformed minister, she grew up with an exceptional knowledge of the Bible and love of the teachings of Jesus. At age nineteen she discovered the only book on yoga in the Los Angeles County Public Library and knew almost immediately that this was a path she wanted to follow.

Since then she has never stopped studying and contributing to the great Eastern spiritual philosophies, practicing their disciplines in conjunction with Western science, especially via the writings of Sri Aurobindo, the Dalai Lama, and Swami Rama of the Himalayan Institute. Starting in 1963 she underwent 264 hours of intensive training in Hinayana Buddhist meditation at Wat Po in Thailand under the personal supervision of the abbot, and later a several-year intensive course in Tibetan Mahayana Buddhist doctrine, practice, and history at the Nyingma Institute in Berkeley, California.

Never relinquishing her persistent focus on the elimination of the suffering of others, she dedicated the last years of her life to writing a series of nonfiction and fiction works for her fellow activists, teaching in the practices how to get what you want by turning what hinders you into tools, taking responsibility for your thoughts and feelings and showing you through self-revelation as well as the example of the great activists of history How to Think If You Want to Change the World.

For more information on Dr. Bayard's life and works, visit www.jeanbayard.org.

Preface

This book is about empowerment. It is meant to enable you to take charge of your own thoughts and feelings and use them to bring about a better world and a happier, more fulfilling personal life for you.

Each of us has the *ability* to do so--each of us has all the potential energy of a nuclear bomb and more, we have all the motivation and energy we need to improve the world.

How can we do that? That's what this book is about--it's the culmination of many, many years of advocacy and efforts to confront the suffering in the world.

I think my first realization that there was terrible suffering was when I was nine years old and witnessed the cruel abuse of a fish, and failed to take action to rescue it. That scene, and my failure to do anything about it, has haunted me to this day.

For many years I struggled to ease the pain that I felt --as a lot of us feel-- because of the suffering caused by war, genocide, poverty, discrimination and all manner of injustice and disappointment, the suffering of animals who are abused and their species wiped out, and the heart ache all of us suffer as we see plant life and even the very rock and dust, air and waters of our earth contaminated and spoiled.

So I became a social activist, fighting for civil rights, an end to war, and the humane treatment of animals. That meant lots of work--endless meetings, demonstrating and marching in the streets, riding a bus for 10 hours to be part of the March on Washington where Martin Luther King delivered his "I have a Dream" speech, writing newsletters, pressuring legislators, and, like Thoreau, getting arrested and going to jail.

But I found the results of all this work to be wildly disproportionate to the effort they took! My friends and I labored mightily and made only minuscule progress which, often as not, was canceled a year or two after we made it. Why did all our work have so little effect? It seemed to me that we needed more members and we needed better strategies to use with the members we had.

So I began to write a book of Practices from which I thought that social activists could learn to be more effective and which would also, I hoped, inspire more people and empower them to make a difference and change the world.

However, I wasn't quite satisfied that I had the whole answer. So as I wrote, I also read hundreds of books, asking of each, "How can we ease the suffering in the world?"

I first studied the works of great activists who had been effective, from the early abolitionists of slavery through Susan B. Anthony, Gandhi and Martin Luther King, Jr. The importance which all these people gave to a spiritual life led me to read the works of spiritual leaders who had also been activists. I reviewed the precious teachings of Jesus which I had absorbed as a child, pondering how they might apply to social activism today. I read about Sri Aurobindo, Mother Teresa, and the liberation theologists. I reviewed some of the great religions themselves and, when I discovered that the goal in Buddhism was the same as mine -- an end to suffering and the coming of happiness for all beings -- and its adherents had never started a war as far as I could tell, I studied it with special care. I gave much extra focus to Tibetan Buddhism because I so admired the way the Tibetan people maintain their commitment to compassion during their oppression by the Chinese.

Everything I read seemed to apply to the problem of alleviating suffering and led me to still further reading. I dabbled in philosophy, history and biology, always asking what they might have to tell me about suffering. As a practicing clinical psychologist I also looked into the various psychotherapies I've used with patients for decades, I read Joseph Campbell's four-volume series on mythology several times, and whole shelves full of books on science for lay readers, looking for answers among the mysteries of relativity, quantum physics, and chaos theory.

I proceeded in this manner for more than twenty years. At last, when I thought the book was finished, I began to read it over-- and was stunned to realize that while I was writing it, my ideas had changed. What I had written was not just a book to help social activists be more effective; it was a set of Practices that could empower anyone to go after whatever she most wanted, and thus help to ease the suffering in the world at large.

But beyond that, I had gained an understanding of what is stopping us from improving the world. Even though we want to and know we can change the world, we can't seem to mobilize ourselves to actually do it, and in the end we become discouraged, bored, or anxious, and resigned to essentially acquiesce in our fate. What's stopping us is the same force that's ruining our world in the first place: *the way we think and feel. The way we use our minds is canceling out our efforts to save ourselves.*

We need to recognize that the way we think and feel, the human mind, actually runs the world, bringing about all the shoddy and the great societies and all the bad and the wonderful things in them. And now, acting together, by the power of your mind and my mind and all of our minds, we human beings ourselves have brought the world to great trouble.

But this can give us great hope, because we can control our own minds, and if we see that we ourselves are doing this wrecking of the world by the way we use our minds, then we can see how powerful we are and how we can use that power to remedy the situation. We see that we can change the world by *changing the ways of thinking* that are making it the way it is. We must learn a kind of jujitsu of the mind, take the very mental powers that are now driving us to destruction and use them to save ourselves instead.

The personal rewards are immense, too. For as you work to decide how the world must change and use your mind to implement that change, you will change too; you will become more courageous, more whole, stronger, more honest, happier. Working to use your mind in this way is a path toward personal enlightenment as well. It turns out that changing the world is changing yourself, too, for salvation of all *is* salvation of the one.

Every one of us has the potential to be a hero, and if we didn't give ourselves to the world we may die with that potential unused. Your seeing that the world has problems and that you must help it gives you a chance to use that potential.

So the goal, and reward, are very high: to change the world to reflect our values, our very identity. Whether we will do it is the question. This is a time of challenge for humanity; let us be thankful for the challenge which calls upon our hidden power, for without it we might never know it, use it, become it!

This book is meant to show how to do this--how to change our ways of thinking so we can change the world, and become happier as well. It is actually the first of a series of books, each going deeper and deeper into the changes in the way we think and feel to be able to change the world and be happy and at peace with ourselves.

*   *   *

The first part of this book describes how it is that so many of us developed the ineffective kinds of thinking and feeling that are harming the world, and why we cling to them.

The second part will present specific Practices you can use to develop more effective ways of thinking, starting with three basic Practices that focus on: honoring your own "daring thoughts," and using your pain and fear to power their translation into action. Further powerful Practices then follow from which you can choose to fit the ineffective thinking habits you most want to change. For each one, I'll first describe a specific harmful thinking habit, show how it hurts the world, and then describe a Practice through which you can reverse it, reclaim the energy that was going into it and direct it to more useful purposes.

Jean Bayard

Part I

How We Developed
Violent Thinking

And Why We Cling To It

I

The Two Ways of Thinking: Courageous and Violent

In the Preface we talked about how all of us cause suffering in the world by entertaining thoughts and feelings that lead to suffering. But that statement has a flip side. All of us also cause happiness in the world by having thoughts and feelings that lead to happiness.

That is, we all have two distinct patterns according to which we use our minds, create our thoughts, feelings and attitudes, and make our decisions.

And the way we affect the world depends not so much on *what* we do, but *which pattern* we're using at any given moment.

In one pattern, we are out of charge and feel helpless, insecure, threatened. It is the attitude from which we get angry, discouraged, pushy, do selfish, petty, cruel things, use people, are thoughtless, worried, unhappy. It leads to pain and problems, first for us ourselves and then, in an outward ripple, for everyone we relate to, and those whom they, in turn, relate to. Because it hurts people in this way, we will call this pattern of thinking and feeling the Violent attitude, meaning harmful or destructive, as spiritual leaders from ancient to modern times have used the term.

In the other pattern, we hold firm against impulses to panic or feel helpless, and stay responsibly with whatever situation we are in. We maintain presence of mind. It is the attitude from which we do generous, expansive things; are decisive, confident and brave. It is based on feelings of unity with and security in the world. It too ripples out to create feelings of well-being and fulfillment for us and everyone we relate to. The Merriam-Webster dictionary's definition of *courage* describes this attitude very well: it is "mental or moral strength to venture, persevere and withstand danger, fear or difficulty;" therefore we shall call it the *Courageous* attitude. It is from this stance that we do good for the world and ourselves.

These two attitudes tend to form two distinct patterns so that, generally speaking, at any given moment you can be in one or the other. You can feel either helpless or able, a pawn or a source, hostile or loving, but not both at once. This makes sense, for we defined the two attitudes according to their effect on the world, and it's hard at the same moment to pollute *and* clean up the planet, hate *and* be generous, make war *and* peace.

Yet at the same time the two attitudes are universal; we all use them both, now one, now the other. We use both patterns, and that means that each of us is *helping the world and hurting it.* The worst tyrant, torturer, terrorist thinks Courageously at times and at those times has a benign effect on his or her own life and the world, and--much more to our present point-- the most devoted helper of the world also does lots of Violent thinking and so pushes him or herself and the world back toward the Dark Ages.

In this last fact is our hope, for if people of good will were already bringing about only good, there would be nothing more they could do to help the world. But if simultaneously with their good works they are also unknowingly making things *worse*, there is room for them to improve, to turn their destructive thoughts and feelings into constructive ones, to make happiness dominant over suffering in our world.

It is important that we learn to catch the Violent thoughts and feelings, in order to *take charge* of the portion of our energy that is going into Violent thinking and feeling, and transform it into Courageous thinking and feeling instead.

*   *   *

We must realize how these negative emotions are not only very bad and harmful to one personally, but harmful to society and the future of the whole world as well.

The Dalai Lama and Howard C. Cutler,
The Art of Happiness, p. 38

The Two Ways of Thinking: Courageous and Violent

All living beings are members, one of another, so that a
person's every act has a beneficial or harmful influence on
the whole world.

Mohandas Gandhi, quoted in Martin Green, editor,
Gandhi in India, p. 180

This conflict within the individual can apply as well to a society and every unit within it--for what happens in society originates within those members and thus exactly reflects the status of this conflict within each one. Every organization and group, every school, every family, every corporation, every nation is also caught between these two ways of thinking. The terrible conditions that so disappoint us--poverty and homelessness, the bomb on Hiroshima, the conflict in Vietnam, letting children starve, genocide, the abuse of animals and the ruin of the earth-- all of these are the society going against its own ideals; for none herald such things as the identity they struggle so hard to maintain, such as Peace, Love, Courage, Justice, Democracy, the Family of Humanity.

*   *   *

How did we develop two such opposing patterns of thought?

Most of us start out with a readiness to be Courageous. As newborns we are entirely open to love. We are unafraid, trusting that we will be taken care of by some higher power. We are decisive; when there's a pin in our diapers, or we're hungry, we know what we want and we go for it as best we can. There's an expansiveness about our attitude, a readiness to embrace whatever comes, and apparently we have not worked out a separation between ourselves and the environment, for we feel a unity and a harmony with all things.

From this expansive, loving base, we build up, within the first few years of our lives, the picture of an ideal world, the beautiful, innocent world of childhood. Even if abuse or neglect deprived us of this world early on, we can know that we all developed it; we can know this because babies grow into this beautiful world through interaction with those who love and take care of them, and if they're not given that love and so do not develop at least some inkling of that world, they die young. You probably wouldn't

4

be here, then, if you hadn't developed, some time, this picture of a beautiful, loving world.

However deeply hidden it may be, we all carry the memory of that long-ago time in our lives. Most adults, even cynical ones, seem to implicitly agree on the value of preserving it in children. We hide the brutal "facts of life" from the children, and present the world to them in terms of all the kindergarten values of kindness and fairness and sharing, of cuddly kittens and teddy bears, of belief in Santa Claus, of faith in their parents.

So there was probably a time when you believed in this beautiful, harmonious world, or at least thought that it could be.

In most societies, though, the child must learn very different lessons before he or she may take part as an adult, and so it is in our society. For all of us, sooner or later, a new learning was superimposed upon our knowledge of the beautiful, childhood world.

The accomplishment of this second learning is a life-and-death project for most of us, and the way we handle it determines much about our later attitude toward life and the troubles of the world. The assignment of this second learning is handed to us by people we trust, and so we can hardly believe it can't be done, but the contradiction is basic enough to bring about a permanent spit in our psyches. For we started out honest and now are taught to pretend; we started out loving, ready to share and be fair, and now are taught to compete, and win, and to the strongest go the spoils. We started out secure and brave; now we are taught to be afraid. It's an impossible assignment; the two views are oil and water and will never blend.

Neither can we choose one view and give up the other one, for we need both, or believe we do. We can all sense, however dimly, that the childhood view of the world is our lifeline, our very core; all our ideals are in it; if we lose it entirely we surely die. But we have also been told that the grown-up view is necessary if we are to survive. We *must* believe them both.

How can we do that? What should a child who's still in the beautiful childhood world do with the news that there's no Santa Claus, that George Washington had slaves, that people test oven cleaner by dropping it in the Easter Bunny's eyes[1], and that all this is *necessary?*

No wonder children are sometimes puzzled and balk at the contradictory new learning. You may remember asking anxious, demanding questions about discrepancies that you noticed when you were making this adjustment but barely remembered afterwards.

> *Why do we go to war to kill people and then send in the Red Cross to help them?*

> *If we love animals, why do we eat them?*

> *If people really believed God was watching them and was all powerful, wouldn't they act differently?*

> *If we love our neighbors as ourselves, why don't we share with the poor?*

It takes each of us years and many crises to learn the juggling act and reach a working balance between the two views of the world – the beautiful childhood world, and the second, more grown-up world. Some of us never do. Perhaps wisely, society goes on formally teaching the second way of thinking for years, right along with the continued teaching--more and more perfunctory, more and more underground--of the ideals of the childhood world.

Thus by adulthood most of us have set our childhood ideals aside in some secret place we are half ashamed of and, with regret, live primarily by the new, grown-up learning.

We can never entirely give up that childhood world, nor can we unite with it again, so we go on as two separate parts. And our life becomes a battleground for the conflict between these two sides of ourselves, for what we knew in childhood doesn't die but is always there underneath, appealing to us, trying to insinuate

---

[1] In the backward days of the twentieth century it was legally required, and still is, that new household products and cosmetics be "tested" on animals. Rabbits were put into stocks in such a way that they could not scratch their faces, fastened by the neck. Their eyelids were clipped off so they could not blink, and then the products, some of them very caustic, were dropped into their open eyes and left there for days. It was not uncommon for the rabbits to break their backs or legs in their frantic efforts to free themselves.

itself into our lives. We never stop yearning for it on the one hand, and being afraid of it, trying to kill it on the other. All of us can feel a nostalgia for the childhood world, and all of us compromise its values every day.

But maybe what's faulty about our situation is not that we have been unfairly deprived of the childhood world, but the way we *interpreted* what happened.

Maybe we've mistaken the message.

Maybe we *thought* the message was, "Here is the beautiful, loving world you should have, that is yours by right, but it is taken from you because the universe is cruel and arbitrary and wants you to suffer, and you are not a good person."

Maybe the true message *is*, "Here is the beautiful, childhood world; mark it well for *this is how you are to create the grown-up world.*" After all, if the great forces behind the universe wanted to direct us to make a beautiful adult world, how else could they communicate their wish than by giving the children a sense of love and beauty and justice right from the beginning? "Here is the beautiful, loving world that should be and is not; this is how you're to *make* it!"

Maybe the beautiful childhood world is not something we were supposed to *have*, then, but something we are supposed to *create*.

Maybe we're not supposed just to long for Eden, but to *make* it.

Maybe we're put here not just to enjoy a wonderful world, but to *create* one and find our enjoyment in the creating.

Maybe the world doesn't owe us fairness; maybe it's our job to *make* it fair.

Maybe we're to be warriors, each of us a King Arthur, not cheated and unfairly wounded but honored to be sent as a champion to reclaim and defend the beautiful childhood kingdom.

II

The Cycling of Courageous and Violent Thinking

It's universal human behavior growing up in a society, then, to use two different patterns of thinking--to think Courageously sometimes, and at those times do good for ourselves and the world, and to think Violently at other times, and harming them.

There is a great illogic about the Violent part of our behavior. We do Violent things in order to survive--yet these very things are destroying us. We're killing ourselves and know we're doing so and yet we don't stop it. Why?

It's not because we're stupid and can't figure it out. We're so smart we've landed a man on the moon!

The reason we do our Violence is out of fear of our own tremendous potential for unity with all there is, fear of our potential for love and creativity— in other words, out of fear not of death but of the life--the kingdom and the power and the glory--of the beautiful childhood world.

Violence is based on hate and fear, and both of these are the opposite of love. Our Violence prevents us from loving, and that's what it's for. It destroys. That's the opposite of creating. Our Violence prevents us from being creative, and that's what it is for, as we shall see later.

*　　*　　*

Fortunately there's more to our situation than this fear. We treasure our beautiful childhood world as well as fear it. We yearn for it the way Citizen Kane yearned after the sled Rosebud. We think of it as the lost Eden, the beloved home we can never return to; we never cease to long for it even as we fear it.

We're caught between a real fear of this lost world and a real longing for it.

In this way we end up in a cycle, vacillating between Violent and Courageous behavior, now hurting ourselves and the world, now helping them. Psychotherapists see this pattern when they deal with people who deeply wish to live but who seem impelled to destroy themselves in one way or another. They see these clients as *trying to hide from some daring possibility* that has come up in their lives--a possibility of becoming happier, more successful, greater than they already are. Some event--a graduation, a birth, a death, or something as simple as walking out of a door into the full glare of the sun--has alerted these clients to something they had forgotten: that they are free to choose a new and wider way in their lives.

In that freedom they might daringly change habits, or jobs, or relationships; they might do something utterly unexpected and creative. Some such daring thought has occurred to these clients, but it was so unfamiliar and came upon them so suddenly that it seems like an abyss; they are terrified of falling into it, and so they deny and try to escape it, just as the whole society they live in tries to deny and escape the implications of its progress.

Therapists understand the danger in this situation, for *the more daring the possibilities* that have occurred to these clients, *the more desperate they will be to escape them*, and there is no limit to what they will do in their panic. They will sacrifice whatever they must; if it seems necessary, they will ruin themselves; they will die or kill themselves, or others; they will commit or submit to any atrocity.

The same is true for the society; our panic in the face of our own possibilities, though natural and understandable, is very dangerous. At such times we are not taking our proper charge of the way the world should go; *there is no one at the helm*. In our fear we are beside ourselves, and we will do anything. We will become oppressors, and let ourselves be oppressed; we will set up extermination camps and let ourselves be marched into them; we will torture and kill and let ourselves be tortured and killed; we will torture and kill ourselves.

A study of the history of societies as well as that of many institutions and individuals therein shows a pattern consisting of periods of great creativity and daring progress followed by periods of decadence, denial and destruction which, as they pass, are followed once more by periods of progress. The destructive period may be seen as a reaction to the progressive one, as an attempt to balance or cancel it, out of society's fear of its own great potential which showed itself in too much progress that was too sudden.

Such behavior was harmful enough when the race was young, but then at least the rest of the world was big enough to absorb our insults every time we took a new step. But our possibilities have expanded now; we could easily destroy ourselves and the planet with us.

We tried to comprehend what was happening and our scientists' findings only confirmed that everything was greater and more relative and far less certain than we had thought. At the same time technology exploded and put into our shaking hands tools whose power, so far as we know, has no limit. Awesome secrets opened to us--secrets of the atom and the far stars and the living cell, and with these secrets, the knowledge of staggering new powers. There is now no wish which we could not fulfill if we dared put ourselves into it –our wish for knowledge, or adventure, for expanding into inner and outer space, for peace, for love, for plenty.

It is too much. From all sides, a vacuum invites us to realize our own terrible freedom and power upon it; we can see no limit to what we could have, do, be, if we dared; we are close to realizing *we run the universe.*

No wonder if we are afraid! No wonder if we backpedal, and attack others and ourselves, and make boundaries, and defend them, and squabble over petty little trifles! We are insisting upon those trifles as *our separate and limited identity* for we have stumbled upon another possible identity of such vast freedom and power that if we acknowledged it, it would burst our old separate self entirely and deliver us to what we think of as death.

The human race is in recoil from a too-sudden prospect of new, expanded identity, and all our self-destructive craziness is an attempt to deny, avoid, escape, pay for, cancel, balance that identity, the terrifying new possibilities that confront us.

*　　*　　*

We tend, then, to alternate between periods of creativity in which we begin to fulfill our potential and periods of destructiveness in which we deny and cancel it.

Is this cycling *necessary*? Is it a balance of nature that must forever be upheld?

We will see in this volume that is not. We can break out of the necessity of cycling between creative and destructive periods, and the first step in doing so is to realize the good news about the cycle. We have said that periods of creativity tend to be followed by periods of Violence, and the higher the creativity the greater the Violence that follows. This sounds like bad news, but there is a jewel to be plucked out of this information, a nugget of good news. For if creativity signals to us that Violence is to follow, then Violence also signals that creativity is potential there somewhere and is only being denied out of fear. And the greater the Violence the better this news, for *the greater the potential creativity we can know is hidden behind it.*

Once we understand this, we can *use* Violence, not only as a sign of hidden creativity but as a vehicle to take us back to it through all the blocks that are holding it down. In terms of this book, we can *use* Violent thinking itself to work our way back to Courageous thinking. In this way we can break the creative-destructive cycle and get on our way to a better world.

That's what the Practices in this book are for.

*   *   *

With this as a base, then, let us go on, and begin as individuals to notice which kind of thinking we're doing at any given moment, with an eye to *changing every instance of Violent thinking into Courageous thinking.*

III

On to the Practices

Our task, then, is to change thoughts and feelings that lead to suffering so they lead to happiness instead.

That shouldn't be too hard, because all of us are already causing happiness as well as suffering. We all know very well how to use two different kinds of thinking and feeling, a destructive one that leads to suffering, and a beneficial one that leads to happiness for ourselves and others.

We can see these two ways of thinking and feeling as forming two distinct patterns, so that at any given moment you can use one or the other. You can feel helpless *or* able, a pawn *or* a source, hostile *or* loving; you can pollute the planet *or* clean it up, hate *or* be generous, make war *or* peace.---but you can't do both at once.

Yet at the same time use of the two attitudes is universal; we all use them both, now one, now the other.

*   *   *

So we are to transform destructive thoughts and feelings into beneficial ones.

Three characteristics of destructive thoughts and feelings suggest a simple way in which we can do this.

The first characteristic is that these thoughts and feelings are always *painful*.

Hatred, fear, anger, guilt are not pleasant; they always involve some degree of pain. Thoughts and feelings that lead to happiness are more likely to be joyous and exhilarating. This difference means that *whenever we experience pain or any kind of discomfort we can know we are harboring destructive thoughts and feelings that cause suffering.*

The second characteristic is that these thoughts and feelings are always *denials* of thoughts and feelings that lead to happiness.

This means that however intense our destructive thoughts or feelings may be, *thoughts or feelings that lead to happiness are never far away, and we can always reach them by changing our destructive thoughts and feelings in some way.*

Thirdly, thoughts and feelings that lead to suffering do not overlap those that lead to happiness.

The two kinds of thinking and feeling form two different and distinct patterns, so that at any given moment you can be in one or the other but not in both, any more than you could walk forwards and backwards at the same time. Each kind of thoughts and feelings has its own characteristics which clump together as a unit and do not occur in the other kind of thinking and feeling. For instance: hostility, a belief that one is unfairly treated, and fear all go together in leading to suffering, and none of them leads to happiness.

This is good news because it means that every instance of destructive thinking or feeling can be used to shift us into beneficial thoughts and feelings, if we learn to recognize when we're using it. Since all destructive thoughts and feelings cling together as a unit, changing any one of them to a beneficial thought or feeling changes them all. For example, if we only change from hostility to good will, the belief that we are unfairly treated and the fear will change as well. *We can move from causing suffering to causing happiness by changing a single destructive aspect of our thinking or feeling to a beneficial one and sticking to that change.*

Understanding these three characteristics, we see that the following general practice can be used to transform thoughts and feelings that cause suffering into those that cause happiness.

Stay alert for feelings of pain or discomfort. Whenever you experience one, know that you are causing suffering; then purposely change one aspect of your thinking or feeling to any thought or feeling that leads to happiness--and stick to it--to switch all of your thinking and feeling so it leads to happiness.

*   *   *

I will go on now, in the next chapters, to describe the Practices through which you can change destructive thoughts or feelings to beneficial ones. Each Practice deals with a particular Violent thought or feeling that I have seen almost everyone fall into from time to time. For each Practice, I will give examples of the Violent thought or feeling, tell how it leads to suffering for you and everyone in your world, and show how you can cancel its destructiveness to find the happy-making thoughts or feelings from which it was derived. I'll present two of the most basic Practices first. *Honor the Daring Thought* can get you started on reclaiming some of the power I believe you have been denying. If you work seriously on this Practice you will certainly meet our great opponent in this work, Pain, and can then tackle the job of transforming it into a trusted ally in the second Practice, *Use Pain to Find the Daring Thought.*

Once you understand these first two Practices, you will be able to choose further Practices according to the particular habits of destructive thinking or feeling you most want to change.

- If you find yourself afraid, practice Holding in the Tension of Fear.

- If you're not clear on what your mission in life is, practice Choosing Your Cause with Utmost Wisdom.

- For a foundation to nurture and sustain your efforts and overcome despair, do the radical practice of Building Beliefs that Support You and Your Work.

- If your energy is easily distracted, practice Going Wholeheartedly into Everything You Do.

- If you're afraid of failing in this or any other project, practice Becoming Invulnerable to Defeat.

- If you have enemies, practice Using the Enemy to Gain Power.

- If you tend to be a judgmental kind of person, practice Changing Judging to Bare Attention.

- If you try to put logic before feelings, practice Caring about Everything, All the Time.

- If you're easily angered, practice Reclaiming the Energy of Anger.

- If you want to grow more conscious of the level of Courage or Violence you are exuding to others, practice Using Courageous Language.

- If you feel driven and that there's not enough time, practice Using Hurry to Take Your Time.

- If you want to become a more wise and effective advocate, the practice of Identifying as "Big You" tackles what limits us and leads us to do Violence.

- If you sometimes get stuck and can't decide which of two undesirable ways to go, practice Resolving Impasse by Welcoming Confusion.

- If you get depressed, practice Becoming Unshakably Happy.

I suggest you skim through all sixteen Practices to get an overall idea of what thoughts and feelings that lead to suffering are like, and how subtle and all pervasive they are, then start by work your way through The Daring Thought and Fear.

After these two, the order in which you do the Practices doesn't matter, so you could choose one or at most two to work on for say six to eight weeks, going on to others as these become habits for you. The goal is to develop the habit of doing all sixteen Practices all the time, without having to think about it. That seems like a big order, but it may be easier than it sounds, for such a habit is our natural bent and in doing the Practices we're only returning to it.

If you're serious about the Practices, you'll need some way of keeping yourself inspired to do them over the long haul. You might set aside five or ten minutes every evening to make note of the times during the day when you caught thoughts and feelings that lead to suffering running off and did or did not turn on some that lead to happiness instead. The record will provide a measure of your progress, and remind and inspire you to keep your project in mind.

* * *

The Practices may not impress you because they seem to make so little demand of time and effort. Don't think them trivial; they are genuine warrior training. Each one requires that you *make a choice* between the two kinds of thinking and feeling--and it is through such choices that we become strong enough for the battle or too weak to engage in it. Each is based on some way in which you currently deny your powers, and so waste them; doing the Practice can free those powers and make them available for your use. And since in doing one Practice you're facilitating the others as well, it has the potential of giving you access to all your hidden Power, the same source that all the great heroes of history drew upon. In doing these Practices you can grow in Power.

These are not namby-pamby Practices, then; they're real and consequential. We're faced with big world problems today, massive problems, and it will take real courage and commitment to solve them. We need the sharpest, best, most effective thinking powers we can get. We've got to mean business. And all the ways in which we're *not* doing these Practices are ways of giving in; they are diluting our energy and going along with a world that we do not want. They're holding us back, and we can't afford them.

So do these Practices with zest and utmost commitment, realizing that every time you transform a thought or feeling which leads to suffering, you're striking a blow for the good of the world and gaining personal power as you do it. The core battle is taking place within you, within your individual heart and mind, every time you decide whether you're going to stand up for a better world or knuckle under.

That's the nature of this battle, that we've all been taught to knuckle under to the conventional world and all its fears, and we do knuckle under, and we've become addicted to knuckling under. It's hard to get over that habit, so don't be upset if you repeat it even though you're working to change it; that's a warrior going down under superior force. Don't waste any time feeling bad about it; just decide you're going to get up and do the right thing from now on. Commit to the work and do the best you can. For the sake of your own well-being and that of the world, persist in the Practices!

It takes a fairly strenuous course of training to attain a mental state of nonviolence. It is a disciplined life, like the life of a soldier.

Mahatma Gandhi, quoted by Paramahansa Yogananda's Autobiography of a Yogi, p. 512

We must assume responsibility for our minds as well as our speech and our physical activities; otherwise our negative mental habits will drag down the entire community of beings.

Robert Thurman, Inner Revolution, p. 27

16

One last word about the use of the Practices. Most of the stories and examples I have given in this book have to do with direct social action bearing on vast, global problems like war, feeding the world's children, civil rights. I apologize for that; when I started this book, I thought that such social action was indeed the only way through which we could mitigate the suffering in the world, and I wanted everyone to join me in marching in the streets, defying wrongful authority, mounting boycotts, and so on.

By the time I finished the book, though, I realized that such social action is only one of very many ways in which we can do good and change the world, and it is not the most essential thing we must do if we want to ease the suffering. To do that we must *change our minds until we are free of mere self-interest and identify with and feel compassion for all beings.* When we have done that, we will be so compassionate and at every moment so aware of our connectedness with everything there is that our every thought, feeling, and action will naturally bear upon every problem in the world, from the "smallest," most "personal" problem to the vast, global ones.

Now let's move on to the Practices themselves, beginning with the first of the two basic Practices, Honor the Daring Thought.

Part II

The Inner Work

Practices to Strengthen Your Courageous Thinking

IV

Honor the Daring Thought

The Practice: *Honor your Daring Thoughts and work always to fulfill them. Welcome your Counter thoughts as signals and guides to help you do this.*

In this chapter we focus on two forms of thoughts: Courageous behavior that we will call the *Daring thought*--the thought that we have the power to be, do, and have whatever we truly want -- and one of the most basic forms of Violent thinking, the *Counter thought*. With these two forms of thought, we play out the conflict between love and fear, between claiming power and denying it, in our daily lives.

It's fairly easy to catch ourselves using both of these kinds of thoughts every day. Most of us, if we reflect for a few moments, realize that we are almost always thinking, that thoughts are constantly going through our heads, and that, in fact, it is quite difficult to stop them from coming for more than a few seconds. Study of these thoughts shows that they often follow a definite pattern--the pattern of a kind of argument in which one side makes strong, confident, positive statements and the other side cancels, or counters, them with negative remarks.

"It'd be a good day to go to the beach."

"I can't, though, because it's a work day."

"Maybe I could go on Saturday."

"But no, it's too crowded then!"

You may recognize the pattern from old stories that go back and forth in this yes-no, good-bad, tit-for-tat fashion.

A man started for the airport so he could catch a plane.

But his taxi broke down.

But a bus came by and he got to the airport on time.

But his plane was grounded.

But another plane became available and he took it.

But a storm came up and he fell out of the plane.

But he landed on a haystack.

But it had a needle in it.

But it was lying flat.

Ad infinitum!

Many of us go through this kind of argument over and over every day; it's as though there were two sides of us; one side forever says Yes! and another, critical and discouraging side says Oh, no!, and the two of them carry on a continual argument in our heads. The argument waxes and wanes, sometimes intense, other times almost matter-of-fact, and for some of us, it can be continuous.

You can get a feeling for these two sides by calling them up in yourself right now. Answer these two questions: First,

"How would you like it if peace came over the whole world this year?"

and then,

"Why is this probably not going to happen?"

Your inner response may look something like:

It would be wonderful if we had world peace! (positive)

But it probably won't happen because...

- *we've always had wars,*

- *human beings are just naturally aggressive*

- *we'll never get everybody to cooperate, or*

- *that's just pie in the sky.* (negative)

This petty argument going on in our heads seems small and inconsequential. However, like a tiny virus that can fell a huge organism, it can be deadly. *This internal conflict is the source of the great, external world conflict between two mighty forces that we spoke of in the first chapter. It is also the potential key to world peace.* We're going to deal with it a great deal in this book.

We will call thoughts on the Courageous side of the argument *Daring thoughts*, because you would like them to come true but you don't think they can, so it's daring of you even to think of them, as it would be daring of a poor child to ask for a pony for Christmas when he or she knows it won't happen. We will call the "sorry-but-it-can't-happen" thoughts from the Violent side of the argument *Counter thoughts*, because they seem always to be of just the right content and intensity to counter the Daring thoughts, cancel them, keep you from acting on them.

Here are some more examples of Daring and Counter thoughts.

Daring thoughts:

> *"I could feed a starving child."*

> *"I'll write a letter. I'll write a hundred letters!"*

> *"Rescue the stray cat."*

> *"Join the protest march!"*

> *"I'll confront the President in person."*

Counter thoughts:

> *"Some just have to suffer."*

> *"It can't be done."*

> *"It's too late."*

> *"It's hopeless."*

> *"It's unrealistic."'*

> *"There's nothing we can do."* (Daring answer: *"There's always something you can do."*)

> *"You can't have it all."* (Daring answer: *"Why not?"*)

> *"I don't have enough money."*

> *"I'm too busy."*

Honor the Daring Thought

And perhaps the biggest:

"It would be so inconvenient!"

If you compare all of these Daring thoughts with the Counter thoughts, you will see that the two kinds of thoughts are radically different from each other. They spring from two very different motives, give you two very different kinds of feelings, and--affect the way your life and the lives of others go in two different ways.

The Daring thought is about something you'd *like* to see come true. You'd like to see the child fed, the cat rescued. You'd like to see success in the cause you're writing letters about, marching about, confronting the President about. So the Daring thought is *wishful* thinking. The Counter thought is about something you *don't* want to be true. You don't want it to be true that some must suffer, that it's too late to do anything, that you're too busy. So the Counter thought is *regretful* thinking.

The Daring thought looks into the future and pictures a way that things could be. There is a *proposal* implicit in it. (Let's *make* this thing happen!) The Counter thought does not propose anything; it merely *reacts to*, denies, the Daring thought. Thus the Daring thought comes first; it is *primary*. It's your initiative speaking. The Counter thought is only *derivative* of it.

The Daring thought is a hopeful idea pressing toward positive change; in that sense it is *new, original, creative*. The Counter thought is *trite*. We've all heard it a hundred times.

A Daring thought tends toward the preposterous, the wild and crazy. It's exciting, joyous--and *unconventional*. Confront the President? Wow! A Counter thought is tame and *conventional*; it fits with all the commonsense, conventional ideas about limits, and what can't be done, and what's appropriate and what won't work that have been drummed into us. "No, that ain't the proper way to do things!"

A Daring thought comes hot from the *heart*, a Counter thought from the cold *head*. I passionately want this! But no, cold logic says you can't have it.

Different *feelings* go with the two kinds of thoughts, too. The idea of a Daring thought's being fulfilled makes you feel *good*, because it's something you'd like to have happen. And the idea of fulfilling the Daring thought yourself is *exhilarating*, because doing that would call out energies that otherwise go stagnant in you, energies that want to be used. The idea of the Counter thought's being true makes you feel *sad*, because it's something you don't want to be true, and it's *discouraging* rather than exhilarating because it says Stop! to energies that have already been alerted and are ready to charge.

At the same time, if we really entertain a Daring thought, it can make us *scared*, and then the Counter thought can give us a feeling of *relief*.

Imagine that you had been invited to speak to all the world leaders at a summit conference. You would probably feel *fear* as well as anticipation about it, and if you then learned the meeting had been canceled, you might feel *relief* from your fear, and also regret--and the regret would be over the cancellation of the daring possibility of using your power.

Daring and Counter thoughts have different aims. A Daring thought aims toward the *solution* of a problem situation. If it were fulfilled, the problem situation would be improved. The Counter thought aims toward getting rid of the Daring thought, and its aim as far as the original problem is concerned is to *keep it the same*. Of course nothing can ever be kept the same, so the Counter thought actually *worsens* the original problem.

"There's nothing we can do" does nothing to help the starving children, and would in fact *discourage* them if they knew of it. It wouldn't make them feel better or give them hope; it would discourage them because it shows we've given up and agreed that Yes, it is too bad but--they are going to starve.

*   *   *

Now, the argument between the two kinds of thoughts doesn't just come into our heads at random nor because that's just the way we happen to think. *Every Daring and every Counter thought is part--a very precise part!--of a distinct sequence of mental events that runs off when something happens to threaten an inner status quo. The whole sequence is exactly designed to protect the status quo and prevent us from thinking Courageously.*

Here's how it works.

Honor the Daring Thought

The sequence starts when a problem comes up for you--concerning news of any sort. Suppose you hear on the news that "Children are starving in Uganda."

That news hurts you, gives you pain; that means it *makes a problem for you.* Now, the first, natural response when a problem comes up for you is *a command to yourself to solve it, followed by a quick first idea of how to do that.* For example, if you set your hand on a hot stove, that makes a problem for you; your inner self commands you to *stop the burning!* and you pull your hand away, fast. Just so, when the problem of suffering children comes up, a command to solve it flashes through your whole being:

"Help those children!"

and then a quick, first idea of how you might do it, perhaps an image of yourself holding and feeding an emaciated child, or the wild thought,

"Bring food to Uganda and feed those kids!"

What a Daring thought! This first inner response to the bad news, the command and the idea of how to fulfill it, comes from the most alive and essential part of your psyche; it represents what you truly wish for in your life. We all want to live and be happy; we all want to feel good about ourselves and other people. *We all basically want to act effectively to take care of problems when they arise for us.* This immediate response is an offshoot of this basic want; it comes from a deep, creative, unconventional, fearless part of you that knows how to live, knows what it wants, and keeps pushing you to fulfill its--your own!--wishes. When a problem comes up for you, it knows what it wants done about it. Solve it!

"Bring food to Uganda and feed those children!"

Wouldn't we all like to do that?

And for a split second the thought thrills you, makes you feel good.

But the problem of the children's suffering gives you much more time to respond than a hot stove does, and in the first microsecond of that time--CAUTION! You see that this wonderful first thought is *too daring* and, shuddering, you come up with a Counter thought that justifies you in dropping it.

"But of course I couldn't do that."

"It would cost too much."

"It's not practical."

"It would be a mess."

How dutiful of you--and how understandable!

Such Counter thoughts are not as basic as the original Command, which comes from the deepest, inborn part of your psyche. Still, they're basic enough; they're meant to protect our practical knowledge about what it takes to survive and maintain our society on this planet. By definition the Daring thought proposes something new that comes from outside that body of knowledge and might change it; that arouses fear, and so the Counter thought cancels it. That's only common sense, no matter how illogical the Counter thought might seem.

"In fact, there's nothing anybody can do."

The Counter thought is based on fear, and by canceling the Daring thought it now triggers *relief from fear*, because now you don't have to do anything. It takes you off the hook. Because of it, you don't have to risk all those strange new experiences, all the inconvenience, the disapproval of others, the danger. What a relief! (It saves you from all that packing, too!)

But along with the relief the Counter thought also makes you feel *sad*, because the children's situation is so hopeless, and they must suffer. It triggers *guilt*, too, because you may feel that in some way you're letting the children down, and maybe you don't feel so good about yourself, either. You're left, then, feeling relieved, sad, and guilty.

So ends one round of the internal argument. Here are the steps:

1. Bad news that is painful, makes a problem for you.

2. A Command to solve it and a first Daring thought of how to do so.

3. A surge of exhilaration.

4. Fear of so much daring.

5. A Counter thought.

6. Relief, sadness, and guilt.

One round is not usually enough to get rid of the Daring thought. Spurred by the sadness, your inner being insists, "The children should be fed!" and a new, more subdued form of the Daring thought emerges.

"It should be possible to do something, though."

And once again the fear arises, and a Counter thought pops up.

"But you can never get the food to those who need it."

This pattern may be repeated for any number of rounds, but the Counter thought has all the weight of the status quo behind it, so usually it gets the last word--at least for the time being. It is taken as true, the Daring thought is forgotten, and you are left in peace, with only sadness and guilt to contend with.

The peace does not last, though! For not all your Counter thoughts can finally kill off the Daring thought, no matter how heavily the society supports them, no matter how frequent, how telling, how "true" they are. The deep, true, fearless part of you that originates Daring thoughts doesn't give up no matter how often or harshly it's been rebuffed. It can't; it's your very life!

Sooner or later another problem will come up, or the same one come to mind again, that fearless part will sound the Command and, in spite of you, a Daring thought will flick through your mind, thrilling and frightening you. Once again you will cancel that Daring thought with a Counter thought, and then feel sad, and guilty--and relieved.

The barrage of Counter thoughts can be so thick and heavy that you may not be able even to remember the Daring thoughts and may think there aren't any, but as long as you live they keep pressing to get through, valiantly springing up only to be beaten down again by the Counter thoughts, a kind of incessant ping pong game going on in your head.

So the cycle goes--and it goes on and on, for *this pattern can never be settled in a final way.* Once in a while, driven by the sadness and guilt, you may pay off with some token behavior-- send a small check to the Red Cross, or collect a few cans of soup for the children. At other times, when the Counter thought seems final, you may firmly tell yourself there's nothing you can do, and try to forget the whole problem. But there's no real commitment behind either of these moves. There's nothing daring about them. The small check is just a sop to a nearly smothered Daring thought, an attempt to forget another stopgap Counter thought. One cycle of the argument follows another, each cycle leaving you feeling sad and guilty, half relieved, never resolved. You are thus unfulfilled, and the world is left--unsaved.

For many of us, this is the pattern than makes up most of our everyday "thinking."

Now, this pattern of Daring-and-Counter-thought-arguing is not real *thinking*. After you do real thinking, something is different; you've come to fresh insights and decisions and are ready to make changes. You could go through this cycle of Daring and Counter thoughts all day long and at the end nothing would be different; no insights would have sprung from it. It's just a spinning of the wheels. You-will-you-won't-you-can-you-can't! Gurus call it "garbage," but it's even worse than that. The inner argument actually *prevents* us from taking effective action in the world; the Counter thoughts block the Daring impulses to creative action and, tied up with this block, we do not move to change things toward the way we want them to be. It's not Courageous. No, *this cycle of thoughts is a form of Violent thinking, designed exactly to prevent us from real, Courageous thinking, and engaging in it at all is bad for ourselves and for the world.*

We can know it's bad for us, first, because of the way it makes us feel sad and discouraged, and secondly, because it's clear that such an indecisive, back and forth way of thinking is a waste of our energy and time. And it's bad for the world, first because the world needs our work, our activism, and this kind of thinking prevents us from giving it, and secondly because it's contagious; our being caught up in this kind of "thinking" presses other people to engage in it too, so that we all become sad and discouraged.

"It's too bad, but human beings are just naturally aggressive." Don't you just naturally feel sad and discouraged and "What's the point of doing anything about it?" when you hear this remark?

What can we do to correct this waste and discouragement?

We can work to change every instance of this kind of thinking to another pattern which leads to good for us and for our world.

Fortunately for all of us, there *is* another pattern of thinking, a Courageous pattern of real thinking, that we can use to do this. All of us know this pattern very well, too, because we all use it as well as the Violent pattern. We wouldn't survive long if we didn't, for this is the pattern according to which we pull a hand off a hot stove--perceiving a problem and going on to solve it in appropriate action. Like the Violent pattern, this Courageous pattern too begins with:

1. Bad news that makes a problem for you.

2. A Command which is your first Daring thought.

3. A flash of exhilaration.

4. Fear.

5. And a Counter thought.

As soon as the Counter thought is called up, though, the two patterns diverge.

This point, when the Daring thought and the Counter thought stand nose to nose, is the moment of truth in your thinking. Here you either *are driven* to hold to the Counter thought or *choose* to hold to the Daring thought. If you accept the Counter thought as a definitive block to the Daring thought, you end up in the Violent thinking pattern we have just outlined in such gloomy detail; if you hold to the Daring thought you go on in Courageous thinking. We'll assume here that this time you've chosen the latter course.

Your whole attitude toward both Daring and Counter thoughts will now be different from what it was in the Violent thinking pattern. Before, you saw the Daring thought as impractical, inconvenient, even threatening. Now you *treasure* it, are grateful for it, even feel a kind of reverence toward it. Before, the Counter thought was an unwelcome barrier; it appeared as a sad and final truth that was forcing you to give up something you really wanted. Now, though, you *welcome* it as a *signal* of the problems you will have to work out in order to get what you want, and a *tool* you can use in solving them.

Until now we've pictured Counter thoughts as real baddies whose only function is to keep us from doing our thing. That's because in Violent thinking they cancel out our Daring thoughts and tell us we can't have what we want. But this is not their natural function; it's only what we ourselves have made of them. The natural function of the Counter thought is to help *develop* the Daring thought and so bring us closer to what we want.

Good thinking can take place only against the resistance of a problem. To play handball, you've got to have a backboard. To do problem solving you've got to have a problem. And the Counter thoughts that echo the original problem furnish that for us. Their function is to make fresh presentations of the problem for Daring thoughts to play against.

Think of the situation as a wonderful game of chess or checkers, and yourself as a player in it. When your opponent makes a move to block you, you can give up the game and feel like a failure. That puts you into Violent thinking. *Or* you can *welcome* the blocking move; you're getting a kick out of the game and you know you can't even play it without your opponent's resistance. You're thrilled to be offered this challenge! You look to see whether or not the new move does indeed block you; if it doesn't, you go on. If it does, you figure out how to get through or around it or, even better, to *use* it to get where you want to go. If none of this works and your opponent wins the game--you start a new game. No matter what, you keep playing. And throughout, you welcome blocking moves as necessary background and facilitation for your own moves.

In the Courageous thinking pattern, then, when the Counter thought comes up and confronts your first Daring thought, you welcome it as a fun challenge and you brainstorm Daring thoughts to come up in response to it.

If it seems irrelevant to solving the problem, simply an attempt to stop you, you decide, "Irrelevant! Just a bluff! Proceed right over it!" Pious platitudes like these are an example:

> *But of course I wouldn't be able to do it.*

> *The poor and starving we have always with us.*

> *It would never work.*

Once you learn to think Courageously, you will laugh for joy to hear such remarks, because you can see right through them and feel powerful because you know they can't stop you. To dwell on them any longer than a laugh would be simply a waste of energy and time. They aren't going to lead anywhere, so you ignore them.

Some Counter thoughts make more sense, though.

> *But it would cost too much.*

> *But you can never get food to the ones who really need it.*

Judging such Counter thoughts as valid, you welcome them and begin to think up ways you can work around or through them to fulfill the Daring thought. Acknowledging that the project would be costly, for example, you begin to think of ways you could get the money it would take.

> *I could get a second job.*

> *I could work through the Red Cross.*

> *I could write a grant.*

> *I could take out a loan.*

> *I could wash windows for the neighbors.*

You let wild and crazy ideas come.

> *I could go to all the local bars and ask the customers for donations to feed the children. (I know of one sweet old lady who did just that and came up with a bundle.)*

> *I could try to develop E.S.P. to guess a winning lottery number.*

> *I could place an ad asking for Dollars for Dinners or start a crowdfunding campaign for children.*

Each of these ideas is a kind of mini-Daring thought, secondary to your primary Daring thought of helping the children, and each will generate exhilaration, fear, and further Counter thoughts. You handle these new Counter thoughts just as you handled the previous ones, either ignoring them or working around or through them, feeling exhilaration and then fear, thinking of further objections or Counter-thoughts, and so on. The big difference from the Violent attitude is that no matter how powerful, intense, and telling the Counter thoughts become, *you do not give up your basic wish, which is to help the children. You do not ever accept the Counter thoughts as the gloomy and final truth and limit and give up your own, creative Daring thought.* You stay loyal to it.

As they are allowed to refine, hone, and develop the Daring thought, the Counter thoughts themselves begin to change character. At first they tend to be simply obstructive, panicky objections, designed to stop you from considering the Daring thought at all. As you *use* them as guides to help you hone the

Daring thought, they *become* better and better guides, pointing out all the places where the Daring idea must be better thought out, and flowing almost immediately into Daring thoughts about possible solutions. You're now in a dialogue of problem solving, if you will.

I'd like to go,

> *but I don't want to get malaria,*

so I'll get shots first,

> *but there are no roads to that place,*

so I'll get fit so I can hike. . .

And so on.

As you continue in this Courageous way of thinking, Counter thoughts and Daring thoughts may seem almost to merge, and new ideas may fall upon you to startle, amaze and inspire you-- ideas even more daring, more apt, more exhilarating than the original Daring thought. If you are very lucky, you may encounter rock-bottom Counter thoughts, Counter thoughts so profound that you can't get around, or through, or deny them in any way, great Counter thoughts only one step removed from very Daring thoughts indeed.

"It would mean tremendous sacrifice."

"I'd have to give up my personal life."

If you took these Counter thoughts one more step by asking, "In what way?" they could carry you to some of the most Daring thoughts of all. You might discover a new life in service to the world. You might find out who you really are. You might give up all that you have and follow after the Lord. You might save the children.

More often, though, your thinking will reach a conclusion before that. This kind of thinking is headed purposively *toward* a decision rather than preventing one, and it need not go on and on in circles as Violent thinking tends to do. Sooner or later, as you continue with the process, you will find yourself coming back again and again to the same Daring thought, trimming the edges a bit here and there, thinking it and thinking it yet again. It will begin to seem too as though you *recognized* it as just right for you, as if it were the last piece of a picture puzzle slipping into place. Sometimes this recognition comes as a subtle but unmistakable premonition that you *are* going to follow through on this idea. The thought of doing so will be at once exhilarating and scary, the way you may once have felt about riding the Giant Roller Coaster at the amusement park, or diving off the high board after you'd learned all the ropes and felt ready but were also scared. You want to do it, you're scared to do it, and something in you tells you that you *will* do it. This is the idea that you go for.

And at first you think, "Oh, no!" And it's scary. And maybe a little piece of you has a small premonition that you *are* going to do this thing and you wait nervously as if a thunderstorm's been predicted. And your mind plays with it, and slowly it begins to seem less daring--but OK--begins to seem like an adventure. And then sometimes, if you're lucky, it may get really exciting, as though now you could hardly wait to do it.

It may take only a moment or it may take months to reach this point of recognition. Gandhi thought things over for two months before deciding on the Salt March; contrarily, when Clara Barton heard there was a battle nearby she knew immediately that she *would* get medical help to the wounded. The time it takes doesn't matter so long as you stay loyal to both your Daring thoughts and Counter thoughts.

Neither is it important to stay with the particular problem that you started out with. In the end, you may decide to do something directly about the original problem; you may decide to turn from it altogether in favor of focusing on some other aspect of the world's trouble. You may end up writing a small check or donating a few cans of soup as you might have done in the Violent attitude. It doesn't matter *what* you decide. What does matter--the *only* thing that matters--is that *you make a decision* about what *you will do* about the problem instead of simply giving in to the pressure of society which tells you it's bad news and you are simply to feel sorry about it--a terrible waste of energy. *You* make a decision instead of being pushed.

You need not worry, either, that your Daring thought will lead you to do something rash or crazy, for if you let it enter into a give-and-take with the Counter thoughts, the two together will hone your first Daring thought into something of just the right daringness for you. Your inner being is not a tease, to send you ideas that would be wrong for you or that you couldn't fulfill. It knows all about what's right and wrong for you, and all about what you're capable of and ready for, and will give you a task precisely within your limits, not too cautious, not too rash. If what you end up with at first isn't right for you, your uneasiness about it will overbalance the exhilaration, and you can know you haven't thought it out enough. You go straight back to the drawing board and use that uneasiness as a Counter thought to develop the idea further until you really feel right about it. Every time you get a doubt, you can sit down and run it to ground until it either adjusts the Daring thought or disappears.

After you have acted upon a Daring thought, the job is of course to continue serving all the further Daring thoughts that will come. As you go through this Courageous thinking process again and again and then act upon your Daring ideas, you will gain confidence and your Daring thoughts will become more daring, your Counter thoughts more sophisticated and effective. It may take all your courage at first to do something as simple as expressing your sympathy with someone, or writing a letter; later you may join a protest march with ease, or lead one, or run for office, and when those things are under your belt, more and more daring ideas will come to you. You'll grow larger and larger into the creative void, happier and happier, because of the freedom-- the prisoner will have been freed!

These are the steps to magnanimous accomplishment, for every working-through to a decision like this frees your energy from hampering chains, and frees the energy that was going into those chains as well, adding to your Daring direction instead of opposing it. As that happens, the limits fall away and you're on your way to having *great* Daring thoughts. With courage, you can do everything you've dreamed of. You're fulfilling your destiny--for we're not here merely to observe things from some cozy corner and feel lucky that we ourselves are safe and secure. We're not on this planet to reiterate pious Counter thoughts, which are irrelevant to all our values. We're here to fulfill our Daring thoughts.

*   *   *

Honor the Daring Thought

Daring Thoughts from great activists:

I will feed the starving!

Leo Tolstoy, <u>Help for the Starving</u>

I will free South America.

Simon Bolivar (at age 23)

My mission will be freedom for India.

Mohandas Gandhi (at age 72)

Exercises to Learn to Recognize and Work with Daring and Counter Thoughts

Exercise 1:

Think of the last time you had an exciting thought--and then distracted yourself with a game, a drink, to see what's on T.V., or by going to bed just to dream about it.

Exercise 2:

Identify that thought, the action it would entail doing, and what you'd be doing now had you not diverted yourself.

V

Use Pain to Find the Daring Thought

The Practice: *WELCOME the pain of hearing bad news, USE it to guide you toward the Daring thought, TAKE CHARGE of the energy that's going into it, and ENJOY it. Refuse to suffer!*

Most of us suffer at least a little bit ourselves when we hear about suffering in the world:

- Students in El Salvador have been gunned down by the military.
- There's a big new oil spill.
- 35,000 children died of starvation today.

News like this makes us feel bad; we feel sorry, or sad, or miserable, or angry, or regretful about it; we feel a *pain*.

As I walked through the living room I passed by my brother-in-law; he was leaning back in his easy chair with the newspaper on his lap, and he had tears in his eyes. I asked him what was wrong, and he said, "Oh, this awful business in Bosnia!"

Some people feel this kind of pain almost all the time.

I guess I have to face it that there will always be a sadness. As a child I did not imagine living with sadness; I rebelled against the possibility. But it is there. When I take a trip and go through a nice town and talk to its friendly folk, and am told there will be a rodeo tomorrow, and think of the horses and cows and calves even now in stalls not knowing, waiting to be harassed and thrown down and dragged about and maybe hurt or killed--or when I meet a nice man, and then hear him remark casually on his shooting of pheasants, and I see in my mind's eye the beautiful, iridescent pattern of the pheasant's feathers, then I feel sad--sad that these pleasant people had a chance to relate to a wider world, to feel their kinship with these other beings, and they missed out--and all they can think to do in relation to an animal is hurt it, prove their superiority upon it--just as some men miss the chance to relate to a woman as a friend and can only think to do a macho on her.

To feel this way when we hear about the suffering of others seems the most natural thing in the world. Most of us are so used to such pain that we just go ahead and endure it; it doesn't occur to us that there's anything to do about it. We may even take a faint pride in such pain because it shows that we are sensitive enough to feel it, and we certainly don't think of it as anything harmful to ourselves or others.

In fact, though, the experience of this kind of pain for more than a few moments is the first great obstacle that can keep us from the Daring thought. It's Violent behavior, for enduring pain is *suffering*--and suffering is itself the very enemy.

The appropriate reaction, when we feel pain, is to act to solve the problem that causes it. You feel "pain" when you sit on a tack; immediately your goal is to ease it, and without analyzing or even stopping to *feel* it as pain, you jump up. That's appropriate behavior, the kind that takes care of yourself and the world as well.

But when the news is very traumatic we tend to give up on the problem and instead focus on how much it hurts. It's as though we continued to sit on the tack while focusing on the sensations of "pain"--"Oh, yes! I'm sitting on a tack and I just feel terrible about it!" When we do that we're *experiencing the pain*, and that puts us in the Violent attitude in which we're destructive to ourselves and the world. The worse the bad news is, the more likely we are to go into this reaction, and we can keep it up so intensely and so long that we become ill or even die of it. One woman I know nearly died; she was worried about the suffering of an oppressed group (and it doesn't matter whether it was children being abused, South American students being disappeared, Tibetan nuns being tortured, laboratory animals being experimented on, African-Americans being bombed as they sat in church, or any other instance of oppression). This woman truly wanted to be happy but thoughts about the suffering tormented her almost continually for many months. She was obsessed with this poignant question: How can I be happy when my friends are being tortured?

As this question stands, it seems unanswerable, but if we translate the complex problem that's torturing this woman into simpler, more immediate terms, the answer is obvious. If she were walking down the street and saw a baby bird being mauled and tormented by a cat, she would know immediately to *do something about the problem* instead of suffering over it. She is unhappy because her friends are being tortured; therefore she should do something to help those friends. Even if in the end she has to join them in order to help, and is then tortured herself, that would be better than just experiencing the pain as she is now doing. *Then*, energy would be surging through her and she would be using all her resources, and she would be happy.

So, how can she be happy when her friends are being tortured? By throwing herself into helping them.

An important question for us here is: Why doesn't she? And why don't we? Why do we go on feeling the sadness, the guilt, the anger instead of working to solve the problem that we feel bad about? Why do we go on sitting on the tack?

It *seems* to us that our feeling the pain is an appropriate, even inevitable reaction to the problem situation, but when we look at it more closely, we see that in fact our feeling bad does not solve anything about that situation; it is *irrelevant* to it, and only our tradition says it's an appropriate response. There seems to be some rule in the back of our heads that says, "When things go badly you're supposed to feel bad." But that's a non-sequitur, as silly as if we said, "When it rains, you're supposed to eat a rotten peach." Our feeling bad doesn't accomplish anything positive for us *or* the problem. The rule doesn't make sense.

Feeling pain *does* make sense, though, if what we want is to stay safe from experiencing the *fear* of our Daring Thought, for that's what our focus on the "pain" sensations actually does accomplish.

At the first news of the problem, all the terrible energy of a Daring thought comes bursting up in you; it's scary, and in your fear you call up a Counter thought to block it. *The collision between the Daring and the Counter thoughts is what causes the sensations you feel, and you interpret them as "pain."*

And although they "hurt," these "painful" sensations actually feel good in one sense; they are *reassuring*. Miserable as they make us feel, they are at least familiar and so give us an illusion of security, and that's why we've made a habit of calling them up and hanging onto them.

In all this we are hiding in the pain because we are afraid to face the Daring Thought that is pressing against it and might emerge if we let go of it. We have condemned ourselves to feel pain in order to save ourselves from having to face fear.

We're experiencing pain *instead of* a Daring thought. The pain is saving us from the Daring thought.

But at a terrible price.

For it is always inappropriate to experience pain longer than the moment it takes to recognize it as a signal. When we feel pain, we are defining ourselves and the world with us as dumb, helpless sufferers bound simply to endure what happens to us--and *that takes the meaning out of our lives.* There's no point in living if you're just a done-to-robot with no initiative of your own. You can't help yourself or the world from that point of view, either.

For our own good and the good of the world, then, we must do something different with the sensations we've been experiencing as "pain."

We must learn to *welcome* them as signals of a problem we are to address rather than, victim-like, taking them as an unpleasantness we must passively endure. We must *use* them to take us to our Daring thoughts. We must *take charge* of the energy that's going into them instead of passively, "painfully" allowing it to leak away. And we must learn to *enjoy* them as a call to action, the way fire-horses used to thrill to the fire alarm.

As soon as we do this and as long as we do it, meaning will flood back into our lives, our "pain" won't be pain any more--for pain and purposiveness are incompatible--and we will become able to help the world and ourselves.

I know that this pain can be so intense that to the sufferer it seems impossible to welcome it, or to take it as a signal or do anything other than *suffer* it--and yet we know it can be done. We've all heard stories about soldiers who do not feel the pain of their wounds so long as they are in active battle. Hypnotists have showed us over and over that people can experience sensations in all sorts of different ways. They can experience cold water as hot, the smell of a rose as ammonia, and the touch of an ordinary pencil as caustic enough to raise blisters. And thousands of people have now showed us they can walk barefoot across burning coals without feeling pain.

All of this shows us that pain is something we create by putting our attention on sensations in a certain way, and that we are all capable of changing our experience of these sensations by placing our attention differently. Let us then no longer be bluffed by belief in the inevitability of "pain;" let us instead *transform* it into a tool we can use in our changing of the world.

The practice with Pain is as follows.

First, *welcome* this pain. Realize how lucky you are to feel it. You were right to feel virtuous about it. Now feel fortunate as well. Far worse than feeling this pain of compassion is to be *unable* to feel it; that's an impairment for which it is very difficult to compensate. To feel pain at the news of suffering in the world is noble. It means you care. It means you are alive. It means you are fit to fight for the world. Martin Luther King saw it as holy; he spoke of "the deep, *indeed sacred* power within each of us to open to the needs and the suffering of humanity." Be glad for it.

But remember that just feeling it is not enough. The pain is just a messenger delivering the news; it's not a bus coming to take you for a ride. It's a signal that you're at a choice point; something is happening and you have a choice of what to do about it. You can either suffer with the pain, or you can decide for yourself what to do and do it. The situation is set up so that only one thing can make it better: your knowledge that you're facing the problem head on and making a responsible decision about what to do about it. We'll talk later about how to make that decision; the point here is that you make it *instead of* feeling pained. Advance into the chance to make the decision; jump into it, seize it. And *refuse to suffer.*

It's not always easy even to *notice* this pain. We're so in the habit of immediately, automatically just *hurting* when these "pain" sensations arise that you can easily suffer, even quite intensely and for a long time, without realizing that you're hurting and wanted to do this Practice when that happened. So you may have to put it firmly in mind that you're going to *notice* the painful feelings you get when you hear bad news. Put yourself on the alert for that feeling of pain; be ready to catch it.

Then, as soon as you've caught it, are aware of it, *switch your attention from the tragic news and the "pain" to the question,*

Use Pain to Find the Daring Thought

"What can I do to solve this problem?" Put at least as much energy into this as you would have put into feeling the "pain."

Any sincere answer to your question will be a Daring thought; you may decide to go to the front lines of activists fighting to solve the problem, or you may decide that you're already putting all of your energy into some other good cause and the best thing you can do for the world is to continue doing that. Both of these decisions would be Daring thoughts; both require a sacrifice from you; both expose you to possible further bad feelings--fear, guilt, remorse, despair--but because both mean that you're facing the problem head on and making your own responsible decision about it, without regard to what other people will think of it, they're both Courageous.

Now you're *using* your energy rather than just *feeling* it as pain.

Do this practice until you can jump into the pain, *enjoy* the challenge of it, until you can say, "Aha!" to it, and, "A pain!" and "What direction is it asking me to go; what problem is it asking me to solve?" "What can I do about the problem?" When you can do that then you will no longer be a victim; you will be in control of the situation; you will have charge of your energy, and you will be able to help the world.

Then, when you hear bad news, your thoughts will follow something like this pattern:

> *This awful business in Bosnia brings tears to my eyes. Aha! My tears are my inner self pressing me to solve that business. What can I do about it? I'll ask my Senator to introduce a bill to help the people (or collect funds to buy medical supplies, or organize a protest in front of the U.N. building, etc.)*

or

> *These days I'm putting all my energy into getting legislation to help the poor. I can do the most good for the world by sticking with that.*

> *I'm so sad because animals are exploited and hurt in the rodeo. Aha! My sadness is a cry from my inner being to do something about it. Thank you for this guidance, Inner Being! Now, what can I do? I'll carry a sign in front of the rodeo tomorrow (or go rescue the calves*

tonight, or substitute myself for one of the horses waiting in the stall, etc.)

How can I be happy when my friends are being tortured? Aha! This misery of mine is pressing me desperately to do something about it. What can I do? I'll start giving lectures and publicizing their plight in every way I can think of (or set up an underground organization to rescue them, or work to reform the torturers, etc.)

*   *   *

Good training for handling the pain of very traumatic bad news is to do this Practice with all the little flicks of any kind of pain that come up for you every day. If you watch for them you can become aware of many little discomforts that arise during your everyday activities--an uneasy feeling that you've forgotten something, a sensation of strain in some part of your body when you've sat too long in one position, a pang of regret because you've unnecessarily hurt someone's feelings with a hasty remark. Consider uncomfortable feelings like these and many others that come up in your everyday life as mini-variations of the "pain" that you feel when you hear bad news. Like those bad-news sensations, they all represent your inner guidance system indicating that there is a problem, and they can all be interpreted either as *pain* and simply *endured,* or taken as *signals* that your appropriate action is needed to solve the problem. If you do this Practice, then, you will decide that every time you feel discomfort of any sort you will not hurt, but will instead first identify the problem that's causing it, and then figure out what to do about it.

*   *   *

This can be a most difficult practice and we shan't fault anyone for not being able to do it, for the habit of feeling pain is deeply ingrained in us, and won't readily dissolve. The kind of pain that we're talking about here can readily become so intense that you *know* it cannot be changed. And yet, no matter; it's still your job to translate it into good works. Be resolute, then. *Refuse to suffer.*

And when the pressure to hurt seems almost overwhelming, remember that that pressure can just as well be applied to power the Daring thought as to block it, and that the moment at which the pain is most intense is also the moment at which the Daring thought is most intense, and the most favorable point at which to switch your thinking. It takes only one wrench, one strong, willful decision, to make the switch, just as it does to jump into a swimming pool full of cold water, but almost immediately when you do make that switch, as when you steel yourself and jump into the pool, there is a reward; energy rushes through you like a fire; you feel suddenly exhilarated and very alive, and know it was right to make the change. Feeling good instead of pained is your signal that you're doing this practice correctly, and already helping the world.

*   *   *

If you follow this Practice, you will no longer feel pain or sadness for more than a few moments at a time, but you will have to deal with fear, for the alternative to suffering is to come head on, face to face, with your fear of the Daring thought. We'll deal with that in the next chapter.

VI

Hold in the Tension of Fear

> The Practice: *Hold firm under the pressure of fear, figuring out the best thing you can do in the problem situation, until fear becomes exhilaration and you become fearless.*

As soon as you refuse to feel bad about some problem in your world and turn instead to the Daring thought of *doing* something about it, a second enemy, more powerful than feeling bad, will arise. Fear.

It will be conveyed to you by Counter thoughts picturing the terrible things that will happen to you if you don't drop the Daring thought.

My professional association had come out in support of a psychologist who had twice been found guilty of cruelty to the monkeys he experimented on. I was incredulous, shocked, and then angry to learn this, and the next day during my daily walk through the neighborhood I tried to think of something I could do about it. As I came through the apricot orchard at the end of the walk it suddenly occurred to me that I could go to the next professional convention and disrupt the meeting of experimental psychologists. I very clearly saw myself getting into the meeting, marching up to the podium, unfolding a large sign denouncing the association's support of this psychologist, and standing there with it until the security guards dragged me away. I could hear the angry boos and insults from the audience. I could understand the possible consequences of my act.

> *"I'll be humiliated."*
> *"There will be no way to get home."*
> *"I'll lose my license."*
> *"I could be shot by some furious researcher."*

And there, standing between the apricot trees, I began literally to shake, so hard that my legs nearly gave way, and fervently wished I had not had this idea.

That's fear. And it will *feel* to you like a fear of whatever the Counter thoughts are threatening you with--inconvenience, or making a fool of yourself, financial ruin, danger, even death. "Disrupting the meeting would cost me everything; I can't!" But if you look to see what this fear would actually accomplish if you gave in to it, you can see that it *is* fear of the Daring thought, for the fear falls away as soon as you give up that Daring thought, and increases as you stick to it. Given that the result of a behavior is the *purpose* of that behavior, we can say that the very purpose of the fear is to get you to drop the Daring thought.

And that fear is very strong. Your Daring thought has behind it all the energy and creativity of your own Power, and your reluctance to face all the unpleasant worldly circumstances that the Counter thoughts tell you about is as nothing compared with your true fear, the fear of this true Power. Death itself can be preferable to the scary project of engaging with that thought and realizing your own power through it; that's why we're so afraid of the Daring thought.

> *Our deepest fear is not that we are inadequate. Our deepest fear is that we are powerful beyond measure. It is our light, not our darkness that most frightens us.*
>
> Marianne Williamson, <u>A Return to Love</u>

We don't ordinarily think of ourselves as being that afraid of mere thoughts, but that's only because we are clinging to other thoughts, ideas about being helpless and not responsible for the suffering that's going on, which protect us from the Daring thought. We need only challenge those other thoughts and we will feel the fear as quickly--and nearly as urgently--as we would panic if our breath were suddenly cut off.

Consider the following statements:

> *"We could have a peaceful, happy world tomorrow."*

> *"We could save the children."*

> *"We could have clean rivers and atmosphere."*

Daring thoughts like these don't sound like anything to be afraid of, do they? We think, "I *want* those conditions; I don't fear them!" But these ideas seem safe only because we're so well defended against them that we think they can't really happen; they're ferocious lions kept in a steel cage. We don't take them seriously for one minute; we discount them even as we hear them, as if they came with a built-in disclaimer, a "yeah-but:" "Yeah-but I know it won't happen; yeah-but it's unrealistic." Think about any of these ideas as a serious, *true* statement and you may feel a faint alarm. Take seriously the thought that *you yourself* might bring about one of them, and you will begin to feel the uneasiness and reluctance that is the edge of the fear. A dozen reasons will occur to you that make the "daring" thought "impossible." If you *dare* to consider any of them further, to start planning ways and means of accomplishing it, the fear will intensify; you will find yourself pulling back as a horse would if it were tugged to jump over a cliff.

I put it to you that painful as it might be, it will be easier for you to accept the world as horrible and full of suffering, and to hurt because of that fact--than to take one of these thoughts seriously. Like the great antlered stag in *Beowulf,* we'd rather be killed by the dogs than plunge into *those* dark waters.

*   *   *

But we must get over this habit of being startled and dubious and hesitant every time we have a Daring thought and then dropping it out of fear, for *our Daring thoughts are the only thing that can get us out of the trouble we're in*. If we're going to change the world, we must learn to be comfortable with these Daring thoughts and honor and develop and fulfill them. To do that we're going to have to overcome fear--and by that, I mean *all* fear, for all fear can be seen as a reaction to a Daring thought--the Daring thought of keeping your head and looking squarely at a bad situation and making your best assessment of what to do about it--and all fear has as its purpose to make us drop that thought. We must overcome all fear.

That need not be as difficult as it sounds. It's not as though fear were some deep, inborn instinct we had to obey; it's just a habit we've learned. We didn't feel fear when we were little, in the beautiful childhood world from the first chapter; we were *taught* fear and learned it when we were too young to know any better.

We gave up the beautiful childhood world under the pressure of this learned fear and, still never thinking it out, we have been giving up that world for it ever since. For even now, when we are so bold as to think a Daring thought, that same fear presses us in the same way, to *give up* what is splendid, daring, beautiful.

But giving up our power in the first place was a betrayal, and as soon as we had done it, our maturational task became to redeem ourselves and *reclaim* that power of the beautiful childhood world from a new, more sophisticated viewpoint *by being loyal to our Daring thought and holding to it under the pressure of fear to drop it.*

And there are at least two things we can do to make this not such a difficult task.

First, we can re-think fear from a grown-up point of view. We learned to feel it when we were small children and couldn't possibly see through the arguments and threats that were used to make us give up the beautiful childhood world, to *give up* what is splendid and daring. We were *taught* to be afraid of claiming too much power and to take fear *seriously.* Now, though, we're adults and, even if that fear still presses us in that same way when we are so bold as to think a Daring thought, we have better judgment. If we take another look at fear we can see that it's quite a sham, and seeing that, dare to work ourselves free of it to reclaim our power.

Secondly, we can prepare ahead of time some ways of dealing with fear the next time it arises. When you have a plan and some specific things to try against fear, you can almost look forward to the next time you will experience it, and that takes some of its power away before you even start.

For the first, then, let's examine some ways of looking at fear that may bring it back down to size, so that we can see it as not such a terrible thing after all.

1. Beyond Providing You with a *Warning,* Fear Is Never Appropriate.

Other than addressing the cause of the fear, *everything you do out of fear is harmful to yourself and to the world.*

The first quake of what we call fear can be a warning of danger, but any fear after that is irrelevant to your basic problems and so is inappropriate. In the most dire circumstances, even if an angry rhinoceros comes galloping at you through the veldt, after the first rush of adrenaline that galvanizes you to action, it is still not appropriate to be afraid. Fear only makes you helplessly freeze, or run off in a panic, or go through some other behavior not directed to solving your problems--and your life's purpose, your *job*, is to *address* your problems.

2. Fear Does Not Further Your Survival but Puts It in Jeopardy

If you haven't thought much about the purpose of fear in your life, you may still think of it as a natural response to dangers that's meant to help you survive. After all, didn't people who were afraid of rhinoceroses and so avoided them survive to have us descendants? Thinking that fear is a friend and furthers your survival, you may take its counsels seriously, and so back away from and deprive yourself of experiences that could be the most growth-stimulative of your life.

For fear itself does not help you survive; it *endangers* you. People who avoided rhinoceroses and so survived didn't do so out of fear, but out of a healthy respect for the rhino's power, just as when you see a Mack truck bearing down on you in the street you don't feel *afraid* of it; you respect its power and step out of its way. Only if you felt helpless to do anything would you be afraid, and then you wouldn't figure out how to cope; you'd *catastrophize*, picture how horrible it would be when you were hit by the truck. That focus on imminent disaster would paralyze you, prevent you from focusing on appropriate action, and so lead you into more, not less danger.

Fear can also push you to act out, in order to escape the tension--to go ahead and *throw* the game, go ahead and *get* yourself arrested, go ahead and *start* the war. That's breaking under pressure, and it too brings you into more, not less danger. It's very different from keeping your head, coolly assessing the situation, and *yourself keeping the power -- yourself purposely determining* your behavior, purposely freezing, purposely fighting, purposely running--always doing what *you* choose to do because *you* have decided that's the best thing to do.

It's probably clear that when you picture the rhino crushing you you've given up and accepted the most disastrous consequences, and that doing that is harmful to you and to the world. It may not be quite so obvious that in dropping the Daring thought of helping the world's children you're doing the same thing. But you are; you've given up on the problem and accepted the disastrous consequence--the starvation and suffering of the children. And you do the same thing every time you drop any Daring thought out of fear. So it's not good for the world for us to go that way.

Once you understand that other than alerting us to danger, fear is *not* a friend, that it does not help you or the world survive but endangers both, you're less likely to fall for it the next time.

3. Fear Is Just a Pressure on You to Give Up a Daring Thought. It Is Not a Vague, Scary, Mysterious Thing with Big Meanings Behind It

When we're feeling fear we're usually so focused on whatever it is we're afraid of that we don't examine the fear itself, just as when someone rushes into a theatre screaming "Fire!" we don't examine the messenger; we look frantically around for the fire. Fear itself, then, is usually unexamined, and that makes an opening for it to be mysterious to us and scary in itself, a vague but powerful and unpleasant force that we don't have control over. But if we do keep our heads and look at exactly what we're experiencing when we're afraid, we see that fear is nothing but a constriction, or tightness, a *pressure*, somewhere in the body. It is predominantly a sensation of *tension*, or *pressure*, the same kind of thing you feel in your muscles when you arm wrestle.

Seeing fear as a pressure fits in with the ideas in this book, too, for according to them fear actually *begins* with a tension, the tension between two thoughts that are coming up against each other. Every time you have a Daring thought, Counter thoughts will arise--that's one of the ways you can be sure it *is* a Daring thought--and the job of a Counter thought is to *counter*, or cancel and kill, the Daring thought. The two thoughts are not compatible, so they come up against each other inside you; if neither gives way right away they then push against each other, energy for energy.

It is this competitive pushing of the two thoughts against each other that makes the feeling of tension we call "fear," and since when the pushing starts you're paying attention to one side of that tension, the Daring thought, you experience the fear as a pressure to switch over and pay attention to the other side of that tension, the Counter thoughts, instead. You continue to feel this pressure of fear until one or the other of the two thoughts wins the pushing contest. If the Counter thought wins then you give up; there's no more pressure, so you don't feel fear. If the Daring thought wins then the erstwhile Counter thoughts now *serve* you by pointing out problems you must solve and you're busy solving them; there's no more opposition and so no more pressure, and you don't feel fear.

Seeing fear in this way, as a simple *pressure* to drop your Daring thought, immediately puts it much more under your own control. Fear is not some big, mysterious thing from the outside with big, mysterious meanings behind it; it's a simple matter of keeping your head, that is, *holding to your own idea under pressure*. You needn't take such a reverent attitude toward it.

If you enjoy imagery you can also understand fear as a pressure in this way: Think of yourself as a hero who wants to reclaim the fire which the gods have stolen from your people. In thinking a beautiful, creative Daring thought you challenge those gods, claim a right to the fire, take some of it back; the Counter thought is an angry god ordering you to *drop* it, and that order coming up against your determination to *keep* the fire makes the pressure you experience as fear. The issue is: are you going to hold firm to your own against that order or are you going to knuckle under and obey it?

4. Feeling Fear Is Just a Habit - And in Some Cases an Addiction

If fear is just a pressure, then dropping our own purposes in order to erase that pressure is a habit just like the habits of smoking, drinking, drugging out. We can get addicted to any of these because it eases a tension, or pressure, but that isn't good for us or anybody else in the world. Better to learn to handle the tension, even *use* it!

5. You Yourself Create the Pressure that Is Fear

When you feel fear you are literally scaring yourself.

When you're afraid it may *seem* that some external thing is causing your fear--the furious rhino, the angry god, or the grim consequences you think might follow if you stick to your Daring thought. But when you see fear as simply the experience of pressure between two opposing thoughts, you can't help noticing that those thoughts are *your own*, that you produce them and that you must therefore be producing your own fear by dividing yourself into two parts and then setting them against each other. It's as though your right hand were trying to push aside your left hand, which resisted it; however hard you press with one hand, the other can block it; there can be plenty of pressure between the two of them but no net gain in any direction. What a waste of good energy! And *you* are producing the whole show. We don't usually let ourselves understand this about fear, but once we do, we can't be afraid any more. Fear can't survive our awareness that it's just something we're doing to ourselves.

6. In Fear, You're Setting Yourself as a Victim

Think about it; in fear aren't you pointing the finger at some *other* person or circumstance as having the power to hurt you because you yourself are helpless? In your fear of the rhino you're pointing at it as having all the power to determine what happens to you; "Look at that thing *over there*; it's going to get me--I'm helpless!" When you're quivering and shaking at the Daring thought you're doing the same thing; pointing at the way the world is-- at the fact that it may visit certain consequences upon you if you fulfill the Daring thought--as having all the power, so that you yourself have none and are helpless. In short, you're defining yourself as a victim. And the victim stance puts you squarely in the Violent attitude; it's one of the several positions we can take within that position (being an oppressor is another one); it *provokes* Violence and so is itself part of the Violent attitude.

7. Fear Is Always an Attempted Blackmail, and a Bluff

It makes a big deal out of things that are NOTHING TO BE AFRAID OF.

I learned this almost by chance.

One night I woke up with a heart pounding feeling of dread and impending doom. I was in such terror that I thought, "Oh, life isn't worth living in this terrible, dysphoric world!" After a while I began trying to figure out *what* I was so scared of. Was I about to die? Did I have some terrible disease? A brain tumor (my standard fear)? Had my husband stopped loving me? Were my children in bad trouble? I even dredged up a fear from my childhood; Is a meteor about to fall on our house? None of these felt like the right answer, and I'd almost given up on identifying my fear when, suddenly, it came to me. I *remembered*, as if it had been a name that I had forgotten but would recognize again as soon as it came back to mind. I had always thought it was pointless to store dirty clothes in a hamper only to have to take them out again before washing them, and I gave my family the daring instruction to simply throw their dirty clothes on the floor in front of the washing machine. It made quite a pile, and the day before a friend had made a disparaging remark to the effect that,

"I see you've got clothes all over the floor again!" My terrible sense of doom was caused by the despairing thought, "Oh, I may come to the end of my life and die and always have had a pile of dirty clothes in front of my washing machine!"

It may seem clear that having a pile of laundry on the floor is not such a fearful thing. What is not so clear is that *all* of the things we are afraid of are not such fearful things; they're *nothing to be afraid of*. We've been trained into thinking them terrible and giving up big pieces of our personhood to avoid them--that's the blackmail--and we've bought the training that they're terrible without ever taking a good look at them--that's the bluff.

The original counsel of fear back in our childhood took the form of a blackmail threat: "There is something called 'death' and it is terrible, and if you don't give up the ideals of the childhood world that's what will happen to you!" It was a bluff as well as a blackmail, for what it threatened us with turns out to be temporary loss of the ego which, when we face it, is seen to be no horrible experience at all. It may in fact be quite strengthening. All the derivatives of that original blackmail, the Counter thoughts that make us feel fear today, are blackmail too: "Drop the Daring thought or you will lose"--you name it!--"House, home, family, friends, money, status, life itself!" They are a bluff, too, for the losses they threaten you with are, in truth, not so horrible. They may even turn out to be gains in the long run

Take for example the following threat: "If you keep resisting you will be sent to prison; you will be tortured." Like me, you may have thought that torture would be almost impossible to stand up to (a real Counter thought!), but Elvia Alvarado, a 48-year-old Honduran villager who became an organizer for the campesinos, found out differently:

> [The sixth time I was arrested by the National Department of Investigations] . . . They tied my hands and feet together and hung me from the ceiling. They kept me hanging there for hours. When they untied me, they threw me on the ground and stomped on me. . .They covered my mouth and hit me harder. Then they covered my mouth and nose so I couldn't breathe. And they threatened me with the capucha, that suffocating hood they put over your head. . .one of the men tried to rape me. . .they kept me incommunicado for three days, with no food, no water, nothing. . .You see this gash on my leg? I've got another one just like it on my behind. It's from the officers' boots. It's

> *from them stomping on me. The first week I was home my*
> *son had to carry me all around because I couldn't walk and*
> *I couldn't lie on my back either.*

Did her experience prove to her that torture was indeed
something to be afraid of? She says:

> *I used to be afraid of the DNI. But now that I've been there,*
> *I'm not scared any more. Now ... I know they can't break*
> *me.*
>
> *I'm sure someday I'll be captured again [and maybe] they'll*
> *kill me . . .that won't stop the others from following my*
> *path. In that sense, I'm stronger than they are.*

> Elvia Alvrado, <u>Don't Be Afraid, Gringo!</u>

She's called the bluff of the threat of torture; now, she's even
stronger than she was before.

*   *   *

We can see fear in these seven ways, then, as *an addictive habit*
according to which for most of our lives we *pressure ourselves*
through *bluff* and *blackmail* into taking the *dangerous* position of
victim in order to suppress the most creative and alive part of
ourselves, our Daring thoughts.

Once you've seen through the mechanisms of fear in this way you
won't be able to take it quite so seriously as you used to. It's
nothing but a bluff; you feel a little silly falling for it again. As
Alice said to the Queen, King and courtiers who were threatening
to cut off her head: "Why, you're nothing but a pack of cards!"

And finally, no longer afraid of fear, you may be ready to see one
last, most important thing about it: that the first quake of fear
can be a signal to you that you *have* just had a Daring thought
and life is about to begin! It signals that you've reached a decision
point; now you're either going to stay in the tension or flee from
it, seize the chance of living all the way or refuse it. You've come
right to the edge between life and death. If you've learned not to
be afraid of fear, then you can feel the glory of that moment. As
the columnist Beaucreau wrote when he was struggling with
AIDS and within a few days of dying of it, "Ah, the terror, the
pain, the exultation of being on the very edge!"

By the time you've come this far, "fear" is no longer fear; it's more like the thrill of recognition when you meet a dear friend you have not seen for a long time, and you do not shrink away when it comes; you know that it is to be joyously welcomed, seized, made much of, as if you were an old-time fire horse and that flick of "fear" were a fire alarm that energizes you and calls you to the action that is your life. For all the rest is sleeping.

*   *   *

Hopefully, looking at fear in this way you've made some sort of decision to conquer it, to go ahead and think your Daring thoughts and not let fear pressure you into dropping them. The story isn't quite over when you've made that decision though, because, as everyone knows who's tried to quit smoking or drinking, until that big decision soaks down into your unconscious and is verified by every part of you, you'll have to fight the battle to make it all over again every time you have a Daring thought. Fear will press you to drop your Daring thoughts until all of you decides you're finished with fear forever. You need some ways of practicing your hold on the Daring thought so that you can stay with it while you're working up to that final decision.

*   *   *

Let's look then at some ways of dealing with fear that you can prepare ahead of time.

One way is to decide that as soon as you feel fear you will simply, immediately, *seize the energy behind the pressure of fear and apply it to your Daring thought instead.* This is what you will do when you are fully committed to fearlessness. To do it, the next time you have a Daring thought and are afraid to consider it, *put your full attention on it* and *intensify it, make it more urgent.*

Remind yourself that your cause is urgent. The children are starving *right now,* and if you dilly dally around being afraid, more will die tomorrow, and tomorrow, and tomorrow.

Pretend you're a surgeon in an emergency, that you're stopping someone's bleeding or re-starting someone's heart, and can't take time from your work to listen to the criticizing remarks of bystanders.

Hold in the Tension of Fear

Imagine that you're busy pulling someone out of a burning house, with flames and falling rafters all around you; you can't afford to be distracted now.

It shouldn't be hard to make your Daring thought that kind of life and death matter, because it really *is* that kind of life and death matter; in imagining these emergencies you're just correcting the usual confused, lethargic view we take of things. In making the Daring thought important in this way, you seize the energy that's being wrongly taken up the Counter thoughts and apply it to the Daring thought instead. Now the real you, not your doubting self, is the one exerting the pressure.

When you get to that point, of course, you can begin to use the Counter thoughts to hone the Daring thought.

> "It can't be done!"
> "Why not?"
> "It's not practical!"
> "What can I do to *make* it practical?"

And by this time, of course, you've conquered fear and made it your ally; you're in the Courageous attitude.

*   *   *

If intensifying the Daring thought is too hard for you at first, simply *holding your focus* on some aspect of the Daring thought may be enough to beat fear. Pick some positive statement, such as, "There's always something I can do!" or "I can do it!" and focus on it, *hold to it with all your might.*

If your resolve is firm, that may be all you need to do. If your resolve is wobbly, if you're not sure that you can or want to conquer fear, a struggle will ensue much like the stare-out contests you used to have in elementary school when it was so difficult to focus on your opponent's eyes. The Counter thoughts will seize upon every remaining uncertainty on your part as a sign of potential loss of focus, and be encouraged by it, and take it as justifying their attacking so ridiculous an idea as the Daring thought. They will become more and more urgent, insistent, and come up with more and more compelling reasons why that thought isn't feasible, dire warnings and put-downs; they will threaten you with lifelong disappointment, loss of love, death, in order to pressure you into dropping the Daring thought.

Don't do it. All the kids are pressing around you taunting, pushing, yelling that you can't hold the stare. Don't let them distract you. Stay there. As long as you hold your focus, fear can't get you; you can't be afraid--but it will seize upon every smallest break in your concentration.

Fear will press harder and harder; the Counter thoughts will rush up to you like frantic, urgent ponies, pulling at you, dragging you, tempting you to jump on them and be carried away into panic. They will urge, demand, plead and threaten, to force you to drop the Daring thought. And you will want to give in to them. You will want to find out that there is *truly* nothing you can do about the original problem--that discovery would be a relief. You will long for a good way to prove that nothing can be done--because it will take you off the hook. You would suffer pain if that happened, but pain is as nothing compared with the fear!

As in those fairy tales in which the hero must remember a secret password or hold to some magical ring because only it will save him, so you hang onto the Daring thought.

If you hold fast, there will come a point at which you know that you have had enough, and you will ask yourself, "Well, am I going to do it or not?" and something in you will answer, "Yes, I am!" Then you will know that no matter how intense the fear may get, you're not going to drop your Daring thought for it, that it cannot bluff you (for this *is* all a bluff). Then the fear will dissolve, and then you can get on with the practical business of deciding what you will do to further your cause; fear has lost its power and you will be able to act on your Daring thought--or, rather, you will not be able *not* to act upon it.

The first time I was arrested at a protest march I was really scared. When I saw the police coming for us I stood there, my knees started to tremble. I kept thinking, "*Shall* I really do this? *Shall* I really do it?" Then the deputy yelled, "If you don't leave in five minutes you'll be arrested," and I thought maybe I would leave and I thought I'd just try walking a few steps away. And my legs *would* not go. They wouldn't take one step. I willed myself to step away and they wouldn't move. Then I knew I was going to stay no matter what, and I wasn't scared any more.

At that point, you've won over fear.

*   *   *

Hold in the Tension of Fear

Another way of holding your focus on the Daring thought is to use the rhythms of fear itself to conquer fear. Once you become sensitive to the pressure of Counter thoughts, you will notice that it is not a steady pressure; like pain, fear washes over you in *waves* and if you stick it out through one wave it can't do anything to you until the next wave.

Try just relaxing when a wave comes, *letting* the terrible Counter thoughts roll over you without fighting them, and then, as each subsides, quickly heighten your focus on the Daring thought, asking your questions, reversing the Counter thoughts, figuring out what you can do about the problem, focusing on your solutions rather than on why they won't work, letting things become clear. If you're too scared even to concentrate on the questions, just stay there with your simple focus on the Daring thought. The waves of fear will wash over you--small ones at first and then, as you still hold to your Daring thought, the waves will become taller, fiercer--great crashing waves--and they will tower over you. Simply let them roll over you without reacting and as soon as one recedes, turn back to the Daring thought and think about what you can do to fulfill it, until the next wave comes bearing down on you.

Do this over and over, until--as you still hold and stay there--at last the Counter thoughts will fall away, and become ashamed, as it were, of their histrionics, and then it will be your turn, to comfort them, and forgive them, and make use of them to hone your Daring thoughts.

*　　　*　　　*

Another, still gentler way of handling fear, if circumstances allow you enough time to use it, is simply to *give it time*. Let it soak. Counter thoughts are urgent, panicky things without much staying power; given a little time they're likely to wear themselves out. When a Daring thought comes, it may well catch you off balance; go ahead and quiver and shake at the scary Counter thoughts and dutifully drop your Daring thought--for a while only! If you are reasonably accepting of your Daring thoughts to start with, negotiations between the two kinds of thoughts can then go on in your unconscious. After an appropriate interval, the Daring thought is likely to come up again, perhaps in improved form.

This is what happened when I was so scared of doing something about the researcher who had been cruel to monkeys. I told you that as I walked through the apricot orchard and thought about protesting at a professional meeting, my knees shook. Two days later I walked in the apricot orchard again and went over the same ideas about disrupting a meeting that had seemed impossibly rash before. They now seemed quite doable. Eventually I established a professional newsletter highlighting research with questionable practices regarding animals, inviting colleagues to share their opinions.

*   *   *

If none of these ways of handling fear works for you, if you're still timid about making Daring thoughts and still can't proudly and lovingly dwell on them when you do have them, it may involve deeper issues that could be resolved by some of the other Practices. Look to your beliefs about what the universe is, and what you are. You may need to develop the knowledge that nothing bad can ever happen to you, that whatever trouble comes, something in you or for you will rise to handle it, to endure it, so you need not be afraid. And you may need to care more, to intensify your love. Exactly how important are the children, the animals, the rivers, the endangered species to you? It is said that perfect love casteth out fear; that means that if your beloved child was in danger you wouldn't even *feel* the fear; you'd do anything, immediately, to save her, as some mothers have done. Well, your beloved human race is in trouble, and your beloved home, helpless animals, the earth; feel your love for these in its full intensity; let it motivate you and cancel out your fear.

Work on the Practices "Build Beliefs that Support You and your Work" and "Care About Everything, All the Time" to strengthen you for the practice of Fear.

*   *   *

Every time you manage to hold to your Daring thought against the pressure of fear to drop it, it will be easier to do the next time. Gradually you will get used to the feeling of fear and be less and less impressed by it, more and more skillful in handling it. And then, when you're comfortable enough with fear, you will begin to feel the *exhilaration* that comes when you let your Daring thought take over.

Hold in the Tension of Fear

I was taking a Sunday afternoon stroll on the pier all dressed up with some rather straight-laced relatives when I saw four or five young boys tormenting a crab that the fishermen had evidently thrown aside. The poor thing was still alive, waving his claws, though rather feebly, and the boys stood in a circle around him, poking him, kicking at him, taking turns thumping him with an old bucket, laughing at how easy it was to hit him without being caught by the pincers.

I would have interfered right away if I'd been alone, but I was *afraid* my rather proper relatives would disapprove if I made a scene, so I held back, and we walked on by. As soon as we did I was sorry I had not intervened, and realizing at the same moment that it was not too late I turned back, rushed into the circle of boys, seized the crab and dropped him through a hole in the planking of the pier into the water several feet below. I saw him begin to swim away, so I knew he was still alive, and such an extremely powerful wave of joy went through me that for that moment at least, the possible scorn of my relatives meant nothing to me.

Every time you feel this kind of joy, this exhilaration, you will be stronger, and more committed to the practice, and more comfortable with "fear".

And finally, as you go on, you will become so steady in your practice that it will become part of you and you will be fearless. There will be no more inner pressure, because Daring thought and Counter thoughts will work together so closely they will be like one; solutions will come instantaneously, free of fear. You will be basically calm and centered no matter what problems arise. And without having to think about it at all, you will behave as you would most like to when the great decisions must be made.

*   *   *

A large family held a reunion on the river bank. Some took a raft ride upstream, and after everyone else got off, one of the women stayed on the raft, playing with poling it about. The current took the raft and carried it swirling downstream, gathering speed as it went. She saw that it was heading for the waterfall and screamed. Her husband shouted directions to her from the bank on how to bring the raft about and reach safety but she couldn't hear him through the roar of the falls. It became obvious that the raft would pass near where the picnickers stood, so he shouted to her to jump to him as the raft skirted the shore. She meant to but at the last minute she panicked and fell back and began to cry instead. Without hesitation, her husband gauged the distance perfectly, jumped onto the raft with her, and held her in his arms as they fell to their death over the falls.

A Dutch baker who risked his life many times to save Jews from the Nazis told what inspired him to begin his rescue work. While out walking in the woods one day, he accidentally witnessed many Jews being herded into a pit and then shot by Nazi officers. What inspired him was this: the sight of a man and a boy, both naked, who stood by the side of the pit about to be pushed in. The man stood calm and tenderly held the boy, talking to him earnestly, stroking his head and every once in a while pointing to the sky.

* * *

Quotes from great activists:

The enemy is fear. We think it is hate; but, it is fear.

Mohandas Gandhi

We have nothing to fear but fear itself.

Winston Churchill

Don't be afraid, gringo!

Elvia Alvarado

Fear thou not, for I am with thee.

Isaiah 41:10

Being afraid takes the spirit out of you.

Mohandas Gandhi

Further Exercises to Free Yourself from Fear

Exercise 1: Do What You Know Is Right but Are Reluctant to Do.

Do you hesitate to make phone calls because you don't want to make a pest of yourself? Require that you make a dozen of them.

Do you think you'll look like a fool going from house to house putting flyers under people's doormats? Make yourself spend a day doing it.

Are you timid about talking with legislators? Volunteer to be the one to do it next time.

If you start doing this exercise with minor fears, it turns out to be easy, fun, and quite effective. Facing down the first few fears *feels so good* that you begin to *welcome* that feeling of reluctance about doing things because you know it will feel so good when you overcome it. Then you can begin to call the bluff of more and more intense fears.

When Goethe was a young man, he wanted to be able to climb the Alps, but, unfortunately, he was afraid of heights. He decided he wouldn't put up with this fear; he ran with it all the way to the top of the highest tower in the city and then made himself step out to the very edge of the parapet over and over until his fear was gone. He climbed many a <u>mountain</u> after that.

Exercise 2: Scare Yourself.

Imagine that you're a child back in kindergarten and the class is making scary masks, complete with scowls, fangs, wild, shaggy hair, menacing claws. Then there's a contest to see which of you can *scare yourself* the most with your own scary mask. Everyone looks at his or her mask and goes into hysterics being scared by it.

Can you scare yourself effectively?

Think up the worst possible consequences that could follow if you acted on your Daring thought. Can you scare yourself into dropping it?

If not, try some more. That's all fear is, *you* scaring *you*.

Exercise 3: When You're Afraid, You're Being Blackmailed By Fear. Use The Blackmail To Free Yourself Of Fear.

When you're afraid, you're being threatened by some kind of loss, and if you *let go* of what you're afraid to lose, you will be free of fear. Use fear to point out what it is you're afraid of losing, and call the bluff of fear--in this way:

When you feel afraid, ask yourself, "What am I afraid of? What's the worst that can happen?" Then ask yourself, "If that happens, what's the thing to do about it?"

"We'll be killed."

Is dying really that awful? Can something every human being has done for thousands of years really be so terrible? What's the thing to do about it? One answer might be: Go into it fully and make the most of it, whatever it is!

"If all my partners die, I'll be left all alone."

What's the thing to do if you're left all alone in the world? One answer might be: Help others who are also left alone.

"People will laugh at me."

You fear humiliation from how others may think after you reveal yourself to them, losing forever the precious image of yourself that you so cherish. Where did you get this image? Did you decide on it, or did someone else make it up? If it's genuinely what you believe, will it really matter to you if anyone disapproves?

Realizing that *none* of the things you fear is so awful and that there's always a right thing you can do if it happens *frees* you to look at possible consequences in the light of your highest goals, objectively, without fear.

VII

Choose Your Cause with Utmost Wisdom

The Practice: *From moment to moment, do only and exactly what you feel like doing to help the world until you're serving because you want to and it's fun.*

Which of the many needy causes in our world should you take as your own? There are so many desperate problems from which to choose: children starving, rain forests being depleted, women being battered, whales being killed off, wars, discrimination and corruption to name a few. Which is most important? Which most urgent?

There is so much suffering, you can hardly choose. If you focus on just one problem the others will be neglected. If you work on them all you're spread too thin and the Counter thought, "I can't do it all!" soon strikes you. You don't want to fragment your energies. You don't want to burn out. And you don't want to feel guilty, but where does your personal life fit in? How do you decide between helping others and having a good time yourself? Between working for the cause and taking a day off?

How can you choose, out of this chaos, which cause or causes you will support? How will you apportion your energies amongst them all?

*   *   *

Finding your own best cause is far too important and complex a matter to be settled by your logical mind, nor must you let it be decided by the people and events of the outer world which put so much pressure on you to support one cause or another. Your best cause can never be determined by logic or the outer world. *You must look within yourself to find it.* Something in you knows of a great cause you would willingly die for; the knowledge of that cause is in you, perhaps smothered by Counter beliefs and thoughts but quite alive, and at a very deep level you *want* to give yourself to it, all the way. But you yourself must find out what it is. Sometimes people discover their hidden great cause in great emergencies as they find themselves risking their lives to rescue their buddies or prevent some catastrophe. Some are called to their work, like St. Paul, who was knocked to the ground until he listened to his call. But in everyday life, if you don't have an emergency or a clear call to pull your cause out of you, you must work to discover it. That's what this Practice is for, to help you, from moment to moment, discover the cause you would die for, so that you can throw yourself into it.

The Practice for finding your right cause is, from moment to moment, to do only and exactly what you truly *want* to. When you can really do this, you'll be following your perfect cause and will find, also, that it's exactly the right activity that best helps you and the world.

It may sound as though that would be easy to do--just do whatever you feel like!--but it is actually the basis of a profound and exacting Practice, because for the most part *we don't know* what we truly want. We've been so trained into wanting to be approved of, to win, to be secure as a separate ego--into all the wants that stem, as the experts say, from the fear of death--that our first answers to the question, "What do I want to do?" are likely to be driven by those trained "wants". They're likely to be simply activities we think will ease various tensions, things we have been *told* will make us happy, or that we *should* want to do; they're dictated by convention, not our true want. The discipline in this Practice is to recognize these trained "I want to do's" as superficial, and move from them to a deeper kind of want. Clara Marie Davis (Davis, 1939) showed in an experiment in Chicago that when very small children are set at a table covered with many kinds of food, they choose--because they want to--exactly the nutritious foods that are best for their health. We know, though, that with a enough exposure they can very soon *learn* to *want* sweets, junk food and drugs--things that aren't very good for them or the world at all.

The job here is to move in the opposite direction, back from our junky wants to what we ourselves, from our freest, uncoerced core in the beautifully childhood world, really *want*. In moving toward this real want we also move toward a perfect activism for the world, for what all of us most deeply, truly want is not just to escape death but *to love*; this want has been pushed down and imprisoned deep inside us by our Violent training, but if we learn to free it and act from it after all we will also fulfill the wants and needs of the world.

> *Gandhi firmly believes that non-violence is actually more natural to man than violence. His doctrine is built on this confidence in man's natural disposition to love. However, man finds himself deeply wounded, and his inmost dispositions are no longer fully true to themselves. In man's disordered condition, violence seems to be the very foundation of social order and is "enthroned as if it were an eternal law,' so that man is called upon by society to reject love and enter into a mysterious 'higher duty,' presented as sacrificial and inscrutable, and demanded by the law of force"*

> Merton, Thomas, <u>Gandhi on Non-Violence</u>. p. 43

The basic skill for getting back in touch with your real want is an exercise I call The Five Minute Want.

The Five-Minute Want

Choose a time--a stretch of several hours or even a day--when you have nothing tightly scheduled and so will be able to take occasional five or ten-minute breaks to do this exercise.

Begin by taking a mental tour of your body and mind and asking yourself whether you feel quite happy and contented, or whether you feel some unease, some uncomfortable or anxious or dissatisfied or disappointed or sad or resentful feeling. In looking for these uneasy feelings pay special attention to your abdominal area, which tends to constrict when things aren't quite right for you and so is a good place to look for uncomfortable feelings.

If your tour shows that you're feeling quite contented, you're already listening to your inner Wanter. That's good, so go on with whatever you're doing until such time as you do experience some uncomfortable feeling.

As soon as you become aware of any unpleasant feeling, though, it's time to do this exercise. Sit down, get as comfortable and relaxed as you can, and then ask *yourself* the question, *"If I were totally free to do whatever I wanted for the next five minutes, what would I like to do?"* Then, remaining relaxed, wait for something to occur to you. Just hold in mind that the answer must be something you can do in five minutes, and it must be something you'd like to do. Would you like to walk around the block and enjoy the weather? Take a bubble bath? Have a screaming tantrum in the bathroom? Go outside and just look at the leaves and the grass for five minutes? If you get answers like, "Finish my report for work," "clean the closets," or any other dutiful activity, you probably haven't got the spirit of it. More likely answers would be:

- Roll around on the ground.

- Continue to relax for a while, right where I am.

- Design a kite.

- Watch the clouds.

- Watch an old favorite movie.

If you have a hard time thinking of anything you'd really like to do, get paper and pencil and list ten things you *might* like to do for five minutes at a time. Just make them up--and be sure to include a few crazy things you've never done before. You could:

- Read a few pages of the latest mystery.

- Sit out on the verandah with a cup of tea.

- Love up your cat, or dog.

- Make that difficult phone call so you could then jump up and down for joy that it's over.

- Get a snack and have a five-minute picnic under the trees-- or maybe *up* a tree.

You may recognize your items as coming from the beautiful childhood world, things a child would be likely to do. If so, you're on the right track.

Make up ten items like this and then lie on the couch with your list and let your eyes just go over it a few times. You will find that some of the items stand out as more attractive to you than others, and as you gaze at them, one in particular will appeal to you the most. (If *none* of these has much appeal for you, just take the least repulsive item. You've got to start somewhere!)

Choose Your Cause with Utmost Wisdom

Then go and for at least five minutes do the activity you've chosen, the only rule being that you must enjoy doing it. If you don't enjoy it, if you feel silly or reluctant and find yourself wondering, "Why am I doing this?", the answer is: you're getting in practice to give your *first* loyalty to your inner Wanter from now on. You are to trust that if you strive faithfully to follow its direction, it will lead you to the perfect, most self-affirming and effective action you can take for the world.

After you've done the favored activity for at least five minutes, go back to whatever you were busy with before you started the exercise, but--only for as long as you are happy and content. As soon as an uneasy or dissatisfied feeling comes up again, sit down, relax, and ask yourself once more, "*If I were totally free to do whatever I wanted for the next five minutes, what would I like to do?*"

Keep at this exercise until you can easily think of fun things you'd like to do for five minutes.

*　　*　　*

Once you understand how the Five Minute Want works and are comfortable doing it, you can use variations of it to make all kinds of decisions.

You can use it to choose the overall, main cause you want to work on. Ask yourself, "If I were totally free to work on any cause I wanted to help the world, what would it be?" And if no sure answer comes, list ten--or eight, or fifteen--problems that you would like to see resolved.

- Abuse of animals

- Disadvantaged children

- Ravaged environment

- War

- Endangered species

- Illiteracy

- Racial discrimination

- Homelessness

- Poverty

Lie down with the idea of choosing one of these general causes; gaze at the list and let that favored one gradually emerge against the background of the others which now seem not quite as right for you. Then use the same procedure to decide what specifically you want to do within that cause. List all the possibilities you can think of, and then let your inner self pinpoint one of them.

- Recruit people for my cause

- Work on legislation for the cause

- Publicize the cause

- Organize demonstrations

- Give direct aid, like Mother Teresa

- And so on.

In this way, you can find your best cause for this particular time, the one you *want* to give yourself to now. Because it has the energy of your want behind it, it will also be the one in which you're more effective and which you will most enjoy.

* * *

Of course, it's not enough to choose your cause and your place in it just once. You must choose them again and again, in an ongoing way. Otherwise even work that you yourself have chosen to do can quickly and slyly turn into a habit and a *should* that you're not choosing at all, and then all the energy of your want and your choosing will drain away from it. That's because neither your cause nor you are fixed or static; both are continually changing. The various problems that cause suffering in the world change over time too; the children get fed, or die, wars end and, perhaps, new wars begin; old causes fade away and new ones move into focus. And as you work in your cause--and *through* working in your cause--you, too, grow and change; your vision broadens, you come to see things differently, and the importance of things shift for you in ways that you can't now predict.

In the 1960's I thought I was quite an activist. I worked in the civil rights movement and had already gone to jail for it. But when it came time to sell our house, I decided that if a Negro wanted to buy it I would not sell to him because that would hurt the neighbors by lowering the value of their houses. Five years later I was amazed and shocked to recall that decision; I had grown so far beyond it that I could hardly believe I ever thought that way.

Years ago I supported the local humane society but cheered and saw nothing wrong with a movie in which John Wayne's men, procuring animals for zoos, dragged them out of the trees by the scrotum and shipped them to America. I was later appalled that I ever thought such a thing, and then saw things very differently.

Thus if you are to *keep* your cause connected to your true want, you must continuously adjust it and your activities within it. As a good driver keeps her mind on the destination and her hand on the wheel, continually changing direction to fit the most efficient route, so must you keep your mind focused on your inner Wanter, and continually adjust your work in the world according to its instructions. When you do so you remain a true and constant activist through all the changes of your character and your cause.

- Martin Luther King, Jr., worked first on *civil rights.* As his vision broadened, he expanded his work to the problems of *war* and *poverty* as well.

- Gandhi honed his cause all the time. After studying the law in London, Gandhi tried out his cause applying justice as a lawyer in his home country. He traveled to South Africa to assist in one case of minority discrimination, then expanded it over a period of twenty-one years to address the plight of the entire Indian population there, then returned to hone his cause to that of Indian freedom from Britain, and finally to abolish the caste system within.

*　　*　　*

The Practice for the ongoing adjustment of your cause as you and the world's problems change is a variation of the Five-minute Want, and uses *the way various activities make you feel afterwards* to help you choose what your action will be the next time. Just as a child is likely to feel solidly good after eating a nutritious meal which his or her whole body wants, and only temporarily satisfied after taking candy or cocaine that he or she has learned to want, so you are likely to feel a kind of full happiness after doing things you truly want to do and only temporarily satisfied after doing things that you've only been trained to want, things that are not quite right for you.

The task in this Practice is to become sensitive to those subtle feelings, good and not so good, after you have gone through an activity (these will be forms of pleasure and pain!). If the feeling after an activity is good, use it as a signal to strengthen your commitment to that activity and its cause. If the feeling is bad, then say to yourself, "Since I feel not-so-good after this work, I must be out of touch with what I truly want to do. *If I were totally free to choose, what would I do for the world starting from this moment?*" It wouldn't hurt to start from scratch and list all the causes and activities you can think of again, or all the possible ways you might act in the disappointing situation next time, including doing nothing.

You don't even have to connect it with your "cause;" *whenever* you get the feeling that what you're doing isn't quite right for you, a feeling of uncertainty that you want to keep doing it, then, even if you're in the middle of a campaign or the whole world is pressing you to keep on with it--ask yourself those questions. "If I were free to do whatever I wanted to do, what would I want to do right now?" As you do this over and over, the lingering pain of having done something that was even slightly not right for you will lead you always to choose again, next time an activity that fits you a little better. Gradually you will choose less and less disappointing activities--that is, better and better ones for you, in which you will be more and more effective for the world because your energy, your true want, is behind them. As you continue to fit your action to your want in this way, your cause -- and you with it -- will gradually change and expand into a better and better fit until the two of you become a perfect, most effective vehicle for serving the world. You will become more and more sensitive to the way you feel about what you're doing so that after acting in your cause you will become aware of a definite body sensation, either a kind of constriction of disappointment or anxiousness or the fullness of satisfaction, a kind of joy because of that action. You are awakening to your own inner being.

Eventually you'll become as sensitive to your feelings as those monks who can smell food being cooked a mile away, and can hear an ash fall. And gradually these "feedback" feelings will come sooner until they begin to come *before* you go into action, when you are only considering it, instead of afterwards. By then, if you find yourself hesitating to undertake an action, you will be able to tell whether your reluctance is because you are afraid of the Daring thought of the action, or because it's not the right action for you. Gradually your Wanter will become more and more outspoken. Sometimes when you think of an action you might undertake you will notice that your lips are smiling or scowling without your having told them to, or that your step quickens or slows, as your inner being uses these ways of telling you what it wants. Sometimes when you think of some scary possible action a kind of knowing will come to you that you *are* going to do it, even though at that moment you are saying, "No!" And other times it will be as if a voice cried out, "No, no!" or "Yes, yes!" when the thought of a possible action comes to your mind. Eventually you will be in touch with your true wants as Socrates was with what the Greeks called his *daimonion* - only even better, for he had an inner voice that only warned him about actions it did *not* want him to take, and yours will also tell you what it *wants* you to do because it will be such a pleasure.

*　　*　　*

As you give yourself more and more fully to your inner guidance, the outer world will of course not drop its pressure on you to follow *its* training. Quite the reverse. It has worked hard to show you the habit, the mold, you are to fit into if you want its approval, and since your inner being is likely to choose activities from *outside* the mold, the outer world is likely to be offended and probably won't take it lying down. It will upscale its pressure on you. Early in your Practices you will want to give into this pressure, perhaps so much that you begin to feel you don't dare to do what you inner being says it wants you to. Thus you can end up squeezed in the middle between inner and outer forces (your inner being and the outer world) competing for your loyalty. The conflict can be severe and the pressure from both sides so great that there seems to be no happy choice you can make. There is one, though.

This is simply the same old choice between following your inner guidance or the outer world that you've made a thousand times since you left the beautiful childhood world. *Every time you choose in favor of your inner being you will feel good afterwards, you will grow, and you will become a little stronger; every choice for the outer world will make you feel a little ashamed and disappointed, will stunt you, and will make you weaker, a little less your own person.* Choose in favor of your inner being as often as you possibly can.

Even while leading a political cause, for one whole day per week Gandhi observed a day of silence during which he could focus on his truth.

In the Old Testament, when the king of Israel asked Elisha whether to slay the blinded Syrian army which had come to capture him but which had instead been duped to go to Samaria, Elisha had a choice between the King's inclination and his God's. He followed his own nonviolent Truth, told the King to give them all a hearty meal and send them back to their masters, never to harass Israel again.

"Witches" have burned for less. Nevertheless, this "right" choice will become easier and easier as you repeat it and it is rewarded with feelings of fullness and satisfaction because you are acting in accord with your own inner guidance.

*   *   *

Your Wanter should definitely have the final say about what your true cause is. However, it has to struggle for your attention against a lot of pressure from the outer world, so it can take many trials and a very long time to find that true cause if following your Wanter is all you do. To give your search more direction and speed the process along, check your current cause against the following criteria. If you find it doesn't measure up to them, try adjusting it so it does and see whether you feel better about it. In the long run, your best cause is likely to be the one that most closely meets these three standards.

1. A Good Cause

Pay attention to how you determine that your cause is *on the right side*, that you're one of the good guys, not the bad guys.

Most causes are mixtures of good and bad, right and wrong elements. Robin Hood wants to help the poor, but robs others to do it. Pro-choicers want to prevent the suffering of unwanted and poverty-stricken children, but kill fetuses to do it. Pro-lifers want to save babies but may condemn them and their mothers to miserable lives to do it. We can, then, assign the various causes a ratio of good to wrong. *Make sure your cause is high on good and very low on wrong.*

Choose Your Cause with Utmost Wisdom

And how can you decide whether elements of your cause are good or bad? Certainly not by grown-up social values; they can't help us decide how good or bad our causes are. But most of us learned some very basic values before we were five years old, well before we absorbed grown up, materialistic values. We learned about being fair and keeping your promises, about taking turns and sharing. We learned to tell bullies from underdogs, and we knew when people were being kind or mean. You need only think back to those early understandings for a few moments to get an idea of where your cause stands in relation to them. Is your cause fair to all sides? Is it on the side of the bullies or the underdogs? Is it a sharing cause or is it greedy? Is it out to hurt others or to help them? Is it more like Robin Hood or the Sheriff of Nottingham? Whom will your cause hurt, and whom will it make feel good?

Suffering is the enemy, yours and everyone else's. Will your cause ease suffering and conduce in the end to the happiness of all beings?

2. A Non-Exclusive Cause

Make sure your cause is not exclusive, that it does not set itself up as the *only* way and so define all other ways as wrong. Seeing others as wrong immediately polarizes things, makes pride and competition into issues, and sets the status quo in concrete, making it that much harder to change things. Is your cause primarily *for* and *to help* some group, as Mother Teresa's and Gandhi's were, or *against* some group, as Hitler's was? Does it love or hate more?

The South African government has wanted to help whites and *exclude blacks*. Nelson Mandela wanted *all* races to be treated fairly. His was the better cause according to the criterion of non-exclusiveness.

When Mother Teresa was asked to join an anti-war campaign she refused, saying she did not want to be *against* anything, but would gladly join a movement *for* peace.

3. A Noble Cause

Make your cause as high and noble as you can.

I once knew a good-hearted and determined woman who spent many hours of the precious time of her life trying to list all the possible moves in Canasta. She wanted to be able to *win* in the weekly card game with her friends. I also knew a writer who spent hours of his working time every week writing lengthy letters to the members of his City Council. He knew they'd have to waste time reading his letters aloud at their meetings, and he wanted to *get back at them* for passing an ordinance that he didn't like.

To my mind, these are cases of good enthusiasm gone awry out of smallness of vision. These two people's purposes were trivial and petty. While they were frittering their time away on them, Mahatma Gandhi was working to find Truth, to correct injustice and to free his people. Einstein was working toward peace of the world. Francis Moore Lappe was working for food for all. Ram Dass was working to serve humanity--and to eradicate blindness from Nepal. And so on.

Check to see where your current cause stands on this scale that goes from trivial to noble, and then connect it to the highest purpose you can think of. You can start from either end. "I'm listing the possible moves in Canasta so I can learn the principles of listing so I can teach them to some little girls so they will realize they can learn math so women and men can feel more equal." Or start at the other end with a high cause and work downward to your specific cause. "My highest cause is true democracy, so I'm working out best ways of communicating with legislators, so I'm trying out the effect of writing them lengthy letters." Once you've done this, hold the higher cause always in mind and from then on *let it mold your activities in the specific cause. Why* you do something matters much more than *what* you do, and this exercise will give your cause a good, broad why.

Ennobling your cause in this way will work to put you in touch with your deepest, true want. You are connected with everything else in the universe in many ways; in that sense you *are* the universe, and pain and happiness anywhere is *your* pain and happiness too. Your truest, deepest want is to ease that pain and bring about peace and happiness for all. Once you truly understand this, you won't be working for petty causes any more; you'll be working to save the whales, to end poverty, to give children a future--to change the world.

I asked what we are here on earth for, and someone said, "To enjoy, enjoy!" That seemed good. Another said, "To praise the Lord." And that seemed good. But still I was restless, and then I heard, in a questioning voice, "To forward evolution?" "To make a work of art, a thing of beauty, an inspiration, of your life?" Then another voice said, and it, too, sounded right, "To help others."

Choose Your Cause with Utmost Wisdom

"But," I thought," if my purpose is to help others, then those others have no role except to *be* helped," and that seemed not right. I decided maybe there was no aim that would be the same for everyone--and the "different" purposes were all the same, basically, all one, and the form mine would take was: To help humanity become more compassionate. And that to follow one path of service was probably to follow all--that to help humanity become more compassionate would be to enjoy, to praise the Lord, and all the other reasons for being here.

*　　*　　*

As you work in all these ways to understand your own feelings and discover what you truly want to do, you open yourself to be taken over by your Wanter, and if you keep it up, sooner or later your cause will grab you. It will take you over, obsess you; you won't want to leave it; you won't be able to leave it; you'll be totally in love with it. At this point, you'll be doing what you *want* to all the time. You will be having a good time. It will be fun. And your service, performed because you deeply *want* to give it, will also be the most effective you can render the world, because all of your want and energy is behind it.

Thus you are led by the pain when you are doing what is not quite right for you, and the pleasure when doing what your Wanter is pressing you to do. Led by pain and pleasure to your proper action in the world.

*　　*　　*

Quotes from great activists:

> *The best way to find yourself is to lose yourself in the service of others.*
>
> Mahatma Gandhi

> *Paint as you like and die happy.*
>
> Henry Miller

How to Think If You Want to Change the World

*It is not our part to master all the tides of the world, but to
do what is in us for the succour of those years wherein we
are set, uprooting the evil in the fields that we know, so
that those who live after may have clean earth to till.*

The Return of the King, J.R.R. Tolkien

*   *   *

Exercise 1:

If we all did what we did because we wanted to rather than
because we had to or out of need, because we were driven, our
whole world would be different and we'd be much happier beings.
Yet people seldom feel that they're doing what they want. Think
about it: Did you do what you wanted so far today? During the
last week?

The assignment in this exercise is to spend an entire weekend
doing only what you want to, using the 5-minute Want format. It
should not involve making anyone else do anything; go on the
premise that *you* are quite capable of satisfying *your* wants.
When you get Counter thoughts explaining that it's not possible
to do what you want, take them as meaning that you have *two*
wants, and use your intelligence (if you're reading this book, you
know that you have plenty of it to do this with!) to figure out how
to satisfy both. The best thing you can do for yourself and the
world right now is to promise yourself from now on to do only
what you want to--which is also to promise you will enjoy
everything you do. You'll have to do a lot of figuring out how to
keep the promise, but after all, that's what your intelligence is for,
and--it will be worth it.

Exercise 2:

All through the day, every time you finish or stop one activity,
you are already deciding what you will do next. You can do this
either with full awareness, or automatically. For this exercise,
begin to catch these break points, these moments of decision,
and stop yourself from automatically going into the next activity.
Instead, ask yourself questions like this:

- What's the most *loving* thing I can do next?

Choose Your Cause with Utmost Wisdom

- Of all the things I could do next, which would be most *helpful* to me and to the world?

- What's the most *noble* thing I can do next?

Exercise 3:

If you have not yet found your true current cause, ask yourself, "If I could save one aspect of the world a day, what would I save first?"

VIII

Build Beliefs that Support You and Your Work

The Practice: *Strengthen your faith in the way you want things to be--and lighten your hold on the facts.*

Our beliefs help determine how effective we are in changing the world. They shape our perceptions, thoughts, actions, and even our ideas about what is real and the truth. We run our lives by them and, according to spiritual traditions, they may even be a medium through which we actually create the "outer" world. It is vitally important for our activism that we learn how to take charge of and use these powerful mental tools.

This Practice is to learn the best use of two essential varieties of belief: *faith* and *belief in facts*. It nearly reverses the way most of us in the West deal with these two kinds of belief, so before we describe the Practice itself we will talk a little about the difference between Western and Eastern approaches to reality and explain why such a reversal is a good idea.

In the West, generally, it seems obvious to us that what we can sense--what we touch, or see, for example--is solid, tangible, and--well, *real*. After all, seeing is believing!

In addition, we take it as being separate from us, as existing in our "outer" world. The very act of sensing something seems to set up a separation between us and it, for whenever we sense something there are always two--ourselves, and what we sense. Thus what seems like an "outer" world of material things determines our inner belief about what is real.

This view of reality *denies our power*. With this view, we have no part in designing or building reality; it simply appears to us through no wish or act of our own.

There's another view, common to many of the Eastern religions, that says just the opposite: *Mind creates matter*. According to it, the basic reality is a vast, intelligent, *non-material* Force which created and still continually re-creates the material world. This Force is not separate from what It creates; It is inherent in every part of Its creation, including us humans, and we share in Its creative power, for our belief in things that do not currently exist in the material world tends to create those things in this outer world. We believe first and then we see.

Create the belief and the reality follows.

William James

. . .all the founders of quantum physics were basically Platonists. That is, they believed that the world of things is a shadowy projection of a vaster, invisible reality that is nonmaterial.

Chopra, Deepak, <u>Quantum Healing</u>, p. 129

If this view is correct, *we're influencing the world through our beliefs all the time* but, because we don't think our minds have any power, our influencing is heedless and unplanned. We would be wise to take responsibility for the way we think, and *learn to believe in what we want to be true* so that through our beliefs, we could create the world we want.

Belief that what we *want* to happen *will* happen is what we call faith.

This view empowers us, for according to it we are doers and shakers. If we believe deeply enough in what we want to have happen, our belief will draw outer reality toward it and actually change the world. Faith is one of the most powerful assets an activist can have.

A man who has solved the problem of identification. . .no longer makes the mistake that perception is flooding in to create his awareness; rather, awareness is going out to create his perceptions. By returning our minds to the depths of awareness, where we are free to make our own experience, yoga opens up the possibility of uprooting all suffering at its source.

Chopra, Deepak, <u>Unconditional Life</u>, p. 113

How to Think If You Want to Change the World

Look at these worlds spinning
out of nothingness
That is within your power.

   Rumi, quoted as frontspiece in Chopra, Deepak, <u>Ageless Body</u>

I believe that both the Western and the Eastern views of reality are valid within their own frameworks, and both can be useful in our work to become more effective activists. They simply represent two kinds of truth--on the one hand the *facts* of the everyday, material world, on the other hand the *wants* and *faith*, or *mental truths*, of the spiritual world. We need them both. Belief in facts helps us get along in the everyday world, and faith supports us in the spiritual world. Both kinds of truth are absolutely essential to full and effective human living and activism.

   . . .the method of non-violence is based on the conviction
that the universe is on the side of justice. It is this deep
faith in the future that causes the nonviolent resister to
accept suffering without retaliation.

          Martin Luther King, <u>A Testament of Hope</u>

Truth and non-violence are not possible without a living
belief in God, meaning a self-existent, all-knowing, living
Force which inheres in every other force known to the world
and which depends on none, and which will live when all
other forces may conceivably perish or cease to act. I am
unable to account for my life without belief in this all-
embracing Light.

          Mahatma Gandhi, 201, p. 49

         *   *   *

How can we develop such faith? Faith begins with pain and passion and matures through struggle.

The pain comes first, with your perception of some unbearable injustice and suffering.

Build Beliefs that Support You and Your Work

- Children are starving.

- The poor are oppressed.

- Corporations are destroying the earth.

- Whole families--grandparents, parents, and children--are being brutally killed in genocide.

Treasure the pain, difficult or unbearable though it might be, because it fuels the faith that you will develop, and the deeper the pain the deeper and more effective that faith will be--assuming that you develop faith.

The passion comes next, the passion of your wish, your earnest desire that the injustice be righted and the suffering eased: "I *want* there to be enough for all!" The intensity of this desire is commensurate with the intensity of your pain.

At this point the struggle begins, for there is now an excruciating discrepancy between your wish and the painful outer reality. You *want* the children to be fed, and in *fact* they are starving. The two ideas can scarcely co-exist; yet you cannot give either up. The fact *cannot* be denied, and the wish *will* not be denied, and you're caught in the difficult struggle between them.

Difficult as it is, this struggle over whether the inner or outer world is to have primacy is necessary to the development of faith; if you don't go through it and finally commit to your wish--while still not denying the facts!--you cannot be said really to have won a faith but only to have bought a conventional belief, as we buy so many of our ideas.

This period of struggle is also a *dangerous* time in the development of faith, for it's possible to stay stuck in the struggle indefinitely, and you may never make it to a faith. The sequel is not at all certain. The outer world will test your new faith's strength by presenting overwhelming evidence that it's invalid, that the painful facts you want to change are stronger than your faith is. Your cause will suffer grueling defeats; Violence and suffering will surround you, pressing you hard to believe they are the only reality. "There *is* suffering!" "There *is* injustice!" Every problem that comes up in your life, large or small, will tempt you to give up on your wish and believe in the problem instead. You will not always be strong enough to hold to your wish. Over time you may become numb, a burned out case, resigned to the injustice of life. You may just shut the painful facts out of mind, as so many of us do, and live on with a shrunken but tolerable awareness. You may do the unthinkable, give up on your wish entirely, and then become so depressed that you die of a broken heart.

Or, after days (or maybe years!) of conflict, you may finally discover a truth beyond the facts, an overall love and goodness about the universe that is greater than the injustice you perceive, and includes it. It may be a belief that things will be better in some future time, or that all the suffering has meaning and serves some worthwhile purpose, or that there is a Higher Power Whose reasons we cannot comprehend but Who works always for the good of us all--or it may be all of these.

> *Here in my heart, I do believe*
> *We shall overcome someday*
> *We'll walk hand in hand someday*
> *We shall live in peace someday*
> *We are not afraid, we are not afraid*
> *We shall overcome someday*

> Pete Seeger, Frank Hamilton, Guy Carawan, Zilphia Horton
> Sung by civil rights activists during the 1960's.

> *When I despair, I remember that all through history the*
> *way of truth and love has always won. There have been*
> *tyrants and murderers and for a while they can seem*
> *invincible. But, in the end, they always fall. Think of it.*
> *Always.*

> Mohandas Gandhi

This kind of belief is what we call *faith.*

> *Children are starving* (fact).

> *I want there to be enough for all* (wish).

> *The Power that sees each sparrow's fall loves and cares*
> *for every one of those children* (faith).

*   *   *

Once you discover even an inkling of such a faith, and you feel sure that it is something good and that it's a right belief for you, nourish it, support it, *do everything you can to strengthen your faith in it!* Work to believe it fully, to give your Wanter, your divine Wish, that power!

Take as your goal a total belief that this thing you now want to believe in is true, a *knowing* that it is.

Make sure that it will not be *blind* faith. Make sure you're not believing something out of social pressure or in rebellion to social pressure. Believe it only because it feels right to you to do so, because it seems to fit who you are. Your faith must be a matter of *your* decision, *your* heart and *your* head, chosen with your eyes wide open, not closed.

I'm talking about the kind of deep faith which a few inmates of Nazi concentration camps maintained, the kind that a Tibetan monk has who, after twenty years in a grim Chinese prison, says that his only fear is that he will stop loving the guards who torment him. Of those who have undergone horrors like these, only a few have been able to keep such faith. But that's the kind of faith the activist needs to have.

You can begin by making a kind of seed statement of faith, describing what you want to believe as clearly, powerfully, and briefly as you can, so you can make a mantra of it.

- The universe is benign.
- We shall have peace.
- People are basically good.

Make your statement broad enough and general enough that the mind will be able to bring it about without opposing too many of your other beliefs, challenging as few "facts" as possible.

I have faith that justice will prevail.

Not:

I have faith we'll win this specific court case.

Make it broad and general enough that there's room for it to be fulfilled in ways that will surprise you.

Make it positive rather than negative, for the unconscious mind does not understand negatives; it simply leaves them out, so that your conscious decision, "I will not" becomes, in the unconscious, "I will," and calls forth the very opposite of the idea you're working for.

Mother Teresa refused to join a movement against war, but said she would gladly join one *for* peace.

Once you have such a clear, concise idea of what you want to have faith in, develop and strengthen your faith in every way you can think of. *Visualize it, commit to work for it, reiterate it, use adversity to strengthen it,* and *be happy in it.*

1. *Visualize* what the world will be like when your faith is entirely fulfilled, and learn to *see* only that world now.

We all see the world through a picture that we superimpose on the world. Your job is to *change that picture*, to dissolve whatever negative is in it and substitute your vision, the world as you want it to become. If our beliefs tend to become reality, it's important to do strong visualizations of the things we want to have happen and *see* them around us now. So work to *see* your truth in the world. Find evidence for your belief--there's always some evidence, if you are open to it - and steep yourself in it.

> *A young woman felt a lot of pain because actions that she had experienced led her to think that people were calloused and insensitive to the needs of people with disabilities. She decided to look for evidence that people are actually loving and caring. After some effort, to her surprise, it didn't take long for her to think of enough things and remember enough incidents to convince her that it was just as likely that people were loving and caring as it was that they were cruel or thoughtless. She chose the former belief because it made her happier; once she accepted that belief, she started to see more instances that supported it, didn't feel the despair she had felt with her old beliefs, and found more opportunities to make a difference.*

2. *Commit to work* for what you believe in, to do everything you can to make the world of facts fit your faith rather than the other way around.

Work out the implications of your faith and dwell upon them. What else must happen, *will* happen, when your vision becomes a reality?

Then promise yourself that you will work to make these implications manifest in this world. Remember that, as St. James said, "Faith without works is dead," and agree that, for your part, you will do everything you can to support your faith with actions.

*If you have built castles in the air, your work will not be
lost; that is where they should be. Now put the foundations
under them.*

Henry David Thoreau, <u>Walden</u>

*While they were saying among themselves it cannot be
done, it was done.*

Helen Keller

3.   Reiterate the statement of your faith like a mantra so that it
      becomes more and more solidly true for you.

You can learn to believe anything you want to, and one way to do
it is to tell it to yourself over and over. Do you remember learning
"facts" like this when you memorized them in school?

Five times six *is* thirty.

Paris *is* the capital of France.

You can make your faith just as true as these "facts" for you.
Instruct yourself to believe it. Stand in front of your mirror and
say, "I *want* this belief and I'm *getting* it;" look hard and repeat
your statement again and again; dissolve all doubts, negatives,
Counter thoughts into a single-minded, unsplit *will* to know that
this belief is true"

Repeat your statement 1000 times and you'll begin to believe it.
Tell it to yourself 100,000 times if you have to.

*Swami Rama repeated his mantra 140,000 times before he
went to demonstrate that he could move a dial from a
distance at the Menninger Institute.*

Elmer and Alyce Green, <u>Beyond Biofeedback</u>, p. 213

4.   Use every instance in which things go badly to re-affirm your
      faith.

Welcome such problems and drawbacks to use for strengthening
your faith even further. Whenever you hear bad news, instead of
repeating that news, even in your head, repeat your faith. Hold to
it against all evidence because, if you are open and look for it, for
every evidence that the world is one way, there is always evidence
supporting the opposite view of the world, and your belief can
affect those around you to make the belief true.

The executives gave themselves huge bonuses and then quit, leaving longtime employees without money, jobs, or pensions.

PEOPLE ARE BASICALLY GOOD.

The election was unfair and we lost.

JUSTICE WILL PREVAIL.

Forty nations are at war right now.

WE SHALL HAVE PEACE.

The victims were tortured to death.

THIS IS A WORLD OF LOVE.

The outcome of every such challenge to your faith affects the strength and efficacy of that faith. Every time you falter and despairingly believe in one view of the apparent reality of a problem--a view which is opposite of your belief -- your faith weakens and the trance of belief in the outer world of facts deepens. Every time you hold to your belief in the good in spite of bad things happening, your faith becomes stronger and you gain one more measure of freedom and power--and *influence the world that much toward your positive vision of it.* If the belief is total and unshakable, then everything that happens feeds it, strengthens it. You don't go up and down with every up and down in worldly affairs; you stay firm.

Within each experience of pain or negativity is the opportunity to challenge the perception that lies behind it, the fear that lies behind it, and to choose to learn with wisdom.

Zukav, <u>Seat of the Soul</u>, p. 237

5. Finally, to put the seal on your true and unshakable faith, *pay off by letting yourself have the reward that was promised.*

For you created your faith in order to stop your pain about the way things were; the implicit deal was, "If I could have this wish--that is, that justice prevail, or the universe be benign, or people be basically good--THEN I will no longer feel the pain; I will be happy."

Well, you now know that your belief is true; you *see* the wish fulfilled, the balance of the world righted. Any breach of happiness compromises your part of the bargain, your faith; you must pay off on your promise by allowing yourself to be happy and that, in turn, will strengthen your faith even more, making its manifestation that much truer. If you are not happy, your faith is compromised.

In summary, then, these are the steps to develop and defend the faith to support you and your work: make sure your faith is in something good and that it is truly yours as you craft a strong, brief statement of it and *see* it as already fulfilled; commit to work for it; reiterate it; take every problem as a challenge to reaffirm it; and become happy. We're talking about a deep commitment here to making what you want be true. You are to compel the world to fit your ideal, not vice versa.

*   *   *

Now let's deal with the other half of this Practice, which is to loosen our hold on the "facts."

Many writers have described the human structure of fact about the everyday world as at once a blessing and a curse. Facts are a blessing because without a body of facts that we agree are true, we'd have nothing in common to base our conversations on and we wouldn't be able to communicate; we'd be in a true Babel. And it forms a stable base of common knowledge that we can stand on in order to change that very structure for the better.

But facts are also a curse, in that once we've set them up, we seem impelled to cling to them and defend them against all other possibilities. Facts then become a prison that limits and stifles us from entertaining the beliefs of faith.

The greatest imprisonment of all is the imprisonment of the mind, and the religious, social and educational systems of this world, with very few exceptions, train people to imprison themselves in their own thinking, and in a restricted belief system.

> Jonathan Parker, The Pathways to Mastership: In search of Enlightenment (first of a 12-CD set)

One, first there was earth. Two, then there was land, sea, and sky. 3. Then there were countries. 4. Then was Germany. 5. [Then there were] East Germany and west

Germany. The categories we make gather momentum and are very hard to overthrow. We build our own shared realities and then we become victims of them--blind to the fact that they are constructs, ideas.

Ellen Langer, <u>Mindfulness</u>, p. 11

. . .opinions all share the same emotional quality: They are strongly adhered to as positions. Having established a position, we accept what matches our position and find reasons to reject what does not match it. Holding to our own opinion may appear to be "independent thinking" but it prevents us from questioning these views.

Tarthang Tulku, <u>Ways of Enlightenment</u>, pp. 117-18

Insofar as you are attached to certain facts as the only truth, your job as an activist is to detach, loosen your hold. *Lighten up!* That's the second part of this Practice.

Consider, for example, that some "facts" may not be absolutely true.

At the medical school graduation ceremony of a doctor I know, the dean announced to his class "half of what we just taught you is wrong; we just don't know which half."

Different societies, starting with assumptions slightly different from ours, have come up with quite different "facts." I've read of a tribe whose members "knew" for a "fact," complete with proofs, that sexual intercourse had nothing to with babies, because they so strongly assumed that babies were spontaneously conceived by women.

So it is good to *hold our "facts" very lightly* rather than settling on them as absolute truth. We could hold them the way scientists hold their hypotheses, as provisional truths to use as long as they are useful, to be replaced when more useful ideas come along. Try this as an exercise: whenever you find yourself stating a "fact," that is, saying that something is so, mentally add, "That is, within my present belief system!"

What we see depends on the theories we use to interpret our observations.

Albert Einstein, quoted in <u>Self-Aware Universe</u>
by Amit Goswami, p. 141

Build Beliefs that Support You and Your Work

. . .the world is a map of all that people agreed to be real,
with the exclusion of all that they agreed to be unreal.

Deepak Chopra, <u>Unconditional Life</u>, p. 232

People one by one come to see that all the separate
problems are symptoms of a set of assumptions about the
nature of reality.

Marilyn Ferguson, <u>Aquarian Conspiracy</u>

The key to discovery lies in accepting no answer as final;
within all we know, many new possibilities await discovery.

Tarthang Tulku, <u>Knowledge of Freedom</u>, p. 26

*   *   *

We can become the master of facts rather than their servant.

This is a position of great power. In Tibetan Buddhism it is felt
that two things are necessary before a Bodhisattva can help
others: her heart must overflow with compassion, and she must
understand sunyata, the Void, the "space" where rules, concepts,
facts, do not obtain. In this space she is not biased by
emotionality and so is free to see clearly how each suffering being
can best be helped and to implement that help.

Getting to that point is a matter far beyond the scope of this
book, but we make a beginning in that direction when we learn to
keep an open mind and reject no ideas out of hand, allowing
them all to come in and stand next to our present facts so we can
see how they might interact and come together to make a larger
truth.

We've settled for life in a mote of dust when the vastness of
the universe is waiting for us.

Tarthang Tulku, <u>Knowledge of Freedom</u>

*   *   *

Quotes from great activists:

Because of your unbelief: for verily I say unto you, If ye have faith as a grain of mustard seed, ye shall say unto this mountain, Remove hence to yonder place; and it shall remove; and nothing shall be impossible unto you.

Jesus of Nazareth (Matthew 17:20)

All of us are chained in such a cave--seeing only shadows on the wall, imagining those shadows to comprise our whole universe. Yet the soul of every man does possess the power of learning the truth and the organ to see it with. If we could but free our perceptions from their shackles, we could at last contemplate reality and that supreme splendor which we have called the good."

Plato

The question is one of faith, of choosing our own "grade of significance." Our ordinary mind always tries to persuade us that we're nothing but acorns and that our greatest happiness will be to become bigger, fatter, shinier acorns, but that is of interest only to pigs. Our faith gives us knowledge of something much better: that we can become oak trees.

Lech Walesa, A Way of Hope

All pain comes from false beliefs.

Ghose Aurobindo

All trouble comes from disbelief in the Universe.

Ernest Holmes, The Science of Mind, p. 498

We can change our beliefs. Usually it happens when our experience is not consistent with our opinion. Another way to change is to just choose another opinion. When you discover that a certain belief is blocking progress, the best way to unlock yourself is to change the belief.

Robert Regis Dvorak, Experimental Drawing

Build Beliefs that Support You and Your Work

Exercise 1:

Play with faith and facts by making up some beliefs that would serve you in the following ways:

a. What beliefs would make you *happy?* Don't put up with any beliefs that make you sad!

> *I have faith that everything will have a happy ending. When bad things happen--men are cruel, children are hurt, people suffer and die--I simply know that's not the end; it can't be, because I know the end will be happy. I don't take the sad "ending" as the end.*

b. What beliefs do you *need* to live and work? Without meaningful beliefs we die.

The activist needs to believe that better things are coming.

She needs to believe there is good underlying the bad.

He has to believe the situation can be better and that his efforts can make a difference.

I have to believe we can change our way of thinking to bring about peace.

c. What beliefs would be *useful* to you?

Physicists hold onto Newton's laws of motion not because they're true (it is now known that they aren't exactly true) but because they're so useful.

List five or six of your major beliefs and ask of each one, "Is this belief *serving* me? Is it useful? does it help or hinder me in working toward my goals?

What beliefs would you hold if you chose them according to their results: the actions they led you to and the results those actions brought about?

Believing you're helpless leads to giving up. Believing there's always a chance leads to hanging on. Which is better for the world?

Ye shall know them by their fruits.

Matthew 7:16

d. What *childhood beliefs* did you give up that you now wish were true?

In the beautiful childhood world from the first chapter, we believed in good things like love, security, fairness, and were disappointed when they turned out not to obtain in the grown-up world. We accepted their loss out of necessity, in order to get into the grown-up world, but it was disloyal of us to abandon them. Our job was and is to defend our ideals like knights defending the Holy Grail, and their turning out not to be "true" is a test of us. Insofar as we don't defend them, we're living by old ideas of limitation; we're like robots. And our work as activists is compromised.

> Can we believe in love?
>
> > Twenty years in prison couldn't stop the Tibetan monk from loving the guards who tormented him.
>
> Can we believe in security?
>
> > I am a precious child of the universe; nothing bad can happen to me.
>
> Can we believe in fairness?
>
> > Justice will flow down like a river.

e. What facts do you *wish were not so*? Find a belief that counters them and let it work for you.

Children are starving! IN THE OVERALL SCHEME OF THINGS IT WILL SOMEHOW BE MADE RIGHT.

Men are cruel and uncaring. AT BASE, ALL MEN ARE KIND AND CARING.

Exercise 2:

Decide on some beliefs that will *protect* you so that you can go on being effective and happy when things go badly. Any old belief can carry you through the good times. The test is in the bad times.

For a long time I have assumed that people are basically good and that any destructive, negative, cruel behaviors that come out are superimposed on that goodness out of some kind of fear. But that's just an assumption. And sometimes that assumption is tested.

I recently had occasion to reread parts of *The Gulag Archipelago* about men who cheerfully compare the different methods of torture they use, about the ingenious ways in which they torment their prisoners, and about Stalin and how millions were killed because of his paranoia--and it gave me a very sad feeling, and for a few moments I doubted that people are basically good. But then, it seemed to me, *what's the alternative?* If we believe that people are basically evil, we might as well cash in our chips right now; life's not worth living. If we believe people are basically good, then at least we have a chance because we can at least try to bring order to our world. So I decide to believe that people are basically good.

Exercise 3:

List a couple of beliefs you feel quite sure about, and for each one ask yourself:

- Is this a belief with heart?

- Is this the richest, most beautiful belief I can think of?

- If I use this belief, will I explore further, or will it be finished? Does this belief offer me mystery and challenge or will it just answer everything and close it down?

Exercise 4:

When you're confronted with an opinion that seems strange and wrong to you, do you automatically defend your own opinion, or do you let yourself feel curious and interested in the strange opinion and consider how it might fit in with or change what you already think? Think of an instance in which you did one or the other and ask yourself: Which of the two makes you feel better?

Defending often makes people feel more secure, but also gradually isolates them in a cocoon. Letting new ideas in is scary but brings its own feeling of satisfaction, even exhilaration. How about you? Do you feel better or not so good when you're defending your own viewpoint? How about afterwards? How do you feel when you're letting a strange new opinion in?

Exercise 5:

Which beliefs, if held by all the people in the world, would lead to a happier world? If everyone believed everyone else was basically good and sent loving thoughts toward them, would the world be better? What if everyone believed there were only enough supplies for a few and everyone else was trying to get them?

Elizabeth Kubler-Ross felt so strongly that belief in an after-life would help the world that she left her job and devoted the rest of her life to spreading the word about Near Death Experiences.

Exercise 6:

What effect do you think you as an individual would have on the course of history if you believed evil was going to win in the world? What effect do you think you would have if you had rock-firm faith that good is going to win?

Exercise 7:

Really believe one of your beliefs.

There's quite a difference between "sort of" believing and *knowing*. If I walk to the edge of a cliff and look over the edge, I *know* that if I take another step I'll fall. It therefore affects what I do. If, on the other hand, I read that the universe is infinitely vast and the nearest other galaxy is millions of light years away, I sort-of believe it, but I don't do much if anything differently because of it.

- What if you *knew* that what you had faith in was *really* true? Would that lighten your heart, make you happier?

- What if we *knew* that our every thought and action influences the world toward war or peace?

- What if now you really *know* you can change your beliefs?

From now on as you move forward, you will work upon the foundation of having *decided* your faith.

IX

Go Whole-Heartedly into Whatever You Do

The Practice: *Purposely put yourself fully into whatever you're doing at any given moment. When you feel a reluctance to continue any activity, immediately choose either to commit more fully to the activity, or put yourself into something else; do not allow yourself to be divided.*

The goal of this Practice is that you *give yourself totally to whatever you're doing, all the time.* As you go through your day, either *go* into each activity all the way or *don't go* into it at all; don't allow yourself to go into it halfheartedly, while not wanting to do it or wishing you were doing something else.

In the morning, when it's time to get up, either get up all the way, with enthusiasm, or don't get up, stay in bed, with enthusiasm; don't allow yourself to get up while hating it, nor to sleep in while feeling guilty. Do one thing or the other, all the way. If you join a protest march, then march with all your heart, with enthusiasm, with fire. Stay to the very end, push it, give it your best shot. And make it you own idea; *you* march; don't be a listless, automatic trudger who's being dragged along; put your initiative into it.

Lots of people want to change the world--*sort of!* Don't be diluted like that; march with a *definite* tread, because you *definitely* want to change the world!

On the other hand, if you're *not* going to march, *don't* march with enthusiasm as well. Do something else, a NOT-march, with all your heart. This is *your life*, and *your world*, right now, so whatever you're doing at this moment is *the most important thing in the world right now.* Put yourself into it with passion. Let yourself burn.

Ordinarily, we do not go fully into what we do. We act, yes--but with only part of our energy, half dragging our feet, like teenagers being forced to clean their rooms. We go to work but with reluctance, not enthusiasm; we want a better world--but not enough to go for it; for every project, we have a dozen doubts and reservations; in every going forward we also hold back. Think of what we're doing to ourselves when we do that! One part of us is saying, "Go ahead and do this thing!" while another says, "No, I don't want to; back off!" so we're tearing ourselves apart inside, *splitting ourselves*, pouring our energy out to *oppose itself* so that obviously we can have little or no overall impact in the world. We all have vast energy but it can't be effective when used against itself and so it is wasted. It's awesome to think of the energy we human beings dribble away by qualifying everything we do--by backpedaling, backing up, being reluctant, doing things but not doing them, thinking of Pat when we're with Chris.

Our conflict between going into and holding back from what we do is one aspect of the Great Split that is at the base of all our troubles and runs through all of our being and our society. It is the same split we saw between our two ways of thinking, and between Daring and Counter thoughts; it is the gulf between the beautiful childhood world and the "realistic" grown up world; it even goes into our physical bodies and brains, affecting our use of our left and right sides. It has become so profound and subtle that maintaining it is almost an instinct with us.

It would obviously be a great benefit to ourselves and the world if we were to heal this split--pull ourselves together!--and all the Practices in this book aim toward that goal. Yet it is a scary thing to attempt it. Healing the split requires that you drop all reservations and qualifications and excuses about what you do and throw yourself into it, all the way--pull out all the stops, *jump* off the cliff, face the great leopard! But that's exactly what society so impressed upon you *not* to do. Society told you to be cautious and hold back, to be afraid of going too far. In your deep, learned fear of the beautiful childhood world you developed this split exactly to *prevent* yourself from going too fully into things lest you become too fully alive, too whole and powerful. That training went deep for most of us, and we're more afraid of defying it than we know. To go ahead with this Practice in the face of it is Daring and can be very difficult. You must be highly motivated to succeed in it.

Look to your motivation then if you undertake this difficult Practice; it will soon be tested. Our whole identity in the world, our "ego," is based upon the split--that is, upon reservations, separations, limits; this Practice aims to eliminate all of this and thus to eliminate ego. Naturally, as soon as "ego" sees what you're up to, it will mount desperate resistances to the Practice which is out to undermine it--and all you have to hold against it is your will. Your motivation. Your stamina. Your persistence. Your determination.

There is a catch, though, in the building up of motivation to become Whole-Hearted. It is this: that you must *want* Whole-Heartedness very much if you are to withstand the difficulties of attaining it, and that's exactly what this ego stresses to avoid--*wanting* anything *whole-heartedly*. We're all halfhearted about wanting to save ourselves and the world, and before we can become Wholehearted, we must *whole-heartedly* want to be Whole-Hearted. Of course, when we reach that point we will already have achieved Whole-Heartedness, so the discipline will turn out to be not so difficult after all.

The *Practice* of Whole-Heartedness and the *wanting* to be Whole-Hearted go together, then; therefore, you must build up your commitment, your *want* to be Whole-Hearted, right along with the direct Practice of Whole-Heartedness itself.

Do whatever you must, then, to build up your motivation. You may be able to do it by remembering what's at stake here: your life, whether you are to live it or be half dead, and your world, whether you are to be effective in helping it. It may motivate you to look forward to what it will feel like when you are Whole-Hearted; there *is* a whole world of joy and power on the other side of the split. It may help to realize that there is an immense driving force dormant in you, the same power, an urgency and a wanting, that you denied in the childhood compromise we explained in the first chapter, and that that power can be awakened. It usually shows itself only in emergencies, when people can sometimes do things they never thought they could, but it's also possible to claim and develop it on purpose. If you can wake it up and connect it to your work for the world you can achieve anything you want.

If you want to do this Practice, then, do whatever it takes to motivate yourself. Build up your intensity and your enthusiasm about *anything*. Realize that giving your whole self to whatever you are doing will save your life. Make it a life and death matter to you, as those monks do who carry rope and knives with them when they do their meditative running in cruel, high mountains.

They commit to hang or disembowel themselves if their commitment fails and they do not fulfill their pledge to run.

A master and his student sat beside a river. The master had long urged the student to increase his motivation but the young man seemed not to understand what he meant. At last the master seized him by the hair and pushed his head under water, holding it there for many seconds while the young man thrashed and struggled to get free. At last he let him up, and told him sternly, "As much as you wanted air when you were underwater, so much must you want enlightenment!"

If we do our part by building up our motivation, then we will be helped from the other side of the split, by our *memory*. For we weren't always half-Hearted. We were all born *whole-hearted*, going for what we wanted without reservation. As babies, when we were hungry or felt a pin in our diapers, did we dilute what we wanted? Did we deny it or worry about what people would think of us, or psychoanalyze it or tell ourselves we couldn't have it? No. We cried out with all our hearts. We *went* for it, all the way, sucking, screaming, kicking with all our might. We were intense and totally committed. Only later were we trained to need the approval of others in order to survive and to hold back in everything we did--that is, we learned the Violent attitude!--and that training has nearly obliterated our recollection of the earlier time. But not quite. The memory of what it is like to be Wholehearted is still there within us all, however diluted, denied, covered over it may be. If you *want* Whole-Heartedness strongly enough, your want will resonate with that sleeping memory and awaken it, and like a hungry lion it will leap up, seize you and unite with your want. Then you will be able to heal the split.

*   *   *

The direct Practice for Whole-Heartedness has two parts. The first is *purposely to put yourself fully into whatever you're doing at any given moment.*

First, of course, you yourself must choose what you're going to do; you may choose anything at all, but once you have chosen, put yourself fully into it. Put yourself into it in such a way that *you know what it is that you're doing* (writing a letter, taking a walk) and *you're doing it on purpose*, so that if someone asks, "What are you doing?" you can say, with definiteness, "Now I'm writing a letter!" "Now I'm buying the groceries!" "Now I'm making a snack to eat while working on my book!" and so on. Thus, if you decide to carry water, you commit yourself to carry water; you do the job vigorously and thoroughly and enjoy it all the way and you don't fudge. If you can't do that, you don't carry water; you do something else you *can* be wholehearted about, so that you're either in or out of an activity, never "in but I don't want to be," "out but I wish I were in."

I once watched a dance troupe rehearsing its routine; from my naive point of view it was doing a pretty good job. Then the director arrived and one glance at the performance told him what was needed; he leaped onto the stage and *ordered* the dancers to put fire, energy, excitement, into their dance. He showed them how he wanted them to *stamp* their feet when they stamped, to *kick* when they kicked, to *slide* when they slid. When they started up again they were like different people; they had been dolls before and now came to life; they developed charisma; they were electrifying. I wanted to cheer, or run down the aisle to dance *with* them. Energy! Enthusiasm! Whole-Heartedness! That's what I want you to generate for yourself in this Practice. Put yourself into your activity or take yourself out of it without holding back. Do it until you're totally one with your action, whatever it is:

> There was a little girl
>
> Who had a little curl
>
> Right in the middle of her forehead.
>
> When she was good she was very, very good.
>
> And when she was bad, she was horrid!

*   *   *

The second part of this Practice is to deal with the "reluctance's" that will arise after you've put yourself into an activity and are working along in it. These will range from mild feelings of discouragement, urges to quit and need for snacks, to sudden fatigue, stomach aches and headaches, and complete, debilitating blocks. One hit me several weeks ago as a sudden, very sharp, never-to-be-explained and completely unjustified pain in the *ankle*. They are whatever comes up that tempts you to split your attention away from what you are doing.

As soon as you catch one of these, stop!

These reluctance's are of course our old friends, Counter thoughts, and *they come exactly when some creative insight or Daring thought about the activity is about to surface and you are about to become Whole Hearted in it.* They are designed exactly to demand part of your attention so that can't happen. Our usual reaction when they come is, obligingly, to split. We pay grudging attention to them while struggling to go on with the activity or, we quit the activity to go gratify them while feeling guilty. Either way, of course, we're longer Whole Hearted in anything. The Counter thought has succeeded!

Don't let that happen. Whenever you catch a reluctance, immediately *choose* either it or your activity and go into that choice without reservation, dropping the other choice completely. *Do not allow yourself to be divided; do not keep on with the activity reluctantly; do not give in to the reluctance reluctantly either.* Do one or the other either all the way or not at all.

*   *   *

The rewards of Whole-Heartedness are great. To mention only three of them: power, invulnerability, and joy--three things that mythical heroes strove to attain.

In a world in which everyone else is double-directed, one who is single-minded has great power. He or she is one-pointed instead of diffused, concentrating all energies in a single, correct direction, like a laser in a field of ordinary light bulbs. The power of such Wholeheartedness frees and enables people to do incredible things. A mother can lift a car off her child. A boy can face down a tank. A guerrilla fighter can go against all his body instincts and mutilate himself rather than betray his cause.

Many years ago a Viet Cong peasant was captured by Vietnamese troops and tortured to force him to give the names of his friends. Fearing that he might somehow give out the names while unconscious, the prisoner took a knife and *cut out his tongue* so he should not be able to betray himself. His captors called a surgeon who stitched the tongue back in. But that night the prisoner *cut it out again*, and this time, it seemed, it could not be replaced.

Wholeheartedness makes us invulnerable to the forces of Violence. Oppressors like nothing better than to see us undecided, in the middle, like donkeys who can't decide between two piles of hay; that way we're much easier to push in one direction or the other. People who are Wholehearted can't be pushed around; they can't be controlled; they serve no other master than their chosen cause and the oppressor has no weapons that can hurt them.

And Wholeheartedness is joyous. It may be that the greatest truth you can know is that feeling of aliveness, rightness, completeness that comes when you've let yourself be carried out of your smaller self in the service of your cause and can throw yourself into action for it. Changing the world is not a duty, that we should go to it grimly and grudgingly and sadly, feeling woebegone and sorry about it. No, it's a call to high adventure, one that will take everything we can joyously give it, that gives us a chance to burn, like great torches, and to feel the joy of the encounter. We can all hear that call; we truly want to be involved in the struggle; we *want* noble causes to throw ourselves into.

I have seen people fight for the rights of blind people. I have seen them compete to become astronauts. To save the world is a cause and an adventure even more compelling, more difficult, more righteous than going into outer space; to throw yourself into it is a joy. And once you've felt that joy, you will always want it again. You will *look* for the injustice in the world, your project, your cause, so you can connect your passion to it again, so that you can throw yourself once more into action. You'll be like the knights of Arthur's court who sought our injustices because they so wanted to commit themselves to their cause.

Oh, for an ocean to drown in! ...

T. S. Eliot

Those knights had melded; they had *become* the desire to redress injustice, and their wanting and their cause were one. That's probably the biggest personal reward of becoming Wholehearted, that *it is so much fun*, that you *want* to give your all to your cause, that when you are not connected to it you feel closed in, imprisoned, like a greyhound kept in a box within view of a long, hard beach upon which it is never allowed to run, and that when you connect Wholeheartedly with your cause again, you are like that greyhound released, so that it can run, and run, and let itself go, all the way, in the work it was born to do.

*   *   *

Quotes from great activists:

Grant thee according to thine own heart, and fulfill all they counsel.

Psalm 20:4

Blessed are those who hunger and thirst for righteousness, because it is they who will be satisfied.

Matthew 5:6

There is in all hearts a desire to live a significant life, to serve a great idea and sacrifice oneself for a noble cause, to feel the thrill of spiritual unity with one's fellows and to act in accordance therewith. We all wish for strenuous action and the exercise of courage and fortitude, to be carried away by the enthusiasm of daring. We all love to undergo a common discipline and hardship for the sake of a fine ideal; to be in good effective order; to be strong, generous and self-reliant; to be physically fit, with body, mind and soul harmoniously working together for a great purpose, thus becoming a channel of immense energies. Under such conditions, the whole personality is alert, conscious, unified and living profoundly, richly and exaltedly. Then one can be truly and gloriously happy.

Richard B. Gregg, <u>The Power of Nonviolence</u>, p. 93

With my whole heart I have sought thee: O let me not wander from thy commandments.

Psalm 119:10

*   *   *

Exercise 1:

Of course we're always doing many things at any one time, most of them without being aware that we're doing them. We can be itching, digesting, blinking, daydreaming, shifting position, and on and on. To *become aware* of these automatic behaviors is to put them under our control so that we're doing what we're doing *on purpose*. It focuses our power.

This exercise is to ask yourself every once in a while, "What are you doing now?" and to answer with any one of the many things you are doing that you were not aware of at that moment. Answer

Go Whole-Heartedly into Whatever You Do

with definiteness so that you're doing whatever you're doing Whole-Heartedly.

"Now I'm rubbing my feet together!"

"Now I'm struggling to write an editorial!"

"Now I'm bringing the spoon to my mouth!"

"Now I'm feeling a pain in my ankle!"

Set reminders when you're starting out--something that will nab you when you've forgotten you're doing this.

Exercise 2:

To be Wholehearted is fun, and conversely, whenever you're having fun, you're Wholehearted. Think about it; have you ever had fun *half-heartedly?*

Write down three activities you do, or will do soon, and then reframe them to be fun by coming up with aspects of their environment or chance encounters they facilitate that you enjoy.

This exercise is to *enjoy whatever you are doing and make it fun*. If you decide you're going to stuff envelopes, travel to Poughkeepsie, clean toilets, as Gandhi did, or confront the president of General Electric, take the project as a great adventure and enjoy it all the way. Being up to your elbows in *anything* is fun.

X

Become Invulnerable to Defeat

The Practice: *Take charge of the way you feel about "defeat," and use this power over your reactions to see your life and all your projects in it as a wonderful game.*

Sometimes the projects you put your heart into for your cause will fail.

You'll put tremendous effort into arranging for a concert to benefit Tibetan refugees, and it will bring in less money than you spent to hire the hall.

You'll put two years of arduous work into getting a bill through the legislature, and the Governor will veto it.

You'll run for office and lose the election.

Black marketers will make off with the food you sent for aid, and the children you were working to save will die of starvation.

Failures like these come to every activist again and again. Because of them, morale can be lost, supporters fade away, the cause be abandoned; we can burn out, become depressed and cynical, give up, and end in worse case than if we had never put ourselves into the cause in the first place. What can we do about such terrible defeats?

*   *   *

The moment of defeat is very powerful. At this time, strong feeling will surge up in you, feeling that can hardly be named. It's not exactly dismay, nor sorrow, nor anger, nor rage; it's not fear, and it's certainly not joy. It's not any specific feeling; it's a powerful general arousal or mobilization. It's *pure energy* coming up in you in response to an emergency. And it can be painfully strong. The more involved you were in the project that now fails, the greater the energy that failure will call up in you. And this powerful energy, this *fire of defeat*, can either burn you out or, if you use it well, forge you into a more effective instrument for the cause.

It is usually experienced as painful, by some of us so much so that we hold back from getting involved in projects at all because we so dread the way we will feel if we lose. I myself noticed some years ago that it was not defeat itself that was difficult for me; when I was calm I could handle that very well. No, what I dreaded was the way I knew I would *feel* after a defeat--the heavy-pounding heart, the sinking stomach, the intolerably tight inner pressure, and the not wanting anyone else to find out about my defeat, as if then they would know I had committed a crime or done some other shameful thing.

Painful as they can be, though, it is good news that *these feelings, and not defeat itself, are what burn us out*. If defeat itself were the problem, we would be helpless to do anything about it, for there is no guarantee that we will meet no defeats. We know, in fact, that we are bound to meet many of them, and the harder we work to help the world, the more of them we are likely to meet.

If the problem is the way we *feel* about defeat, though, then we can solve it, for we *can* control our feelings. The energy that surges up in us when we see that a project has failed is ours to use, and we are free to interpret it in whatever way we choose. We can experience it negatively, as a painful thing, or positively, as something useful and even pleasant.

You can learn to do the latter. You can learn to change that energy of defeat which at first is so painful--change it in such a way that you are not hurt and discouraged but exhilarated and empowered by it. You can in fact learn to be exhilarated and empowered by *every* outcome, regardless of whether it be defeat, victory, or a draw, simply because it's the touch of life.

It is essential to take charge of the way you feel about defeat rather than let the outer world determine that feeling. This Practice is to teach you how to do this. Its two components are (1) to *take charge of the way you feel about "defeat,"* and (2) to *use this power over your reactions to see your life and all your projects in it as a wonderful game.*

*   *   *

In ordinary life, if you haven't gone through this practice, you probably feel good only if your projects succeed and bad if they fail. But in doing this you are letting your state of mind be determined by events in the outer world; if those events go one way, you're happy; if they go another way you're sad. Notice that all four "failures" described at the beginning of this section were brought upon you by what other people did or did not do: other people didn't buy tickets to your concert; other people vetoed your bill, voted for someone else, made off with your supplies. If you were to let any of these defeats upset and discourage you, you would be letting events in the outer world, such as what those other people did, determine your mood. You would not be in charge of your own feelings. *If you let events in the outer world direct your energy in this way, "defeat" will surely burn you out.* Even worse, you will have been untrue to yourself and to your cause. Your state of mind is not your own to give away in this way. It represents your moral force, your great weapon in activism. You must not put that at the mercy of the little ups and downs of your cause. It's your *job* to keep your weapon clean and sharp and not let the outer world take it away from you.

This Practice, then, is to *notice* when you feel chagrined or discouraged about a defeat, *realize* that in doing so you're being run by the outer world, and then *purposely take charge of your own mood,* staying calm and shifting your attention from the "defeat" to what you will do next.

This is probably best learned by practicing on the small and petty defeats we all suffer every day, and working up from them to handling bigger defeats. Let's define defeats as things not going as you would like; if we do this we will all have plenty of them to practice on--a broken pencil or fingernail, another car cutting in front of you on the freeway, the computer malfunctioning or running out of batteries on your smart phone when you need to use it, the weather's being too hot, or too cold, not getting the seat you wanted at the concert, and so on. Every such small defeat offers you a chance to practice; learn to take it not as an insult and loss to feel chagrined or discouraged about, but as a welcome challenge and guide to future behavior.

First of all, recognize that no matter how calamitous the loss, it's *always* best to keep our heads, feel the way we want to (and we always *want* to feel good), and focus on what we are going to do next. It's fairly easy to see that feeling bad about a broken pencil is a waste of energy and actually prevents you from taking effective further action; the thing to do when your pencil breaks is to thank the universe for telling you that you were pressing on it too hard, and then sharpen it, resolve to use a more appropriate pressure next time, and get on with your projects; any chagrin or complaint is only a waste of good emotional energy. When we can see this clearly about small failures and defeats, we can begin to see that it applies to larger failures and defeats as well.

*   *   *

Secondly, once you understand how to take charge of the way you feel in this way, you can go further and learn to *see your life and your projects in it as a wonderful game.*

I once saw the great cellist Pablo Casals make a mistake during a major concert that was being televised live around the world. There was simply a sudden jangle and discord in the music; he had obviously played the wrong notes. I remember my own pang of dismay and immediate sympathy with him because he had spoiled his performance and would be humiliated before the whole world. I remember with equal clarity the surprise and admiration I felt the next moment at Casals' own reaction. I cannot say what he felt on the inside, but what appeared on the outside was no change at all in his utter relaxedness, and *a delighted chuckle.* He seemed *thrilled* at his mistake.

It struck me then that he was not at all focused on us, his audience. He was preoccupied with a great, zestful game with something larger than us, like the universe, or life itself, or his art. He had thought he had this mighty opponent all figured out and subdued, and then it caught him in his moment of complacency, nudging him with that mistake; that's how it told him the game wasn't finished and challenged him to wake up and re-join it.

If that is how he felt, then Casals *welcomed* his mistake because, like a playful shove from one puppy to another, it invited him back into an exciting game, gave him a chance to throw himself into the play. And in that play he was not at all focused on any worldly outcome, on doing well or poorly for an audience, on winning or losing; he went into the game *for itself,* because he so enjoyed it, because it is a privilege and honor to be allowed in it, because his life was fulfilled just by being *in* it. And within that game, he was invincible by the outer world; he was above it, he was superior to it, he was his own master, and he could take whatever "victory" or "defeat" that outer world handed out as just another invitation to play.

We can all thrill to worldly "failure" or "defeat" as Casals did. We can do it now because we used to do it all the time, long before we learned there was any such thing as "*real*" defeat, back there in the beautiful childhood world. Do you remember playing a game outdoors in the late summer evenings when you were allowed out after supper? Do you remember how you could hardly stay in the house long enough to eat that supper because you were so impatient to get outside and into the game and play on, and on, and on? There were "victories" and "defeats" in that game, then, too, but we hardly noticed them in our eagerness to start the next game and play! play! before the fireflies came out and we had to go in.

At times we're likely to forget how to *play* in that intense and joyous way, especially if we become activists and understand all the suffering that "defeat" may mean for our friends in the outer world. For their sake as well as our own, we must re-learn that pure joy of the game, so we can become impervious to defeat. When we were young we'd rather play than watch or rest or eat any time; we lived in the challenge, not just in the winning, and not in the security, either. We were like a certain small boy, six-year old Jimmy, who looked very glum and uncertain as his father escorted him to his first day at a new school, but who brightened up as soon as another boy, hiding behind the schoolroom door, gave him a raucous raspberry. The teacher, of course, scolded the other boy for this aggressive greeting, but Jimmy understood it; he *recognized* it as the challenge to play, to tussle, to lose himself in the joy of the game, and so he welcomed it.

This is how we must learn to meet all "failures" and "defeats" of the outer world, as challenges to re-join a high-spirited game.

*   *   *

This game has certain characteristics that make it truly a game. One of them is *uncertainty of outcome*. Although Casals did not focus on winning or losing in the outer world, his game does have a focus and can definitely be won or lost: he can keep his proper state of mind or he can lose it; he can hold or he can break. His involvement in the game is tied to this uncertainty of outcome; it wouldn't be a game without it. Notice, though, that it is an *inner* outcome, and Casals himself is in charge of it; it is not controlled by the outer world.

Further, the goal in this game is so high as to be *never finally won or lost*. It amounts to a loyalty to one's own ideals, an elusive, abstract thing that must always be re-tested; thus the game is never *over*. You can always re-join it, and no matter how often you win or lose in it, the next outcome will always be uncertain; it can go on forever. In that sense, there *is* no defeat; there are just moments of decision: whether to feel bad about an outcome, or to look past it to the next step in the game. To give up or get back on your horse.

We can play the Wonderful Game all day, everyday, and all our "defeats" and "failures", major and minor alike, are incidents within it. Of course it wouldn't be a game if we didn't lose sometimes, that is, fall for the worldly illusion that it's not a game at all, that our "defeat" is real and final and therefore we should grieve, be upset, depressed, discouraged. Some defeats are so grievous to us that human heart cannot hold up under them, and we do lose faith, and despair. Even the greatest activists have done so. Gandhi did when his people used their hard-won freedom to kill each other off. Einstein did when his wonderful discovery was used to bomb thousands of Japanese.

Let us be tolerant of ourselves through this "despair in extremis" which we can't help but feel simply because we're human. But even the time of such despair is good for more than sulking in your tent; even through the worst of it some small part of you *is still playing the Game*, and goes right on *using* the energy of defeat to make Daring thoughts about what you can do next for your cause. Be tolerant of yourself when you despair, then, but also hold yourself ready to hear those Daring thoughts, to be inspired by them, to hone them--and to act again.

Eventually, you won't have to work on handling any but the gravest defeats. You will take most "defeats" simply as moves by your opponent in an engrossing game and automatically look beyond them to decide upon your own next move. And sometimes, when you've begun to take the game for granted, have become complacent and perhaps a little bored with it, a "defeat" will wake you up and invigorate you, as Casals' mistake awakened him. Then an event which other people see as a defeat can become, to *you*, a sign that you haven't used your full power; you can thrill to discover that your opponent is real; as if you had thought you were playing with a small child and held back out of consideration, but suddenly realized the "child" was a black belt karate master; the realization will surprise and delight you, and call you as if by thrilling trumpets back into the Game.

Think of what it would be like to be a pro baseball player and have to spend the whole season on the bench, just watching and waiting. Suppose that then you suddenly saw the coach waving to you to *join the game*! Would you stop to worry about winning or losing? I think not! You'd be so happy about getting to play, getting to be part of the rush and tumble of the game, about getting to experience the winning and the losing, that *everything* about the game would thrill you through and through; you would appreciate it as the touch of life.

And what if you'd been living in such a way that you could never tell whether you "won" or "lost," so that your life was flat, with no ups or downs, always the same--and suddenly you achieved the vision to know victory and defeat? You would probably be so glad to see it, to be part of the push and pull of life, to feel yourself a serious, solid part of the universe, that whether it was winning or losing you saw would be a matter of indifference to you. Every outcome would thrill you, before you ever judged it as pleasant or unpleasant, good or bad, defeat or victory.

That's how I want you to experience every outcome. Feel zest for *every* experience, because it is the touch of life.

*   *   *

When you have learned this Practice of seeing it all as a game, you can begin to reap the uses and benefits of "defeat". We would not purposely court defeat in order to get these benefits, but once we have lost in spite of our best efforts, they're definitely there to be called out.

One of those benefits is that *you can learn from defeat how to do better next time*. My mother used to say that even a donkey doesn't step in the same hole twice; if that's true, donkeys may be smarter than human beings, for I can repeat a mistake again and again. But if I take defeat to mean I must take some different direction, and study what that direction could be, I can turn defeat into a good learning experience. I'll bet Casals never made his concert mistake again, but rather *used* it to tell him to go home and practice that very section of the music until he knew it six ways from Sunday. In other words, part of this Practice is to make *use* of defeat by studying how you lost, and learn enough that you become more effective in your cause than you were before.

Using the defeat in this way, to guide you in another direction, you may even win a greater victory than was lost in the original defeat.

I was never so proud of my daughter, Dona, as when she suffered the painful defeat of flunking out of nursing school. She failed because of her poor organizational skills, so she concentrated on those skills while working as a nurses' aid, and returned to take the semester over again. This time she passed easily, but realized that nursing wasn't for her and parlayed her newly-developed skills and training into a very successful career she much preferred: orientation and mobility for people who are blind or visually impaired.

Jimmy Carter suffered a cruel defeat when he lost the election for a second term as President. He changed direction, though, and went on to found the Carter Foundation, through which he may have helped the world far more than he could have as a second term President.

Another benefit of defeat is that it *enables you to grow*. Once we're past childhood, we can grow intellectually and spiritually only through experiences that break up faulty aspects of our picture of the world. Such shatterings of our hopes and expectations are often disappointing and painful--in fact they are what we have been calling "defeats"--but they are absolutely necessary for our growth; if you never experienced "defeat" you wouldn't grow, and if you died and went to heaven St. Peter would send you right back down to earth, because you wouldn't have lived yet.

> *[L]eaders and managers must encourage risk and embrace failure. [As] General Omar N. Bradley, five-star general and former chairman of the Joint Chief of Staff stated, "I learned that good judgment comes from experience and that experience grows from mistakes."*
>
> Ralph Heath, <u>Celebrating Failure: The Power of Taking Risks, Making Mistakes, and Thinking Big</u>, pp 16-17

Each experience of "defeat" can help you by pointing out some block or constriction in your belief system that has been limiting you. As Aurobindo puts it, "Every sorrow is caused by a narrowing of consciousness"--and so can be used to point out that narrowing so you can work on it.

If you examine your own feelings of chagrin, shame, hurt, or despair over a defeat, ask yourself exactly what it is you're upset about and why it upsets you. You can eventually see that every such feeling is based on a limiting and therefore incomplete belief. It's possible to *widen the belief* until the things that so upset you appear as trivialities, like broken pencil points over which you had a tantrum all the while knowing in your heart that they weren't important.

I once knew a young man who wanted to kill himself because his high school team had lost a football game. I knew a woman who fell into such despair over the fact that her maid quit that she had to be hospitalized. I thought they were overreacting to what seemed to me to be quite picayune affairs. But to some very wise beings our despairs over *any* worldly affairs, even those that we give the highest value to, must seem just as foolish. We can despair over them only if we think this world of matter is all there is, death is terrible and the end of life, harm to our bodies harms some permanent part of us, this life is our only chance to live, and so on--the same old deal we fell for in our childhood, when we lost the beautiful childhood world. Let's try to understand their viewpoint, and adopt it. Let's broaden our view so that we see all defeats, big and little alike, as picayune, simply part of what goes along with getting to play the game, and be glad for getting to experience them.

Don't shrink in defeat then, nor let it burn you out, but instead let the feelings of "defeat" show you where your picture of the world was constricted, and then widen it. This widening of belief is a kind of insight, or enlightenment, a growth of your identity; it empowers you to become a more effective activist than ever; like Anteus, the giant who became stronger every time Hercules threw him to the ground, you too are strengthened rather than diminished by "defeat."

When Gandhi was sentenced to hard labor his friends worried about his health, for he was sent out on strenuous details like road construction and scavenger work. But for him it was a test of his moral strength as it brought him closer to God:

Become Invulnerable to Defeat

> *"The greatest good I have derived from these sufferings was that by undergoing bodily hardships I could see my mental strength clearly increasing, and it is even now maintained,"* [Ghandi] *wrote after his release. "The experience of the last three months in prison left me more than ever prepared to undergo all such hardships with ease."*

Sexton, Bernard, <u>Gandhi's Weaponless Revolt in India</u>

Yet another benefit of this Practice is that in a very real sense you become invincible. When you see "defeat" as part of a great game, it puts the defeat to its best possible use for your work. Nothing in the outer world can destroy you and your opponents will be confounded. After they "win" over you they may expect you to be glum and shamed and to give up; such a response on your part would strengthen them, and when they don't get it, it worries them.

In this Practice you maintain equanimity and steadiness of resolve through all outer "defeats;" for you the struggle is always a Game in the inner world and there you can lose only through your own actions, and even if you do, you can always start the Game again and redeem yourself, so nothing they do can shake you. This gives you a surefire power to further your cause.

Eventually, when you're fully in the Game you can achieve a high enough perspective that you can *enjoy* defeat. Then it really has no power over you.

When Aldous Huxley's house burned down, his treasured collection of books burned too. Friends were concerned for him, and one of them went to the site of the burning house and commiserated with him about it. Huxley said quietly, "The books are gone. Let's sit down and enjoy the fire."

A final benefit of defeat is that, if you take it in the spirit of this Practice, the defeat is *an honor* because it means you're in the Game; you *went* for something; you dared. You were an activist. I don't know of an activist who hasn't gone through defeat; all the great ones suffered many grueling ones, and the greater the defeats the more honor they are to them, for the greater were the Daring thoughts that led to them. We could almost say that the only activists who are ever defeated are the ones who dare; the only way to avoid defeats is not to join the Game in the first place, not to dare. It is in this sense that defeats are badges of honor that can be won only by activists, and your defeat brings you into that fellowship. And the rule may be that as part of your training to be as effective an activist as you want to be, you must rack up a certain number of defeats, the higher your goal, the more the defeats required. You may need 300 defeats or more; Edison needed *thousands*.

So rack up each defeat you face as one more credit toward your total--and be humbly grateful for it. It was the only way you could get that much closer to your Truth, and it makes you one of the company of seekers after Truth.

*   *   *

Quotes from great activists:

It's not whether you win or lose, but how you play the game.

Adage taught in British schools.

My imperfections and failures are as much a blessing from God as my successes and my talents, and I lay them both at His feet.

Mahatma Gandhi

Therefore, arise, thou Son of Kunti! Brace
Thine arm for conflict, nerve thy heart to meet--
As things alike to thee--pleasure or pain,
Profit or ruin, victory or defeat.

Bhagavad-Gita, Chapter II, verse 129-133

*   *   *

Become Invulnerable to Defeat

Exercise 1:

Think of the most recent defeat on the road to achieving a personal goal you went through that made you lose heart. Then, choose an activist you admire, either some of the really great activists from Jesus and Buddha through Gandhi, Mother Teresa, Nelson Mandela, Martin Luther King, and so on, or one you may know personally.

If put in your shoes, how would the spirit of this great activist move from that point onward, in view of your overall mission?

Exercise 2:

If the Practice of Becoming Invulnerable to Defeat is hard for you, it may be because you have not taken care of *worry* that you may be defeated or fail in your project. Worry is your inner being saying it's afraid and insecure, and you need to have it feeling safe and confident, so reassure it before you go into the battle.

To do that, think of something you're worried about. First check over your preparations for the engagement. Worry is often based on the subtle knowledge that you haven't prepared as thoroughly as you should have. Review your plans until you're sure you have. If you're still worried, make a plan for what you will do in case of the worst possible outcome. Worry is more often based on a fear of being helpless and having to make decisions from that position than on fear of defeat itself. If you make a back-up plan for the worst possible scenario you won't *be* helpless even if you lose, and your inner being will know that and be reassured.

Once you've made the plan, you can forget the worry and put *all* your energy into the work. This is what we call taking care of yourself.

XI

Use the Enemy to Become More Effective Yourself

The Practice: *See the fault of your enemy in your own side; then find it within yourself. Decide how you're going to eliminate the fault in yourself, and begin doing so. Once you can see both parties as basically good people who made a mistake, deal then with the "enemy."*

When things go badly in our causes we tend to point the finger at some *other* person or group in the outer world as causing the problem. When we do that we're setting that person or group apart from us as a bad guy, while we claim credit as being the righteously good guy. In this we're setting up good and bad sides, as an "I" and a "them". In short, we are creating an enemy, the other side, such as:

- The oil company that pollutes the ocean.
- The military-industrial complex that supports the bomb.
- Whatever country we're at war with.
- The iron-handed dictator who oppresses the people.
- The terrorist who kills innocent people.
- The landowner who exploits the peasants.

It's very satisfying to be able to point the finger at an outer enemy in this way, for we human beings are addicted to having villains and heroes and the contests between them. We seem driven to make all things into sports events, two sides that fight each other. That clarifies everything for us; it's simple, straightforward, and gives us closure in otherwise complicated situations.

I remember how, when I was a child and listened to stories or saw movies, I couldn't really relax and enjoy myself until I had *identified the good and bad guys*. It was easy to do. The good guy was the one the story was *about*; by definition I was on his (seldom her) side. The bad guy was anyone he was against and also anyone who was cruel and hurt people or did bad things like lying or stealing. So Mordred, the dragon, and King George were bad guys, enemies. King Arthur, St. George, and George Washington were good guys, heroes.

Even as I began to grow up it was still easy to make this distinction for a long time. Nazis were bad, of course, and so were dictators, oppressors, slave owners and torturers. I and those with whom I associated saw chemical companies and the National Rifle Association in the same bad light, while Greenpeace and the Red Cross were good, and so were resistance fighters, the poor and oppressed, the tortured.

I don't quite recall when the clear-cut line between these two groups of good and bad began to fuzz. Maybe when, incredulous, I learned that George Washington was a slave owner. In the repercussions of that discovery, I took another look at the bad guys, too, and saw that they weren't all one thing either. Hitler, I read, was kind to his dogs. Chemical companies polluted the earth but they also supported Big Brother for fatherless boys. The NRA and its guns--well, what about the heroes who used guns? Shane? And John Brown, who used guns in what he thought was a noble cause? And is a gun all that different from a sword? King Arthur and Lancelot themselves would probably have used guns if they had them.

And so I began to question my habit of looking for good and bad guys. Such a habit confused the issues more than it clarified them. It seemed to be taking the easy way out; it may have been that all it did "for" me was to save me from having to sort out the facts and think for myself. Maybe everybody was both a good and a bad guy. And *maybe seeing an enemy in the outer world at all was a big mistake,* by which I was actually denying my own responsibility and power, handing them over to that very "enemy". It was as if I said, "There's a villain--over *there*," and by implication, "not here"--and so set up the "other" side as having the power and myself as merely reacting to it. I was actually aiding and abetting the "enemy," and conducing not to peace and a better world, but to war and a worse one.

Today it seems to me that the people I used to call "bad guys" and "enemies" were at most only *opponents*; things had turned out in such a way that they and I opposed each other in the Great Game, but they were no more "bad" nor "enemies" than was the person with whom I played a game of checkers after supper, or who was on the other side from me in a game of tennis. It was my job to play the best game I could with them but it was not appropriate to feel hate or anger toward them any more than it would have been in these games. In fact, insofar as I did see them as bad guys I sharply limited the facts I could see and so weakened myself and became that much less effective as an activist. I probably won fewer games, too, than I would have without such an emotional bias.

*   *   *

Step 1:

Once you've identified the trait in your enemy with which you so acridly disapprove, the first step is to *see that fault among your own side.*

Remember Walt Kelly's Pogo Possum saying "We have met the enemy and he is us"? That was quite an achievement on his part, for finding the fault in your *us*--your own beloved race, or country, or family--is very hard, the harder the more you love it. To see fault where we thought there was good in those we care about can be a terrible blow. It's easy to see Mordred and King George as bad guys; they're long ago and far away; so now are the Nazis, and the Soviet Communists, all safe to tag as villains because we do not know or love them.

But as we look closer to home it becomes more painful to see the fault; the discovery that your own country, or place of worship, or profession is doing wrong can force you into making a painful choice, either to deny the fault you know is there so that you don't feel the pain and so you can keep the peace and stay intact, or to let your very self be painfully shattered so you can see the truth. The meaning went out of life for many, many people during the Nazi Holocaust, when they let themselves realize that their race, the human race, was capable of such horror as was perpetrated there. It was as if they had found out that the beloved father who kissed them to bed every night was really Hitler--they reeled; the world reeled around them at the discovery. I believe some died of their very realization.

A naive woman friend of mine was surprised and dismayed to learn that commercial products like laundry bleach and oven cleaner were routinely "tested" by being put into rabbits' eyes.

She saw this as terrible cruelty and assumed that if people only knew about it they would rise up and stop it. She was arrested for blocking the entrance to the animal laboratory and gladly went to trial feeling sure that the jurors, who to her represented the people, would support her. When, instead, they found her guilty, it meant to her that her race, human beings in general, did not care that some of their conveniences were based on terrible suffering. From then on, she refused to identify as a member of the human race; she wanted to die and thought she *was* dying; she was in despair, and within two years she developed a serious immune system disorder.

So it can be difficult and painful to discover fault in the race, the country, the corporation, the political party we love. We must do it anyway; we owe it to our own to *see* it when we think they do wrong. Bearing witness to the crimes of our own is the essence of democracy; mindless approval and following of those we love doesn't help them and is not loving in the long run; it is more of a mutual security pact. Good parents teach their children to do right, and good friends deserve the same.

Find comfort, though, in knowing that this step is the most painful part of this Practice. The changes you undergo in the next steps ease the agony of this one and are fueled by it.

*   *   *

Step 2:

The second step of this Practice is to *find the fault you noticed in the enemy and in your side within* <u>*yourself*</u>.

Seeing the fault in your side does not cut close enough, for in doing that you are still pointing the finger outside yourself; you can still say, "I weep, I die, because *someone else* is gassing human beings; *they* are shooting peasants, abusing children, torturing animals, desecrating the earth." If he's to be an effective activist, Pogo Possum must take it one step further and say, "We have met the enemy--and he is *us*." And indeed your identification with the people and institutions you love presses you to do that yourself. Once you've discovered the guilt of your beloved race, or religion, or country, or family, or organization, it's only a small step, since you so identify with them, to realize that you, too, bear this very guilt. Only after you have done this will you be able to reap the great benefits this Practice can bring.

Your tool in the search for your own, personal fault is the knowledge that, when it comes to wrongdoers, "It takes one to know one." You couldn't recognize the fault of the others *as a fault* if it didn't live somewhere in you as well. Every time you notice the "enemy's" fault you can know that in some way or another you are doing the same thing the "enemy" is and that your doing it is hampering you in your work for your cause. The job is to find that fault in yourself.

Begin by staying alert for your own pointing of the finger of blame at the outer world. Whenever you think of any person or group as bad, or as an enemy, you're doing it. Whenever you feel disgruntled or dissatisfied, whenever you tut tut ("Oh, it's too bad that. . ."), you're doing it. And always, you're doing it without fully understanding what you're doing.

When you catch it, be glad; it's an achievement to become aware of what you were doing! Then sit down and make a statement describing the bad person's fault in very general terms--not, "he batters his wife and abuses his kids," but, "he bullies helpless beings." Not "they let oil spill all over the ocean, killing the birds and ruining the environment," but "they are careless out of greed for profit," or, "they ruthlessly take what they want without regard for the rights of others," or, "they selfishly take more than their share even though others then have to go without." If you don't easily find such a statement, just use this general statement, which covers just about everything we blame others for: "They unfairly hurt others."

Now search your own memory until you find an instance in which you did the same thing. You can depend on this: if you noticed the fault in others, you've committed it yourself at some time or other; you couldn't understand it as wrongdoing if you hadn't.

When you find one, reconstruct in your mind how you came to commit it, what "made you do it." Do your best to really *understand* why you did this wrong thing. Stay with it until you do.

At a time when I was infuriated by men's sexual harassment of women, I found that I, being a woman, could not imagine being one of those men and harassing a woman. It seemed to me I would not have done it. So I tried to make a general statement describing the wrongdoing I saw in those men. I saw that it was men who had worldly power over the woman, either physical strength or some position of authority, who harassed them, so my statement became, "They demonstrated their power over others who were weaker."

Then I looked to see how I might have done just that myself at some time. At first I was sure I had never done it, but then I remembered how only a few days before I had "played" with my cat, Lani. I had wanted to snuggle her on my lap but she wasn't in the mood and kept jumping off. I found that by putting my arm out at just the right moment I could catch her in mid-leap and set her back on my lap. It was almost like catching a baseball; as she jumped off and her hot little body slapped into my hand I felt a thrill of achievement and--I had to face it--superior power. I *enjoyed* letting her try to get away from me and then snatching her back again in mid-flight, as if to prove that she couldn't get away from me, that I was indisputably in charge here.

After a few such catches I was ashamed and let her go, and apologized and tried to make it up to her. But now, thinking about men in positions of power harassing women, I realized I could not throw any stones of blame at them. I had to first take responsibility for my own harassment of a being unfortunate enough to be in my power. And when I asked myself *why* I had done it, I saw that it was exactly because I was unsure of my power and wanted to prove it upon Lani. I saw too that that attempt could never succeed; I could prove my physical power over her but I would never be able to force her will. I could put her on my lap but I couldn't make her like it. My "proving" my power over her only "proved" that I did not in fact have real power at all. If I had, I wouldn't have had to "prove" it.

Then I asked myself what would have to happen before I could stop wanting to bully a weaker being in that way. I would probably have to learn to guard against my tendency to use force against helpless beings, and meanwhile develop my real, inner power until I was sure enough of it that I no longer needed to prove it on them. It seemed to me that that was what the men I had been angry about needed too.

At this point you can begin to *understand* the enemy.

*   *   *

Step 3:

Step 3 is to *decide how you're going to eliminate the fault in yourself,* and begin doing so. Once you've become fully aware of it and understand why you did it, you can't do it automatically any more; your awareness of it gives you a button by which to cancel it. In doing this you're taking further charge of your own behavior and you gain power accordingly.

A mother brought her young son to a swami and asked him to tell the boy to stop eating sugar. The swami told her to wait three days and then come back. When she returned he duly told the boy to stop eating sugar, but the mother was curious and asked why he had asked them to wait three days.

"I had to stop eating sugar myself before I could tell the boy to do so," said the swami.

*   *   *

Step 4:

You can do Steps 3 and 4 at the same time. The job in Step 4 is to *make sure you can see both of the erring sides--the enemy or beloved institution and yourself--as basically good people who made a mistake.* You've just put energy into seeing the fault in everybody, in both sides, but nothing effective can be done from such a negative view, and it doesn't feel good, either, to think that you and everyone else are bad. In order to be more effective and to feel good, then, *take charge of the way you see things*, your perceptions, and put it in your head that we're *all* good and erring people. And before entering into any action, any encounter in your cause, pause to make sure you feel only positive regard and good will toward your opponents.

In four steps, now, you've come a long and very important way from the original pointing the finger at a bad guy. The attitude you're in now could change the world. Consider what it may have done for the relationship between a little boy and his father in this family.

A worker in child protective services was concerned about a five-year old boy in her care, and came to a psychotherapist for advice. The child's father had been sentenced and sent to prison for various wrongdoings, including assault and stealing cars. The boy loved and identified with his father and wanted to know where he was and why he was gone. The worker dreaded having to tell him his father was a criminal--that is, a bad person--and was therefore in jail. The therapist advised her not to use the word "bad" at all, but rather to tell the boy that his father was basically a good man, who had made some mistakes and was going to jail to make them right, because that's what good people do when they make mistakes: they make them right.

At this point you'll be able to identify with the worst offender, even a Nazi, a terrorist, a torturer; you'll recognize the humanness of whatever the "enemy" did. You'll be able to feel the weight of his or her wrongdoing, and be grateful you don't have to bear it. The psalmist says it is not ours to judge and condemn others -- that is up to God: "Vengeance is mine, I will repay, sayeth the Lord."

You'll be able to wish him or her well. You'll reach the attitude of fellow feeling and good will that lies underneath all the hating in the world. This does not mean that you will approve of what the enemy is doing nor that you will hold back in dealing with it; it means you won't let it determine *your* feelings and actions; it means you are free to do what you decide is best, which is basically, always, to care about the other, to love. This part of the Practice is to develop and strengthen this goodwill and caring. It has to be stronger than the "enemy's" Violence, outlast it, drown it.

When you've reached this point you'll experience the great relief of being able to love the "enemy".

All through my childhood I was immensely proud to be an American, one of the free and the brave. Even as an adult, when I lived in a foreign country for a while, I burst into tears of love, nostalgia, devotion at the very sight of the American flag. Then it was borne in on me that my country had sinned; it had slaughtered Indians, oppressed "slaves," and dropped the first atomic bombs in history on defenseless civilians. In a terrible disappointment I turned against it, and *hated America.* Years later, though, I realized that I *am* an American and so am *myself* responsible for these terrible mistakes. The realization was painful, but freeing. I had not liked hating the country I loved; I *wanted* to love it. It was a relief when I was able to do so again.

My woman friend who had wanted to die because people used conveniences based on suffering had been trying to believe she was not part of the human race for many months when it suddenly struck her that she was living on the same conveniences as were the rest of its members, and so was as guilty as any of them of "not caring." Surprisingly, this idea brought her peace; she could now identify with people instead of being disgusted with them, and she began active work on projects to help people develop compassion. She was especially happy that she could once again feel an undiluted love for others rather than disgust and hatred.

*   *   *

Step 5:

Now, able to feel good will, you're ready for Step 5: *deal with the "enemy."* You can do that much more effectively now than you could have before, for pointing the finger sets other people's Violent behavior in concrete, while pointing at yourself as responsible, being a Courageous stance, leaves a space in which they can change.

You can see that "enemy" clearly now, see how much of what you perceived in him was the projection of your own fault upon him, as opposed to his true wrongdoing. All the energy you were putting into hate, fear, resentment of the enemy is now freed for your use in figuring out the best solution for all; you are free to be creative, firm and fair.

You'll be far less likely to decide on a fight, but if you do you'll be more likely to win it because in place of that Violent distraction of energy, you'll maintain a basic compassionate good will throughout.

*   *   *

Work on the five steps of this Practice until nothing anyone does can make you want to point your finger in blame nor change your feeling of positive regard for all living beings. Work on it until nothing can push your buttons--until you *have* no buttons.

Properly done, this Practice brings many benefits.

You learn you can control your perceptions and your feelings.

You grow in real power, because when you take back responsibility for a fault you had attributed to someone else you also get back the energy and power you had attributed with it. And your new insight into the fault expands your awareness so that you are more in charge of your own behavior. Once you've caught out the fault which was hidden and automatic in you before, it cannot so easily run off again; you will be self-conscious about committing it next time, and so be able *not* to do it if you wish; you have gained that power.

And the Practice enables you to fulfill another deep human longing--the wish for a hero. Having heroes in the outer world is as confusing as it is to have villains. It's very easy to pick out a hero and then follow him or her; we have a deep human longing to do that, and it feels good. But human heroes turn out to have embarrassing faults that we don't feel like following them in, that dilute their hero-ship for us. Martin Luther King is said to have cheated on a school exam. Gandhi used young girls to prove Brahmacharya. Probably even Mother Teresa picked her nose in private.

Taking responsibility for the enemy's fault in yourself is an act of courage, for it involves the fearful sacrifice of ego, so the moment you do this Practice you become not just part of the villain, but also the good guy, your own hero. Finding out your faults and *changing* them to make them right is exactly what makes you a *hero*, so you don't have to worry about being embarrassed by them. And Pogo can now say, "We have met the hero--and it's *me!*"

*   *   *

Quotes from great activists:

> It is the essence of non-violence to hate the sin--but love
> the sinner. This is the most difficult part of non-violence for
> me.
>
> Mohandas Gandhi

> If only there were evil people somewhere insidiously
> committing evil deeds, and it were necessary only to
> separate them from the rest of the us and destroy them.
> But the line dividing good and evil cuts through the heart of
> every human being. And who is willing to destroy a piece of
> his own heart?

> During the life of any heart this line keeps changing place;
> sometimes it is squeezed one way by exuberant evil and
> sometimes it shifts to allow space for good to flourish. One
> and the same human being is, at various ages, under
> various circumstances, a totally different human being. At
> times he is close to being a devil, at times to sainthood. But

his name doesn't change, and to that name we ascribe the whole lot, good and evil.

Socrates taught us: Know thyself!

Confronted by the pit into which we are about to toss those who have done us harm, we halt, stricken dumb: it is after all only because of the way things worked out that they were the executioners and we weren't.

Aleksander Solzenitzkin, <u>The Gulag Archipelago</u>, p. 168

How can you say to your brother, 'Brother, let me take out the speck that is in your eye,' when you yourself do not see the log that is in your own eye? You hypocrite, first take the log out of your own eye, and then you will see clearly to take out the speck that is in your brother's eye.

Luke 6:42

The nonviolent resister seeks to attack the evil system rather than individuals who happen to be caught up in the system. . . our aim is not to defeat the white community, not to humiliate the white community, but to win the friendship of all of the persons who had perpetrated this system in the past.

Martin Luther King, June 4, 1957

It saddens me so,
those fingers ever pointing,
from the first evil gesture
to the point of near extinction.

. . .(And) Jesus said, "Love thy neighbor,"
and Jesus said "Love thy enemy,"

And so I guess the first step
is to take my own finger
and put it on a button tritely marked,
"Love is the answer!",
take my finger and with my own blood sign a treaty
permanently disbanding my own formidable army
of hatred and illness and fear,
make a corny pact with myself that says,
"Peace in the world starts with peace in the heart."

Use the Enemy to Become More Effective Yourself

Take this step and try to remember
there are G.I. Joes in every uniform of every country
who are all an equal part of the One God
whose eye is everywhere and whose finger does not point.

Tomas Fuentez

on earth Peace, good will toward men.

Luke 2:14

*   *   *

Exercise 1:

Don't think that just because we're talking about good will this is a namby-pamby, easy Practice. It's not. Gandhi found hating the sin but *loving the sinner* to be the hardest part of his non-violent approach. Sometimes it's as though one's very body revolts when asked to generate positive regard for certain people. If you can't do it before time for an encounter with such people, for this exercise at least get yourself into a neutral position so that you no longer feel dislike, disgust or anger toward them.

Identify any ill feelings you have toward a person in particular. Ask yourself whether these feelings are what you want to invest your life energy into, and say firmly, "*I don't have time for such trivialities!*" From now on, simply *refuse* such feelings as you would refuse any petty, irrelevant interruption when you were in the middle of an important job. Hatred, dislike, anger, having enemies have nothing to do with why you're on this earth; they're irrelevant to your cause and therefore a waste of your time and energy.

Exercise 2:

The next time you meet someone, especially a person whom you don't like or are tempted to see as an enemy, ask yourself, "How can I show my respect for this person?"

126

Exercise 3:

Looking to heroes in the outer world can be as destructive and confusing an enterprise as looking to villains. If you currently idolize someone, look for ways in which your assumption about his or her perfection is limiting you in being yourself when creating solutions. Realize that we're *all* good and *all* bad, and don't expect a leader to be perfect any more than you'd expect him or her to be all wrong. Think for yourself!

XII

Change Judging to Bare Attention

The Practice: *When you catch yourself disapproving and criticizing, look at the offending object with bare attention and then ask yourself whether it hurts anything. If you decide it does not, welcome it into your world. If you decide it is harmful, do something about it.*

Very few of us are judges in courts of law but very many of us are wonderful and severe judges in our minds, eagerly muttering, "That's bad" under our breaths about the things in our lives-- other people, their habits, their clothes, their ideas, the weather, the traffic, the service. We seem to think it's our job to be judges, or critics, to scan every scene and prove that we know what's wrong with it. And we do the job so skillfully that it becomes automatic, a *habit* of criticizing and disapproving that runs off by itself without our being aware of it.

We may even think we do not have this habit, but I believe most of us do. I say this because I believe myself to be remarkably non-judgmental, and yet as I am writing this, a few seconds of thought are enough for me to remember within the last two days mentally shaking my head in disapproval as a friend told me how she handled her dog, and feeling critical and condescending toward someone else who made the grammatical error of saying "raise" when it "should" have been "rise." I remembered that I have some peeves, too, and peeves are simply such disapprovals and criticisms solidified, made permanent. I dislike little white fences made of plastic, and dishes with too many scallops around the edge, and people calling to sell me something by phone, and. . .

But wait! Suddenly I notice something here.

So far, the little peeves and disapprovals I'm recalling seem harmless. To dislike scalloped dishes is such a small thing--just a little moment of irritation, a little put-down, perhaps not even expressed out loud, just in my head, so harmless it is sometimes called a *pet* peeve. But this small dislike, this critical and *judgmental* attitude I take toward scalloped dishes, using the word "raise" incorrectly or handling their dog differently from the way I think they should, is the baby form of destructive blaming, contempt, and prejudice.

It took me only a few more seconds, once I had started recalling instances of this attitude in myself, to add, "people who dawdle when they cross the street in front of me," and to recall the following incident:

I was driving somewhere in a hurry and had to stop at a pedestrian crossing while a crippled woman dragged herself across the street in front of my car. A flash of impatience, irritation, feeling abused shot through me and the indignant thought, "She should *get out of my way!*"

Whoa! What happened to compassion? My thought was arrogant and unfair and will certainly have negative consequences for the world even if I only *think* it (for I can't keep my thoughts entirely separate from my actions). And *it is of basically the same structure as my dislike of scalloped dishes*. In both cases I set up two sides and decree one (myself) to be somehow right, good, and superior, and the other (all the people who make or like scalloped dishes, and the crippled woman) to be somehow wrong, bad, inferior. *That's the Violent attitude! All* of such judgmental irritations, dislikes, criticisms, peeves, snobberies, rejections, ignorings, disapprovals, whether they seem harmless or not, are forms of Violence and conduce to suffering in the world.

And essentially *all* of us think thoughts like this regularly.

Why?

There's a reason why we become such disapproving judges. We do it in order *not to see* things that don't fit into the picture we already have of who we are and what the world is. We all have such a picture and strongly tend to identify with it, as if it were our essential self. That makes our mental picture very important, and most of us will do just about anything to keep it and reject new ideas that might disrupt it. It's hard for a member of one political party such as a Democrat to see the truth of an argument from someone of an opposing party such as a Republican because doing so would shake up the picture of his or her self as a Democrat.

We keep these threatening ideas out by *sorting* instead of *seeing* things. We hold the idea or thing that might jar us up against the picture we already have of how things should be and throw out any parts of it that do not fit that picture. In doing that we do see the *discrepancy* between the old picture and the new thing, but we don't see the new thing itself. We see only *what it is not* (it's *not* like the picture) and thereby miss the truth of it, *what it actually is*. We're just sorting, like chickens picking corn out of pebbles. They "see" the pebbles only as much as it takes to know they're *not* corn, and so to ignore them. We see things that might jar us in the same way, only as much as it takes to know they do not fit our picture, and so we don't see the truth of what they are, any more than you'd "see" a rusty tin can if you came upon it while you were looking through a pile of trash for a gold watch.

What is a table? When you hear that question you may think of a flat, rectangular top with four legs, of an appropriate size for people to sit at. Now I used to have in my office a little, round, three-legged phone table with a carved top. If you were presented with that round table *as* a table and you didn't want to go to the trouble of enlarging your definition of tables, you might feel a small shock of disapproval and think, "Hey, it's NOT rectangular, it's NOT four-legged, it's NOT flat topped, it's NOT of a size people can sit at. That's not what *I'd* call a table!" That is, you would see what my table is *not* rather than what it *is*; you would reject it as a table. Then you could relax because your old picture of what a table is--and your identity, your picture of who you are--would be safe from having to change and expand.

So we can use sorting to keep strange new things out of the picture we have of ourselves and our world. And it's when the things we've managed not to see won't stay invisible, and begin to insinuate themselves into our field of vision anyway, that we push them back down by criticizing and disapproving.

That's what I'm doing with a person's saying "raise" instead of "rise," which doesn't fit my idea of how a person should talk. That's what I'm doing with the crippled woman, who doesn't fit into the tight, hurried schedule I believe I should keep. Now I can relax, safe in my old, familiar world.

At a cost, though! For *I'm not seeing what's out there, reality, the Truth!* I'm seeing *what-is-not* instead of *what-is*. That's bound to have some pretty undesirable consequences both for me personally and for my work as an activist.

One consequence is the way I feel: not very happy. Life as a disapproving judge is a pretty somber affair. It's full of disappointment because things don't live up to the standard in my head, and resentment because I think they *should*, and sadness because the world just seems to be going to the dogs. So I don't enjoy as many happy, light-hearted moods as I might like, and that can even hamper my effectiveness as an advocate.

I don't learn and grow, either, while I'm disapproving. Strange new things that don't fit what I already know are exactly what I need if I am to learn and my mind grow, and my judgmental attitude keeps them out. And as things forever change in one direction or another, if my mind doesn't grow it will stagnate and decay, starved for lack of anything new.

And the world I live in gets smaller and smaller with my every critical judgment. When I criticize, I have divided the world into two parts--gold watches and tin cans--and that I'm automatically rejecting tin cans, without noticing that every such rejection narrows my focus that much more, and certainly not comprehending that the life and vitality I need are in the tin cans and not the watch. Every tin can I *don't* see because I'm sorting, everything I shake my head at in disapproval, is rejected from my world which then constricts around me more and more tightly. Keeping three-legged tables *out* shuts me *into* a world of four-legged tables only, please! Excluding new, different things from my picture of myself and the world impoverishes that picture while it locking me into it. If I keep on rejecting everything that that doesn't fit, I can end up in a world of Counter thoughts, a pretty small, confined, and dried up place--a prison.

And, perhaps most harmful of all to my activism and the world, *my judgmental attitude prevents me from dealing appropriately with the person or thing I disapprove of.* When I criticize I have only a single goal in mind: to protect my identity and my picture of the world, and all I see of the strange new thing is that it doesn't fit that picture. I don't notice whether that thing is merely different, or truly harmful. And this failure to discriminate, this blanket disapproval of the merely different as well as the truly harmful prevents me from dealing appropriately with either. I don't deal appropriately with merely different harmless people and things.

White plastic fencing and scalloped plates may not fit my picture of what should be, but they are not harmful; they don't cause suffering, and *it's unfair of me* to criticize them because in so doing I'm implicitly labeling people who make and like them as wrong and inferior, and *they've done nothing harmful*. The unfairness of my labeling, even if I only think it, seeps out of me into their world and hurts those innocent people, and so conduces to war, not peace. This is even more obvious it it's *people* I'm criticizing because of harmless differences they can't help--their color, their physique, their gender, their background. Indulging in these snobbish prejudices is always harmful to the world and so inappropriate. Much better to catch them and use this Practice to *look* with a more open interest at the people or things they're aimed at.

Disapproving is not an appropriate way to deal with truly harmful things, either. Our aim when we disapprove is to *reject* and get rid of the disapproved thing; once we've done that we can haughtily turn away. But our job as activists is to *engage* with what is wrong and work to change it. When we merely criticize we cheat the world of the energy that should have gone into actually taking care of the problem; we merely confirm our passivity. Skilled wrongdoers laugh at our disapproval; they seem to know that if we stop to shake our heads and purse our lips then we won't do anything effective to change or stop them. We disapprove *instead of* acting effectively.

So the judgmental attitude is harmful; because of it we miss out on the truth, innocents are unjustly hurt, wrongdoers are, if anything, encouraged in their wrongdoing, and energy the world needs is wasted.

Yet, beneath our habits of judging lies a real treasure for our taking. If used properly this critical and rejecting attitude can lead us to good things instead. *Every instance of sorting in order not-to-see, every criticism and disapproval can show us where we're indulging in Violence and remind us to respond differently instead.* We can *reverse* the energy that's going into this destructive attitude so that it leads to seeing not less but *more* of the truth of things. We can *use* it to break out of our passivity and into the action, to enjoy goods we do not now enjoy, to fight bads we do not now fight. We can use it to become bigger and more fair persons whose interactions with others conduce to peace, not war.

So let's change the habit. That's what this Practice is.

*   *   *

There's nothing wrong with sorting in itself, nor with making right-wrong judgments either; in fact, we must do lots of both if we are to be effective activists. What matters is *why* we do these things, whether we sort in order to further our cause or in order not to see the truth, whether we decide something is bad because we see it causes suffering or in order to protect a constricted identity.

This Practice is to change all instances of criticizing-in-order-to-protect-constricted-identity into *considered* judgment in terms of whether something that jars you is truly harmful or not. Its goal is a free, unbroken flow of Truth into your mind.

Be on the alert, then, for that crucial moment when something doesn't fit the way you think things should be and you get that little shock of disapproval, that feeling of righteous indignation at the audacity of this thing to show itself, and then your inner comment of name calling, put down, should, or negativity.

> *"Dummy!"*
> *"That's stupid."*
> *"They shouldn't be doing that!"*
> *"That's no good."*

As soon as you catch any part of this sequence, *turn off your disapproval, reserve judgment as to whether the shocking thing is bad or not, and turn a full and loving attention on it as something new that has come into your life.*

Now look at exactly what it *is.* Mentally investigate the offending thing; never mind what it *should* be and simply look at it with bare attention. There may be a tension when you do that, like the tension of fear; just feel that and let it be, and relax, and go ahead and examine the offending thing dispassionately. Do what artists do, who also must learn to "see." One way they do it is to focus on and draw the *negative* spaces, the spaces *surrounding* the subject they are drawing or painting. So look at what you've been excluding--the pebbles, the rusty tin can, the crippled woman, instead of just the corn, the gold watch, the conventional way things "should" be, the "norm."

> I see that this dish has exactly sixteen scallops; each one is edged in gold and has a little flower painted on it. Someone has thought to put a different flower on every other scallop. And the whole thing has a touching kind of old-fashioned look about it.

> *This person is wearing a blue dress and scuffed, boot-like shoes. One of her legs seems to be shorter than the other. She's pulling herself along laboriously, but sagging a little as though she were tired. She's leaning so heavily on her crutches that they seem to jut painfully into her underarms. She's looking at my car fearfully, as though she's afraid it might start up again and come at her.*

It's not easy to *see* like this, simply, as if you were taking an inventory of facts; it's hard because to do it you may have to give up prejudices deeply ingrained since childhood, even infancy, and all of us, even the greatest, have failed to do that many times over in our lives.

A psychologist dreamed that God defecated on a church; he interpreted this to mean that God was saying the church is dirty and no good. However, if it were not for his prejudiced belief that feces are dirty, he could just as well have interpreted it to mean that God was saying feces are holy. After all, it's just another form of the food a godly person blesses in prayer before partaking of it.

Continue your looking until you have a feeling of *understanding* the offending thing. It will come like the slow opening of a blossom. You may be able to *feel* your mind opening. Insights may come.

> *This dish isn't fussy; it's ornate. It's giving me a feeling of elegance and gracious living just as my simple, modern dishes do.*

> *Ah, I represent a kind of threat to this crippled woman! That's why she has such an anxious expression!*

Now, when you've *seen* clearly what really is, the bare facts about the person or thing you had been criticizing, you can better deal with it. You're ready to make a *considered* judgment as to its true harm. That's a very different thing from your earlier, merely critical judgment. At this point ask yourself how, according to your own unique way of thinking, the offending things hurts anything. *Did it jar you because it's truly something harmful or just because it's different and doesn't fit your learned ideas about what should be?*

If it doesn't hurt anything, drop your old, preconceived notion, let your world expand, and welcome the new event in. *Enjoy* the openness you'll feel. A new possibility has been added to your world.

If you decide it truly is a harmful thing, stand up for what you think is right; continue to look at it and lovingly, as if a beloved child had come to you with a sore finger, and decide what remedial action you will take. Then take it.

Either enjoy the offending object, or fight it; don't allow yourself merely to dislike it.

*   *   *

You can use this Practice to catch and eliminate habits of judging you never knew you had; you can follow it until you can look at *anything*, even the worst atrocity, without criticizing, for that is the goal here: the free flow of Truth into your mind so you can see what-is without the obstruction of prejudice.

You can learn to see the bare facts and truth of events in the outer world, and so be better able to decide how to handle them. You can reclaim the energy, too, that used to go into maintaining your old prejudices, your *pre*-judgings, so you will have that additional energy to power you. You can now be free of the dragging weight of having to approve and disapprove, and experience the relief and lightness of your freedom from this duty and the new expansiveness of your world. And because to see outer events as they really are is to identify with them, as we practice from the chapter "Use the Enemy to Become more Effective Yourself," you will see something of yourself in everything--and find nothing totally alien to you. In all this new power, and freedom, and understanding you will now be able to help the world more effectively than before.

One morning as I stepped out of the house I was struck by one of the most beautiful patterns I had ever seen, right at my feet. Delicate fawn color drifted through a field of creamy white and then melted into a darker shape of something like burnt umber, the whole thing describing a perfect balance of shapes and colors. I stared at it in absolute wonder and admiration for a few seconds before I realized it was a dropping from one of our ducks who made a habit of sunning themselves on the doorstep.

*   *   *

Change Judging to Bare Attention

Quotes from great activists:

When we talk about wisdom we ordinarily think it has something to do with discursive intellection whereas it really has no connection. Wisdom means pure understanding in the present, of reality in the here and now. It is impossible to accumulate it. The wise man has the ability to see the truth as the truth, and the false as the false. Not only that, he is capable of loving all beings without discrimination, as they really are, and hence, has the power to eliminate suffering.

Donald Swearer, Secrets of the Lotus

Be innocent of judgement, unaware of any thoughts of evil or of good that ever crossed your mind of anyone. Now do you know him not. But you are free to learn of him, and learn of him anew. . .learning passed away, and left a place for the truth to be reborn.

Quoted by Marianne Williamson in A Course in Miracles, pp. 602-3

*   *   *

Exercise 1:

In judging, we're looking at the world through right-wrong glasses.

Do this: Imagine that you have two pair of glasses and can see through only one or the other of them at a time. One is an approving or "That's right" pair; the other is the disapproving or "That's wrong" pair.

Now walk around for say ten minutes with the "wrong" pair on and *find something wrong with everything you see.* Find the places where things are dirty, or misplaced, or sloppy, or incorrect, or bad. Pick up a good book and read some ideas and disapprove of all of them. Ward off everything as being no good. Don't allow yourself to find anything positive, at all.

Then for the next ten minutes go over the same area with your "right" glasses on and find only beautiful, good things.

136

If you see a rose bush in your first walk around and it's covered with aphids and its leaves with black spot, notice those things and condemn them and see how bad they are. Then, when you take the second walk, looking for good things, notice how the rose bush springs out of the ground. Notice how it's trying. Notice that even the black spot makes a beautiful pattern on the leaves. Notice that the aphids are such interesting little green creatures. Notice the pink rose in full bloom.

Do this exercise until you understand exactly how you go about setting your mind to disapprove or to approve. Then, take off the glasses. Once you know how to set your mind, they become just a pair of glasses, things you can use when you want to but not part of your eye. Use this exercise to *take charge of your constant judging* so that in the future, *you choose* whether to disapprove, approve (much more fun), or simply, at first, to observe the facts with bare attention.

Exercise 2:

When we meet another person, we immediately, automatically notice many ways in which he or she is different from us and therefore of either superior or inferior status in the conventional social world. We're superior, for instance, if we're more educated, or physically stronger, or better dressed, or a WASP; we're inferior if we're disabled, or very young or old, or stutter or have brown skin. Within a split second of meeting we have a fully formed, precise picture of how we two stand relative to each other on many counts. We see all this with bare attention, as a fact.

However, if this assignment of superiority and inferiority contradicts some bit of status that we identify with, we will struggle to maintain or re-gain that status by proving we're better (or worse!) than the other somehow. We will try to protect and reinforce the status that we identify with. This is Violence, and it informs a great many of our social interactions as we contest with each other to prove we're not inferior (or superior).

"It is so!"

"It is not!"

As an old therapist of mine used to ask me when I tried to prove my importance, "Would you rather be right--or happy?"

Think of someone you have considered beneath you in regard to a particular tendency or trait, and someone else you considered above you in another trait or tendency. This exercise is to *notice* these differences in social status between you and any other being *without feeling superior or inferior* because of them. Let them simply be fact, recognizing that they describe only *social* superiority and inferiority and have *nothing* to do with yours or the other's basic worth. The goal is to end up with no status at all, so you recognize your equality with every other being. Have no investment in your status at all, so you simply *use* the differences as tools in your activism and do not feel defined by them at all.

Exercise 3:

The sorting itself easily becomes terrible Violence. It can become science, technology, government, personal relationships that ruin our world because they are not guided by positive values.

Joseph Conrad, in *Heart of Darkness,* tells how Europeans scrambling for ivory in Africa were blind to the mystery, the grandeur, the true riches of the people and the place, and how those people and that place were utterly wrecked by that oblivious, unseeing greed.

Don't let the exhilaration carry you into focusing on unrelated or even destructive projects. Don't do things just because they can be done (as development of technology tempts us to do) or even because you may be the only person in the world who could do them. Don't let changing circumstances leave you obsessed with a project that was once Courageous but has turned Violent. Remember how J. Robert Oppenheimer started work on a bomb to defeat Hitler and help the Jews, and finished it to destroy two Japanese cities and the civilians in them? It may be that the great joy of creating this new thing pulled him inexorably into continuing with it even after he understood, at some level, that "physicists have sinned."

It's great to be so taken over by your projects that you see nothing else. Wonderful, admirable, thrilling *focus* may be the most exhilarating thing in the world! This exercise is to *hold your true course in mind through this exhilaration*. If you have not already, draw up a specific project that is important to you, define that course now, and *hold yourself to it*.

XIII

Care About Everything, All the Time

The Practice: *Learn to be interested in and care about everything.*

All the world's troubles revolve around issues of *caring*. We all need to care about others and we need to know that others care about us, too, and it's when these needs are denied that we do Violent things, hurt people or feel hurt ourselves. The worst we have to fear is not pain nor death nor even the loss of loved ones, but finding out that *nobody cares*. We can endure through many tribulations but when there is no caring we wither away.

Yet there is a great lack of caring today. If we are to have a better world we'll have to bring much more caring into it.

To do that we're going to have to learn to care against our strong tendency to turn off our caring.

*   *   *

Most of us habitually turn off our caring in order to avoid the *pain* of it.

We all know about that pain.

We know how painful it is to find out that people don't care about us. Any kind of trouble is made worse for us by the knowledge that we are hated and not loved. The Jews suffered greatly during the Holocaust; the knowledge that they were hated by the Nazis and that for the most part the rest of world stood by and let it happen must have sharpened that suffering. Jesus on the cross complained not of the pain; not the death, but of being abandoned, not cared about. The suffering of the poor, the starving, the persecuted of today is bad enough in itself. What makes it worse is their knowledge and ours that the rest of us are letting it happen--that *we don't care enough* to help them.

Care About Everything, All the Time

We know how painful it can be to care about others, too, know how vulnerable that caring makes us feel because it exposes us to the possible deep pain of loss. Many of us were brave enough to care about President Kennedy, and John Lennon, and Mother Teresa, and Princess Diana, and suffered such pain because of our caring for them.

Many of us know too what may be the worst pain of all because in it we are the most helpless: the pain of seeing someone we care about suffer when we cannot help. This is the terrible pain of parents when a beloved child is sick and dying. The best of all definitions of caring may be this: that if another's suffering makes you, too, suffer and feel helpless, then you care about that person. Beginning activists feel this pain because they see the world's suffering everywhere and do not yet know how to help it.

*   *   *

We know about the pain of caring, then. And we all know how to *not-care*, to turn off our caring. "I don't care!" we say.

Some of our non-caring is a direct reaction to the too great pain of caring, as if we said, "If no one cares about me, or if my loved ones must suffer and I can't help them, then I'm not going to care." This kind of not-caring has a desperate feel about it, as if we had given up in the face of more pain than we could handle and went numb around it, took Novocain so as not to feel the bad tooth which, however, we know is still there.

Most of our non-caring is something quite different, though. It's a turning off of feeling *before* we have felt the pain, in order to avoid it. It's based on *fear* of pain. And *most of us turn off our caring in this way most of the time*, in the face not of extraordinary stress but of plain, ordinary, everyday living, as if caring were something too difficult to do for very long, like holding our breaths or doing a high jump in the Olympics, and we had to turn it off and save it for special occasions.

When we have turned off our caring in this way we become mechanical people, robots--for what is a robot but a functioning human being who *does not care*? We go through our lives automatically and as if the only important thing in them were our little daily businesses. We don't relate to our surroundings or the people in them in any meaningful way; we don't even *see* them. We pass by other people in a supermarket, say, and do not see them at all, or if we do, see them only as obstacles in the way of getting at the tomato sauce. Not noticing what a remarkable thing is happening, that two living bits from the same star, two sentient beings with an electric charge toward each other, are approaching each other and about to meet, we pass each other by as *indifferent strangers.* Sometimes when I'm feeling really good I smile at these strangers and they do a double take, as if wondering whether it would be appropriate to smile back. "Do I know you?" Sometimes one of them smiles at me first, and then I, too, startle, shaken out of my not-caring trance for a moment. (But how it affirms me, when they smile at me!) Then we close up again, drop back into our numbed out, automatic lives, closed off to everything but our familiar reactions, roles, routines.

At such times, we look at what's in our world not with interest and care but *in terms of its use in keeping us safe from caring,* in terms of our own all-important *security.* We see land merely as real estate, trees as lumber, animals as beef or pork, other people as things in our way, as sex objects or consumers or gooks or employees.

And we neither perceive nor really care about the suffering of others. We can let our car motor idle while we're waiting somewhere because the world is made for our convenience and comfort and we do not see the hole in the ozone that the exhaust makes wider. We can build a bomb to be dropped on other human beings and write on it, "Send them the best!" because it's right and fair that others be killed to protect our way of living. We can pass a homeless person on the street and not falter because *we're* not homeless. We can see someone crying and turn away as though we did not see it at all because we're here to take care of our *own* problems.

And our uncaringness is contagious and presses others to feel uncared for and to become uncaring like us, so that unless they are strong they too take on the I don't care attitude and become, like us, the walking dead. And everything either of us does from this uncaringness is Violent and hurts the world.

We are feelingless machines going after the wrong things.

*   *   *

A feelingless machine is not a bad thing to be in itself. What's bad is to be a feelingless machine *set to go after the wrong things.* If we're to be effective in the world we must all become feelingless machines when it's time to execute our plans because then we need to look at things without emotion, simply in terms of how they can be used to forward our purposes; we're making practical decisions and need to base them on practical questions. For example, a surgeon who wants to take the best possible care of a patient becomes a feelingless, skillful machine when it's time to do an operation, seeing everything without emotion and solely in terms of its use in the work. What's important here is not that she becomes unfeeling during the operation but that well before the operation *she is SET to take CARE of the patient rather than to USE him or her in some way to serve her own ego and its fears.* Once she is set, her caring informs all her behavior as a feelingless machine.

Because caring is so important for the world and because it's in such short supply in our times, it is of utmost importance that we reclaim all the caring we have turned off, so thoroughly that caring then informs all our work as feelingless machines to execute our plans. This may not be easy to accomplish, because we all fear the pains of caring. Fortunately, we also all want to care and know we're cared for, and our want is stronger than our fear.

We want the robots to come back to life.

That's what this Practice is for.

*   *   *

If you're reading this book you already care, probably in many ways, but you may still benefit from this Practice for its goal is that you come to care about *everything* and *everybody*, *all the time.* Even if you care a great deal already, reaching this goal is likely to require some broadening or expanding of your caring, and even the smallest such broadening will be of benefit to you as well as to the world. For you were born to be interested in and to care about everything and through this Practice you can reclaim that birthright to do so. Remember how interested an infant is in every little thing, and how eager to interact with it? Did you know that three-week-old infants already show signs of caring about others, taking on distressed expressions and crying when they hear another infant cry? Strong interest in and caring about the world is built into them, and it was built into you, too. Only as you grew up did you learn to be so cautious in your interest and your caring as most of us are. In that learning to curtail caring you were deprived, and reclaiming the right to care about everything will enrich your life as well as make you a more effective activist.

That original caring is still potential within us all and so can be awakened through serious work. No matter how it has been suppressed or denied, it's always possible to find it again and then develop and broaden it. The Buddhist peace activist, Joanna Macy, has been able to tap deep wells of compassion even in people who said they did not care about war or the state of the world. And the most brutalized of men have sometimes showed that caring was still a possibility within them. Several of the *executioners* at Auschwitz once noticed that one of the victims they had just gassed, a young woman, was still alive. *Something about her struggles touched them*; they took her in and did everything they could think of to revive and take care of her, but finally realized they did not know enough to do so. They then consulted the officer in charge, asking how they could take care of her, and were of course ordered to kill her too.

If you're human the seed of compassion still lives in your heart.

You can learn the Practice of Caring through four exercises designed to help you awaken from the trance of not-caring and reclaim your original interest in and caring about everything.

*   *   *

Exercise 1: Imagine You're the Other

Set aside ten or more minutes to get into this exercise. Arm yourself with paper and pencil and then make yourself comfortable in some place where you can think quietly. Relax yourself and take a few easy deep breaths so you can settle down.

Do the exercise the first few times with *things*. Look around you and pick out one of the things you see, to work with--a chair, a jar, an old apple core, a crack in the wall--whatever you eyes light upon. It does not matter at all what you choose; you can always do the exercise again with any of the other things you see, so make your choice lightly.

Now gaze easily and softly at what you've chosen, *imagining that you ARE it*, and begin to write a description of yourself as this "thing," using the word "I." List every detail of how you look and what your past was like and what your future is likely to be and what it's like to be you right now. The first time I did this exercise I chose a piece of crumpled up paper that I had thrown on the floor during my studies. My description went something like this: "I'm a piece of crumpled up paper. The sun makes lots of shadows and bright white places on me and I'd be very hard to draw. I've been crushed up and thrown away. Sometimes I begin to expand a little as my creases open up. I used to be pristine white but now I'm all marked up. I once was a tree in a Norwegian forest. . ." And so on.

When you start to slow down in your description, stop and read over what you've written, asking yourself at every item, *How does it FEEL to be this way?* and answering your own question. "How does it feel to be crushed up and thrown away? Well, I'm glad I was used in a good project, but yet it makes me feel sad to be thrown away, but also there's a freedom about it. . ." and so on.

If you stay with the exercise long enough three things are likely to happen. You will discover that *the "thing" you have chosen leads to every other "thing" in the world.* My piece of crumpled paper led me to the precise and beautiful shapes of lights and shadows, and their origin in the sun, to the idea that light always seems to be balanced by dark, to loggers in a far-away forest, to what it was like to be a tree--or any plant, to all things made of wood, to concern about the rain forests, to seeds that may first have developed before the Ice Age, and finally to the realization that *everything in the universe really is connected to everything else.*

You may notice, too, that *the way you look at your "thing" when the exercise is over is quite different from the way you looked at it before it started.* I know that I was strangely reluctant to throw my crumpled paper away when we had finished--and even now, my using the pronoun "we" to describe the exercise shows the comradeship I had come to feel with the paper. It was no longer "just" a "thing." We had gone through too much together. I know a man who did this exercise with a rock he picked up off the roadway and who ended up keeping it the rest of his life. You too may feel a little of what he and I did and realize that *you have recovered some of your original caring about things.*

After you have done the exercise a few times you may find, too, that every once in a while, *something in the world suddenly appears to you in an especially clear and immediate way.* As you're walking out of the house, for instance, the yellow of a dandelion in the lawn, or the shape of the space beneath a tree, or the expression on a friend's face may *strike* you as extraordinarily vivid, as if it had risen up and hit you. This sudden vividness of the things around you will happen because you have considered a few things in all their detail in this exercise and are now more ready to see all things in that way. *You are breaking out of the not-caring trance* in which you passed most things by without noticing them.

*   *   *

Exercise 2:

After you've done the exercise with "things" a few times, begin to do a variation of it with people. This is likely to be more difficult because people aren't as predictable as "things;" you can't tell what they're going to say, and they won't sit still for you the way things did, and they look back at you in disconcerting ways as things did not. However, their unpredictability is part of the reason why we all turned off much of our caring about people in the first place, so an exercise that will help us *enjoy* that unpredictability could go a long way toward helping us care again.

For this exercise look around you just as you did in the exercise with "things," and pick out some *person* to work with. Then just begin to *notice details* about him--simple, obvious details such as what he says, how he acts, his expressions and gestures, his clothes, how he sounds and smells. It probably won't be convenient to write them out as you do it so just do it mentally with anyone in sight, even with a person on TV. Simply a running inventory of the details, in your head: "He has on wrinkled brown boots; now he's pursing up his lips; he's screwing up his eyes; a lock of hair is hanging over his face; his elbow is dirty . . ." and so on. Then, after you've detailed him in this way, sit down and write out the details you noticed by memory, to let yourself know you're taking the exercise seriously.

When you've learned to do that with some ease, move on to times when you're talking with someone else, and do the exercise of *listening* to what that person says. Focus on it so closely that you could re-phrase every remark in your own words and can recall and write most of them down later. Most of the time we focus not on what the other person is saying but on what we're going to say next, how *we* look and sound to her, how *we* might best compete with her, or impress her, or prove that she's impressed *us*, and so on and on and on. This focus away from the other person and what's happening right now effectively shuts off our caring. We don't even *hear* the other person. I myself once introduced myself to the woman sitting next to me at a conference and proceeded very politely to compliment her on her dress and ask her name, what kind of work she did and where, and so on, only to have her remind me we had just had lunch together and that I had made these same polite inquires of her less than an hour and a half before. It's very nice to be that preoccupied with one's own little affairs because it keeps one so safe from the risks of caring, the possible pain of being put down, or seen as inadequate, or not being liked, or being liked and then rejected, and so on. But it's Violent behavior, and we hurt rather than help the world when we indulge in it. Much better to do exercises like this and learn to *notice* and *listen to* and therefore *care about* people and things, so that you *are* wherever you are and don't walk around in that kind of uncaring stupor. It makes us feel better to do this, too, because then we can know that we're in charge of our own behavior, and that's a power.

As you grow in skill at noticing details about people and "things" and at hearing what people have to say, insights will begin to come to you about what other people are feeling and what their motivations are in various situations; that is, you will become more empathic. By the time you reach that point you'll usually be able to be with people without being afraid of their unpredictability; instead you'll be *interested in understanding it.* And with understanding you're far along on the way to the kind of caring we're working toward in this Practice.

*　　*　　*

Exercise 3:

The final exercise for this Practice is designed to help you care about people you do not care about now, either because they leave you cold and you're indifferent to them, or because you actively dislike them. It's needed because our goal is to wake up and be interested in and care about *everything* and *everybody*, and for most of us there are at least a few people we have real trouble caring about. Every such failure-to-like is a *block* in the current of caringness that flows through you, a block that's costly for you to maintain and which tips you over into the Violent attitude every time you stumble upon it. It weakens and brutalizes you as an activist and conduces to Violence in the world. But it's also a treasure; *some of your ability to care is locked inside every such block* for you to find and reclaim if you will earnestly search for it.

Begin the exercise by sitting down in some comfortable and private place and settling yourself there. When you're ready, close your eyes and begin mentally to *send love* to the people in your life. Send it to one person at a time, starting with the people closest to you and moving on toward the periphery of your circle until, if you get that far, you're sending it to people you only know *of*, people in the news, or historical figures. Spend time with each person and send love until you really wish him or her well, until you can honestly think, "Oh, I just *love* this person!" and "I truly want this person to be happy and succeed in everything he or she does."

The exercise proper begins with the first person you think of to whom *you can't send love*, for whom you can't develop that feeling of, "Oh, I just love him!" or, "I just love her!" At this point you've hit a *block* in the flow of your caring, a place where your caring is shut off and the Violent attitude has taken over.

Remind yourself, in one short sentence, what it is about this person that you can't love, what action, what way of being, what habit bothers you.

Now imagine that you are that person, go into his or her life and, *as that person*, think back into the past to figure out what led to your doing that deed, having that habit, showing that characteristic that makes it so hard for you to be loved.

If you do this seriously you will soon begin to understand how your person developed the offending characteristic, but you may also come to *another* person who seems to you to be *responsible* for person number one's having done the thing you disliked. For not-liking can't survive the light of careful thinking about it, and when your dislike for one person is exposed, it can flee to some next person to shelter itself. Now you dislike that person and must repeat the exercise with him or her.

A woman I know was in so much pain when thinking of her conflict with her son that she felt helpless in sending him love or wishing him success in his projects. Then when she imagined she *was* her son--who she adopted as a child--and went back into his past as if it were her own, she remembered how his biological mother had left him when he was young, and in exploring what that had felt like she began to understand his behavior and feel the stirrings of an ability to send him love.

But she now felt a resentment toward the mother for having deserted her child, and so she went into the mother's life. She had very little information about that life but she did know that the mother was a beautiful woman who lived in a country that was occupied by foreign armies, and that women had few rights and little status in that country. She must have had a fairly secure life for some time, for she was married and had her small son, but then, her husband deserted the family. So there she was--everything had changed. She had basically nothing.

At that point my friend began to understand why the mother had left her boy with his grandparents and become a camp follower of the foreign army; it must have been the only way she could see to have a life. Now my friend could understand her and wish her well, but was left with anger toward the husband who had deserted the family in the first place. Now she went into his life and tried to understand why he had done this.

All she knew about him was that he was born in a country whose men, it seemed to her, had been emasculated. It was being run by foreigners, its traditional values had been canceled, and it could hardly offer the men work to do. They had no roots to grow families on. She now began to understand why this husband did what he did, and was able to send love to him.

If you follow your dislike from person to person in this way, you will find that this exercise can lead you anywhere in the world, just as the exercise of Describing Things could. It takes time to do it so my friend stopped at the third person, the husband of the mother of her son, but she could have gone on indefinitely, through the foreign armies that "caused" the husband to desert the family, through the commanders and governments of those armies, through all the tit-for-tat political problems and so on, until she had gone into the lives of a thousand people and forgiven them their part in her son's behavior.

Had she done this she would have found that every block of dislike, or resentment, or blame, is part of a *chain* of blocks, and that all the chains are linked together to form a great web which connects each block to every other. And she would have seen that this web, made of blocks of dislike, is a web of Violence, and that once you plug into it at one block you are connected to the whole world of Violence *and you can begin to unravel it.*

That's the great treasure hidden within your not-caring; that by following the trail of your own dislikes and canceling them as you go you can unravel *all* of them, until there is no dislike left at all and you care about everything.

* * *

There is a prickly aspect to this exercise that I haven't mentioned yet. As you go through it you may think of many people you can't send love to because *they* have offended *you* in some way, and for these you can cancel your dislike in the ways we have talked about. But as you're pondering other people's unfair treatment of you, you will suddenly remember that part of it was in reaction to cruel and uncaring things that *you* did to *them*. You will remember this past cruelty of yours with surprise, because you will have forgotten it for a long time, and yet you will recognize it immediately it comes to mind again, and cringe to think of it. You will not want to admit what you did to anyone. And *you don't want to send love to the people you did it to* because that would jar with your shame and guilt, and because you are not a suitable giver and, deeper down, because you want to continue to think of them as having done the hurting and to dislike them for it, to save yourself from feeling responsible.

Working with such memories is not easy, because we are so ashamed of them. Yet, it is an act of courage to remember your own wrongdoing in this way, and if you remembered it you're ready to deal with it, just as you're ready to deal with the dislikes that come up for you.

For each such memory of your own guilt, go into your *own* life, figure out what led to your doing this hurt to the other person, and why you did it, and think of how you might make up for it, until you can forgive yourself and so can once more love the one you hurt.

Thus you can use the exercise to cleanse yourself of all not-caring about other people either because they hurt you or because you hurt them, and you will be able to be interested in and care about everything.

Call Me by My True Names

Do not say that I'll depart tomorrow,
Because even today I still arrive.
Look, deeply. I arrive in every second
To be a bird on a spring branch
To be a tiny bird with wings still fragile
Learning to sing in my new nest.
To be a caterpillar in the heart of a flower
To be a jewel hiding itself in a stone.
I arrive in order to fear, and to hope.
The rhythm of my heart is the birth and death of all that are alive.
I am the mayfly metamorphosing on the surface of the river.
And I am the bird which, when spring comes, arrives in time to eat the mayfly.
I am the frog swimming happily on the clear water of the pond
And I am also the grass snake who, approaching in silence, feeds itself on the frog.

I am the child in Uganda, all skin and bones.
My legs as thin as bamboo sticks
And I am the arms merchant, selling deadly weapons to Uganda.
I am the twelve-year old girl, refugee on the small boat,
Who throws herself into the ocean after being raped by a sea pirate.
And, I am the pirate, my heart not yet capable of seeing and loving.

I am a member of the politburo
With plenty of power in my hands
And I am the man who has to pay his debt of blood to my people dying slowly in a forced labor camp.
My joy is like spring
So warm it makes flowers bloom in all walks of life.
My pain is like a river of tears
So full it fills up four oceans.
Please call me by my true names
So I can hear all my cries and my laughs at once
So that I can see that my joy and my pain are one.
Please call me by my true names
So I can wake up and so the door of my heart can be left open
The door of compassion.

Thich Nhat Hanh, <u>Being Peace</u>, p. 63

*   *   *

Quotes from great activists:

A compassionate heart is more effective against evil than an army.

Gary Zukav, <u>Seat of the Soul</u>, p. 72

'Our goal is to have kind consideration for all sentient beings, every moment, forever.' And when he talked about sentient beings he included the chair, the pen, the floor, a table.

Natalie Goldberg, describing her teacher,
Zen master Katagiri Roshi in <u>Long Quiet Highway</u>, p. 136

Spread love everywhere you go: first of all in your own house. Give love to your children, to your wife or husband, to a next door neighbor. Let no one ever come to you without leaving better and happier. Be the living expression of God's kindness: kindness in your face, kindness in your eyes, kindness in your smile, kindness in your warm greeting.

Mother Teresa (quoted in <u>Bragg's Apple Cider Vinegar</u>, p. 18)

Let the entire universe be flooded with compassion. Let this compassion radiate outward from every part of your body, and let us together send our power and energy to all beings so that they may overcome their obstacles and become healthy and happy.

Tarthang Tulku

. . . the single most destructive aspect of the existing society (is) the willingness to pursue one's own fulfillment without concern for the fulfillment of one's fellows.

. . . at the center of our movement stood the philosophy of love.

Martin Luther King, Jr.

Care About Everything, All the Time

Let me say, with the risk of appearing ridiculous, that the true revolutionary is guided by strong feelings of love. It is impossible to think of an authentic revolutionary without this quality.

Che Guevara, in Pedagogy of the Oppressed by Paulo Friere,
pp. 77-8

Bhagavan, Perfect caring is the root of all the Dharma. For those for whom there is no such caring, the whole of the Buddha Dharma remains far distant. Bhagavan, when the highest caring is active, though the Buddha may not presently be living, the Dharma continues to speak softly from the sphere of space and even from walls and from trees.

Zhechen Gyaltsab and Padma Gyurmed Namgyal,
Path of Heroes, vol. II, p. 161

A man was once given a chicken by his guru and told to go and kill it where nobody could see. The man tried and tried to find a place where he could kill the chicken without anybody's seeing and finally gave up and went back to the guru. "Why couldn't you find a place where nobody would see you kill the chicken?" asked the guru. "Because everywhere I went, the chicken saw," said the man.

Sikh Story, Paraphrased by Ram Dass

During an early visit to the United States, the 5-year old Venerable Kalu Rinpoche was asked what, as a high Tibetan lama and meditation master, he could do. Could he read minds? Walk through walls? Fly in the air? He said, "No, I don't do those things, but I can have compassion for all sentient beings."

Spirit Rock Meditation Center Newsletter, February-August
1996

May all beings be happy.

Buddhist saying

*   *   *

Exercise

A teenager cried because a little bird's nest had been destroyed and then said that it was painful and embarrassing to her to be so sensitive, such a bleeding heart. I asked whether she would want to change and become *not* sensitive, and she exclaimed, "No!" explaining that this painful sensitivity was also precious and to be deprived of it would be to become cold, as if set out alone on a desolate plain.

Think of an issue about which you feel you have grown numb, and then close your eyes and recall the earliest incident you can remember that had to do with this issue and affected you in a similarly negative way.

Then ask yourself: is avoiding an incident like that worth losing a part of your connection with the world?

XIV

Reclaim the Energy of Anger

The Practice: *Take charge of the energy of anger and apply it to work on your most worthwhile projects.*

Anger. Every activist gets lots of provocation to it. There are always oppressors who won't change their ways, victims who won't stand up for themselves, people who won't lift a hand to help out, workers in your own movement who let you down; some of these actively cheat and hinder and work against you besides. There's plenty to get mad about, and I've heard many angry denunciations of the "other side" and quite a few angry quarrels among workers in the field themselves. Many activist tempers have been lost, many times.

That's too bad, because "getting mad" is always a mistake, always harmful to you and your cause. More than that, you've missed out on an opportunity, for used properly your anger *could* have been a tremendous help and ally in the work for your cause.

Anger is a powerful *energy* that is ignited and rises up in us when we perceive an injustice. Depending on how galling that injustice is to us, the rising of the energy can range from a mere unpleasant twinge in the pit of the stomach to such a mighty surging through the body that we hear a noise as of whole troops storming past and feel with awe the blood rushing behind our eyes, the heart powerfully pounding, and a wonderful, exhilarating, terrifying mobilization of our whole being. This terrible energy is the kundalini, or serpent power, of the Eastern philosophers, and when it rises it sweeps away all the hindrances to noble action that they talk about, all the scared little conventionalities, the prissy inhibitions, the politeness, the fears and doubts we've been living with, to make way for its own uninterrupted, impetuous flow. It is the same energy that we long ago pushed down, telling it, "Stay hidden so that I, the ego, may survive!" and it's as though now at the sight of an injustice it cried out indignantly, "This is too much; the deal's off!" and rose up to sweep away the inhibitions that said injustice was necessary to our survival and so OK.

And what it works to clear away is the whole system of Counter thoughts, so that to the extent it succeeds we become pure Daring thought.

*   *   *

There are two different kinds of things we can do with this great energy of anger. We can *waste* it or we can *use* it.

Very often we waste it by "getting mad," and then we either *suppress* or *express* it; these are the behaviors we think of as "anger" in the everyday sense of the word. If we *suppress* it we stand there simmering and sputtering, trying to hold back from saying or doing the destructive things that have occurred to us. The waters are close to breaking through the dam; we manage to hold them in but just barely. Suppressing involves a lot of tension and the cost is strain on the body as the struggle between keeping in and letting go rages within it.

If we *express* it, we let fly and lash out at people or conditions in the outer world; we blow up. The waters have burst through the dam and as they roll mightily past we don't even try to stop them. There's no tension involved here but there's a cost in terms of damage somewhere in the outer world. When water breaks through a dam, a tension is relieved but the uncontrolled waters can destroy the countryside, for there are no channels for them to run in.

Both of these ways of handling the energy of anger are ineffective and can actually do harm to you and your cause. When you're going through one of these ways you may feel very powerful and think that you're impressing others with your power too, but you are probably wrong; for all the upheaval, the sound and fury "getting mad" may involve, it demonstrates to others not strength but weakness.

Years ago, at a time when we couldn't think of anything to do and had nothing but an old game board to do it with, my husband and I used to spend day after day playing checkers. And although I thought I was pretty smart, I was not able to win a single game. For a while I was a good sport and made nothing of it, convinced that if I tried harder I *would* win. Nothing doing; no matter what I did I continued to lose every game. Still I kept my cool about it, even when it was sorely tried by my husband's sympathetic commiseration. Finally, though, after six straight days of losing, I lost yet one more time and it was too much. I leaped up in a rage, seized the game board with all the checkers on it and smashed it to the floor with all my might. Checkers flew, and my husband sat there astounded.

At that moment I felt power surging through me (as indeed it was) but--was I actually demonstrating strength or weakness?

Both expressing and suppressing waste the precious energy; when it's expressed it surges recklessly out into the world with no more direction than a sneeze; when it's suppressed it wears itself out in the locked inner conflict, one aspect of you against another; in both cases it uselessly dissipated--and it's *your energy* that's wasted and lost, so that you are disempowered.

Your getting mad is a bad thing for the cause you're working in, too, because when you're mad you're not in control of yourself and become manipulable. Your weakness becomes evident to friend and foe alike and makes you a danger to your own side. I remember that the activists who developed a French underground during World War II would not accept volunteers who were "angry" or "emotional" about Nazis. And here is what a character in *The Godfather* thought of an opponent he had originally thought to be unbeatable but whom he now saw "get mad:"

> *Hagen listened patiently. He had expected better from a man of Woltz's stature. Was it possible that a man who acted this stupidly could rise to the head of a company worth hundreds of millions?. . .The abuse bothered him not at all. Hagen had learned the art of negotiation from the Don himself. "Never get angry," the Don had instructed. "Never make a threat. Reason with people."*

> Mario Puzo, The Godfather

*   *   *

Contrary to the way it appears, "getting mad" is based on the belief that you are *helpless*, a poor victim who's stuck and can't do anything about a bad situation. Some kind of fairness or justice that you trusted in, that you thought you had a right to expect, has been withheld, and *you feel helpless* to implement it. We tend to think the person who's mad is aggressive and ready to fight, not helpless, but think about it: if some unfairness bothered you and you knew you could do something about it wouldn't you *do* it instead of getting mad? Don't you get mad exactly *because* you don't see any way to make things turn out your way? Doesn't getting mad really mean that you've given up on solving the situation in any other way and so are helpless?

But feeling helpless and getting mad in this way is childish of us; we're acting more like sullen children who think the world should take care of them than like Courageous grown ups and warriors who are responsible to take care of it. We're being disloyal, because an ideal of fairness that we care about is being violated, and we're not hurrying to rescue it but are backing away and feeling helpless. In getting mad then we're being disloyal to our ideals.

Anger is the energy of the Daring thought of rescuing our ideals running up against our frightened determination to stay out of the fight; we get mad in support of that determination. If we look at it this way we see that "getting mad" is a strong claim to being helpless and not responsible, and so is Violent.

The Courageous way of dealing with the energy of anger is to *use* it.

*   *   *

Water breaking through a dam doesn't have any particular direction in mind that it's going to take; it's just pure, raw, mindless energy and goes wherever it's directed. The energy of anger is the same way; it's raw, mindless energy that's suddenly showed up for you to use in getting out of a bad situation, but it doesn't point out any direction you should take. It's as though when you thought you were hopelessly stuck and couldn't get out of some trap, a great, powerful racecar were to draw up beside you, *your* car, ready for you to use in dealing with the problem. You called up this car by seeing something as unfair, and it's meant to be your vehicle in handling that unfairness. You *could* just dutifully reach in and pull up the parking brake; that would shut it down as when you suppress your anger. Or you *could* reach in, open the throttle and then just stand there watching while the car crashed around destroying everything it ran into. That would be like expressing your anger. But the best thing to do if you want to be an effective activist is to get in the driver's seat and steer it where you want to go.

Reclaim the Energy of Anger

Here's how to do that.

First, begin to think of the energy as a great treasure instead of something to be afraid of. Think of it as the genie of near infinite power whom you can command if you are brave and wise enough. *Want* it and be willing to work to learn its ways; give yourself to it; then you can learn to use it well.

Begin to catch yourself when you are starting to "get mad." That's likely to be when something or other bothers you; you'll know it by its familiar and unique signs in your own body, perhaps the catch in your breath, or a sort of breathlessness, the knowledge that *something* is about to happen, and the felt sense of something expanding or rising within you. The energy is beginning to rise. When you feel it, be glad and welcome it and stay as open as you can to receive it. Encourage it to come--but *do not get mad.*

Remind yourself that nothing in the outer world can get to you unless you let it, that you are never helpless, that there is always something you can do, and then just stick with the wonderful feeling of this energy coming up in you. When you have yourself well in hand but are still feeling the energy, begin to *plan how you will use it.* Remind yourself of what your highest goals are, what you want to accomplish in your life, and figure out how you can put this energy into it. Don't be surprised if the thing that originally bothered you doesn't have anything to do with your true goals, and don't put energy into it if it doesn't, for if you're in the habit of suppressing the energy on important occasions it often rises in response to petty little annoyances instead, and you don't want to waste your precious energy on them. Make sure you don't spend any of it on a game of checkers, as I did. Figure out some way you can apply it in the project that's most worthwhile to you.

While you're figuring out how you want to use it, the energy will continue to press up in you with urges to flail out in action. Don't do it; just keep your head and *wait* until you're sure that what you're going to do is good for your cause. There will definitely be a tension about this waiting; it's as though you're holding the great car in neutral so you'll have time to decide what direction to take, ready to take off--and a whole crowd around you is yelling at you to *go*! It takes a good driver to know when it's time. Hold the car there until you're sure; then *go*--when *you decide to*, and *use* the great energy of anger to power what you do.

As you practice this you will begin to find that you can direct the energy in ways that *you* want it to go, so that your reaction to everything that happens feeds into and sharpens your work, and no one and nothing can make you mad. What a freedom there is in this! Here's how one student experienced it:

Another time I feel the freedom is when someone is grumpy to me, as a cable salesman was just now. Instead of coming to the door and ringing the bell he had the nerve to try and push into the house. The inner door was locked so he couldn't get in and he stood there pushing at it and muttering, "You supposed to push in here?" (grump, grump). I distinctly *felt* the invitation to get mad, but that's all. In the old days I would have told him off, but not this time. It did not touch off any grumpiness in me at all. I, myself, truly didn't care. I was able to be cheery and pleasant myself, feeling no resentment, feeling *in charge of myself*--a good feeling.

When you get this far you're well on your way to transforming a timid experience of helplessness into a brave determination to make things different. There is hardly a limit to where you can go with it.

*   *   *

Quotes from great activists:

Student: What should I do about getting angry?

Meditation master: Don't get angry.

Meditation Class at Nyingma Institute

I think there is clearly a kind of anger that is healthy. It is the concentration of one's whole being in the determination: this must change.

Barbara Deming (Meyerding),
We Are All Part of One Another.

[Non-violent resisters] are trying to discipline and control the emotion of anger and the instinct of pugnacity in the same way and to the same extent that military discipline controls the emotion of fear and the instinct of flight.

159

Therefore, under this new discipline, violent words and actions directed against the opponent or his interests are to be made as traitorous to the cause as desertion is in the army. Anger is as disgraceful and socially reprehensible among nonviolent resisters as cowardice is among schoolboys or soldiers.

Richard Gregg, <u>The Power of Nonviolence</u>, p. 88

In the composition of the truly brave there should be no malice, no anger, no distrust, no fear of death or physical hurt. Non-Violence is certainly not for those who lack these essential qualities.

Gandhi, <u>The Infallible Remedy</u>, p. 45

*　　　*　　　*

Exercise

Crying is also a Violent reaction to a frustrating situation; it may be the feminine form of anger, and maybe we could say, in paraphrase of the old saying, "Men must get mad; women must weep." But we can learn to react differently. Mother Teresa didn't do much crying. She certainly dealt with potentially frustrating situations, but she went cheerfully into action to change them instead of crying, and she insisted that her aides be cheerful as well.

If you tend to cry when you're frustrated, begin to catch the feelings that tell you you're about to start crying, perhaps a tightening of the breath, a stinging around your eyes. As soon as you feel them come, make a mental switch of attitude and *focus on what you can do* about the frustrating situation. *Stay* with the situation; don't run away from it in tears.

This exercise is thus to move directly from the feelings of frustration and "I'm about to cry" to planning what you will do about the situation. Practice it until you don't cry any more, until nothing can make you cry. It can be done! When you're this far in charge of yourself you will feel the wonderful freedom and power of it.

I don't at all mean to denigrate your despair; I've spent a lot of time in it myself. But there *are* better things to do with our energy.

Stop and think of an activity you normally undergo or in which you would like to engage which, if you added a bit more intensity to it, you know for a *fact* would make a difference to your cause. This could be something rote like stuffing more envelopes to donors, self-enriching like picking up that book from the shelf you've been meaning to read about your cause, or creative like writing more articles. Whatever it is, once you have decided that activity, notice how you feel about doing it right now.

Finally, think back to the last thing that made you so frustrated you wanted to cry. As you do, take some deep breaths. it's almost impossible to cry and breathe deeply at the same time. Remind yourself that you are never helpless; there's always *something* you can do. Start to *reallocate that energy to figuring out what it is,* by first envisioning the frustration, then your feeling about the onset of that activity, one after the other, in increasingly rapid succession.

Repeat this, as necessary, until you start to see and viscerally feel the connection between the two - and until you can't *wait* to get to that activity with *double* your resolve.

Now you are in a position to *Rechannel* the Energy of Anger, and be back in control of this indispensable tool in your arsenal.

XV

Use Courageous Language

> The Practice: *Catch those parts of your speech that derive from the Violent attitude and change them to more Courageous forms of speech.*

In this book we've divided our ways of thinking into two broad categories, Courageous and Violent, and said that by using Courageous thinking, we can help the world and ourselves. Let's now do the same thing with our language, and see that there are also two type of language--a Courageous one and a Violent one-- and that by using the Courageous language we can help the world and ourselves.

Just as we say we have two ways of thinking, then, so we could say that we have two kinds of language.

In fact, our speech patterns are a major way we maintain the Courageous or Violent attitude, and changing Violent speech patterns into Courageous ones is a simple and effective way of changing our Violent thinking into Courageous thinking.

A Daring thought begins as a first-person singular wish, or want, and an intent to do something to fulfill that want.

> *"I want such and so, and I shall do such and such to make it happen!"*

> *"I want the children to live, and so I'm going to feed them!"*

> *"I want clean rivers and so I'm going to clean them up!"*

These are the language forms of the Daring thought and of Courageous thinking. They are characterized by a first-person singular pronoun, indicative, statement of wish, and intent.

The wish is sacred. Be careful about what you wish, or want, because it will be your job to fulfill it! In the 'Courageous attitude you say "can" and "will" in response to your wish.

This Courageous form of speech reflects Courageous thinking, which comes first and is basic. Violent thinking is then merely derived from it.

Counter thoughts arise to block the Daring thought; they are expressed in language forms that take the responsibility and the sense of agency out of the Daring thought and define you as a victim. These expressions deny the Courageous statement.

They will use such pronouns as "you", "they", even "we" instead of "I". These words are Courageous or Violent depending on whether they are used to *express* agency and responsibility or to *deny it*.

> *I'm going to do this.* (Courageous)
>
> *You should do it.* (Violent)
>
> *I'm taking responsibility for this mess.* (Courageous)
>
> *They did this.* (Violent)
>
> *I can do it.* (Courageous)
>
> *We should do something about this.* (Violent)

Generally, use "I" when you're describing what you want, and use "you" when you're listening to someone else. This "you" is really an "I" in that when you really listen, you're imagining that you *are* the other person and describing how you, as that other person, feel. "You're pretty tired," then, means, "*If I were you*, I'd be feeling pretty tired."

Counter thoughts dilute and deny Daring thoughts, so that our energy goes round and round inside instead of flowing outward into action. They are energy leaks. Following are some forms of Courageous language which express Daring thoughts and avoid counter thoughts.

Use "Does" Instead of "Is" When Describing Others

When we tend to say, "So-and-so *is* a good (or bad) person," this usage describes the person as fixed with a permanent characteristic of goodness or badness. This sets him in concrete, dehumanizes him--makes an object of him--for the essential quality of human life is that the person forever changes. If he "is" a certain way, what's the use of his trying to change? It's what he *is*.

So, when you notice yourself using "is", stop and instead describe what someone "does":

"He does Violent things."

"He has done a good thing."

"Sometimes he acts Violent."

This kind of usage leaves open the possibility of change and, because it could be applied to any of us, brings him back into the human race.

Use Statements of Responsibility Instead of Questions

Some types of questions, or questions we disguise as statements, can reveal certain Violent thinking in their assumptions, including shoving responsibility upon others (as in the last example below):

"What will happen?"

"I wonder about this."

"Why isn't the government doing something about this?"

Changing them to sentences is the first step to revealing the thought behind them, more clearly revealing its Courageous or Violent nature.

"I'm not in control of what will happen."

"It's up to someone else to interpret this for me."

"The government should be responsible for this."

Use Positives Instead of Negatives and Words Ending in the Contraction "n't."

Negatives are always a denial of some other idea that came first, and that *prior* idea is almost always true! Further, the mind does not understand negatives.

If you say, "It's not so!" you're first giving "it" reality, bringing up the possibility that "it" does exist, in order to refute it; you're thus supporting a *refutation*, something that doesn't exist--a negative. You're also setting up two opposing sides, a true and a not true, and so have entered into Violent thinking.

Avoid Pejorative Words that Deny

"Ugly", "bad", "hate"--these are all denials of a positive by comparison.

- "Ugly" denies beautiful
- "Bad" denies good.
- "Hate" denies love

There are many expressions that put someone or something down more subtly, such as the examples below. All of them support the Violent attitude.

- Sick

    Society would have it that we're all sick and in need of healing. A recent study showed that 97% of American families are "dysfunctional." I'd like to see all of us get the help we need but I also think we're doing an overkill on claiming to be sick and so *denying our own power*. Don't join that part of the healthcare movement!

- Pathological
- Stupid

Use Active Voice Instead of Passive

We're not made just to be passive observers of what happens; we're made to be active participants, so the original Daring thought is our urge to do something about the bad news situation. The passive voice denies that urge, denies responsibility, agency, sets me or someone else up as merely done-to--and serves as a statement that I'm not going to honor the Daring thought.

I was shafted.

She was raped.

Use Intransitive Verbs

Anything that tends toward separation smacks of Violence; anything that tends toward love and unity tends toward Courageousness. Transitive verbs set up two entities, a subject and an object. Intransitive verbs are statements of pure being; I AM. Of the two forms, then, intransitive verbs tend more toward the Courageous end of the spectrum, Transitive toward the Violent end.

Focus on the Present Tense over the Past

The past is the land of events about which you can't do anything. When speaking of a problem, pose it in terms of *now*, which brings a fresh immediacy to a condition upon which you can act: "The boat went off course." becomes "This boat *is* off course."

Replace Doubts and Qualifiers with Direct Statements

I'm afraid that such and so.

I'll try to do such and so.

Maybe I'll come.

Not bad! (instead of "Great!"; do you hear the double negative in this one?)

This category of phrase elements diminish your commitment to your expression and thus ultimate responsibility for it, an indication of the Violent thought pattern.

Replace "Should", "Ought-to", "Have-to", "Need" and "Must"

These words introduce coercion and deny responsibility. They imply that some other force is making a person do something; the person isn't initiating it him or herself. When you find yourself expressing such a position, revert closer to the truth by using the word "Want" instead.

Courageous and Violent Vocabulary

Some words imply an expansive world of vitality, love and harmony; others imply a limited, materialistic world. The first kind, being Courageous conduce toward a loving world full of values; the second to a merely practical world without them.

The chart on the following page shows examples of the former category on the left, the latter on the right:

Adventure	Expedient
Romantic	Realistic
Courage	Measurement
Loyalty	Hard and cold
Honor	Machine
Ideals	Competition

Avoid Name-Calling

You pig!

You jackass!

There's a double insult involved here; it first expresses contempt of pigs or jackasses, and then puts whomever you're scolding in the same category. Ask yourself, "What exactly did pigs or jackasses do to me that I should put them down?"

Think about similar terms we use to take *our* anger out on others:

Nigger!

Wop!

Bitch!

Using language that re-creates the Violent split and denies the Courageous attitude can create what we don't want! Simply noticing and reversing them is a powerful practice that can be used to get back to Courageous thinking and make ourselves more effective.

So this Practice is: *Notice the Violent forms of your own speech and change them to Courageous forms.* You don't even have to *mean* the new statement. When you change "should" to "want", for example, you'll feel a kind of discrepancy; there will be a sort of tension between your old, habitual way of talking and this new way; it will jar. You don't have to resolve that discrepancy or do anything about it; just continue with the Practice, and the old habit will change to fit the new way you speak. And as you change the way you talk, the way you think will change to fit as well. If you talk Courageously you will soon think Courageously, as Luke Skywalker learned in the movie *Star Wars: The Empire Strikes Back* when Yoda corrected his Violent language in "I'll give it a try" with the emendation, "Do. Or do not. There is no try."

The project, then, is to clean up your language and through that work, clean up your thinking as well.

*   *   *

As a start, I suggest that you pick one of the following eight speech habits to work on at a time. For each one, I have listed below a Courageous way of talking followed by its Violent counterpart. The Practice is to *notice every time you use the Violent form of speech and substitute the Courageous form for it; say the Courageous form instead.*

Each of the Courageous forms below is a form of taking responsibility for something; if it's appropriate, after you have switched to the Courageous form, take that responsibility and follow through in action. If it's not appropriate for you to take action on what you ended up saying, figure out what you *do* want to do, and do it.

- Use *I*'s instead of *you*'s.
- Use statements instead of questions.
- Use positives instead of negatives.
- Use neutral or approving terms instead of pejoratives.
- Use active instead of passive sentences.
- Use present instead of past.
- Use direct beliefs instead of doubts (Say what you do believe, not what you doubt).
- Use "want" instead of "should", "ought to", "have to", "must", etc.

I once committed to use only positive expression for one month, and can tell you that it's quite possible to do, although it does mean coming out with some awkward forms of speech. Nowadays I do use occasional negatives, and if you pay attention you will find instances throughout this book; I consider the word "only" in the sentence above to be one. The important difference that makes the experiment a success is that I have been more *aware* of how I'm speaking ever since.

*   *   *

Exercise 1:

After you've worked through these eight patterns, think of another and write it down. Language is so rich, and our society so hooked on duality and opposites, that you will find plenty of Violent speech habits to work on.

When you come up with an example of a statement and are unsure whether it's Violent, here's a way to tell: if it would be appropriate to follow it with the expression, "That's too bad!"--it's probably Violent, part of our society's attempt to keep us split, passive, victimized wimps. Rephrase it!

Exercise 2:

Choose one of the language patterns from above. For the rest of the day, look for instances of each one of these in your own speech, both in your internal dialogue and aloud to others.

Then for the next week, add at least one pattern each day on which to focus, converting each instance of Violent language you notice into its Courageous counterpart, until you come to automatically craft your means of expression in the Courageous form.

If you are feeling particularly Courageous, commit to focusing on this for a month thereafter.

XVI

Notice Your Hurry to Find an Inner Peace

The Practice: *Watch for the impulse to hurry and use it as a signal to return to yourself and take your own time, go at your own pace.*

Do you remember those endless summer vacations of childhood that seemed to go on forever?

We were unhurried then. It was a long, peaceful time, with no pressure.

By comparison with those summers, grown-up life--at least in the West--seems hectic, hyped up, driven. We're often in a hurry, pushing ourselves to reach our goals, busy and a little breathless because there's so much more to do, to have, to strive for. And we hardly have time to savor the fruits of all our effort, to enjoy our families, our gardens, our food, ourselves. It's called "the rat race."

A Tibetan lama who had spent some time in China negotiating with the government came to visit the United States, and an American interviewer asked how he liked it.

He said, "It's beautiful, all the cars, beautiful houses--but it's too much like Communist China to me."

"Oh, Rimpoche, what do you mean?" his American companion asked, shocked to hear his country likened to a regimented Communist regime.

The lama said, "Well, America is much nicer, and you know, you have much more wealth, but America is just like Communist China in the sense that everybody, the whole country, has no time, totally just rush rush rush, work work work. I go to the house of even a wealthy person; they're talking on the phone at the table. They say, "Rimpoche, sit down;" then they run out the door and they've got to get to a place--nobody has any time. . .in

China they rush around; production brigade, sixteen hours a day, seven days a week, rush rush rush, march march march. I don't know what it is with the both of you."

Robert Thurman, videotape set <u>The Dharma</u>.

Of course, it's a good thing, fun and exciting, to be busy, to be in demand, to have lots of things to do--*as long as you're running your own activities.* When it begins to seem that they are running you, so that you feel pressed and anxious and hyped up about them, then you've slipped into the hurry habit, and that's not so good. For in the long run the hurry habit is harmful to us as individuals, and to the world.

It's harmful to us as individuals in several ways.

<u>Hurrying is bad for our health.</u> Most of us suffer more or less stress from hurrying, and in the extreme we can become Type A's and develop ulcers and heart problems because of it. Then it's called "the hurry sickness." The Chinese written characters for "busy" are "heart" and "death."

The body cannot help the mind by its tension, and it injures itself.

Annie Besant

<u>We're less effective when we're hurried.</u> Hurry actually *slows us down* in the long run.

- In the movie *The Searchers*, Indians have carried off a beloved girl, and the young man leaps on his horse and races after them. The older, more knowledgeable man, though, methodically prepares for an arduous trip, gathers provisions, makes sure his horse is sound, sets himself for the long haul, and then starts after the Indians. Two days later he passes the young man, whose horse has foundered, and he goes on to rescue the girl.

- There is a certain medical operation which must be completed within three minutes or the patient will die. And it is said that a surgeon can do it within that time *only if he does not hurry.*

Our attempts to be efficient can even backfire if we're hurried.

Even as I was writing this chapter, I stopped working to telephone a company I had some business with. I heard the phone ring, and then an urgent, man's voice came on saying something like, "Sdanelpyu!" I said, "I didn't catch the name. . ." The answer came back: "Dan." What he had really said was, "This is Dan; how may I help you?" but the courtesy implied in that question was completely lost in his efficiency and haste. It made me less rather than more likely to buy his product; his hurry nearly lost him a sale.

We miss out on a great deal, often the most important things when we hurry.

Imagine that you're a professional dog-walker and you have two dogs to walk, first one, then the other. The first dog spends the whole time pulling at the leash, Huff! Huff!--dragging you along, her hind legs straining to get ahead. So that's that dog's walk. The second dog walks along in a joyous but leisurely way and smells everything he comes to. Sometimes he puts his nose in it; sometimes he may pick up a leaf or an old food wrapper or the thrown-away tip of an ice cream cone; he notices other dogs that come by, other people that walk by--he's alert, aware, and yet relaxed, just smelling and looking at everything.

Which one do you think got more good life experience out of the walk?

Of course, I am hoping you agree that the second dog did. Why didn't the first dog get more out of the walk? Because she never *was* where she was. When she was passing a nice bush covered with all sorts of good smells, she scarcely noticed it in her eagerness to get ahead. She wasn't content to stay in the present moment, with the present tree or post. She was forever straining to get to the next post, some *other* post, and once she got there, she strained to get to the still further one. She was too driven to stay with anything long enough to experience it, to enjoy it. She missed everything of importance.

We're presented with an interesting new fact and the reaction is an immediate, "OK, I've got that; what next?"

Eckhart Tolle, The Flowering of Human Consciousness

I had an appointment and wanted to hang up the clothes before I left, in a hurry. And I missed--I missed being with the laundry as I hung it up. I missed that enjoyment. I missed all the squishy feelings of the wet clothes as I slung them over my arm, and I could feel, even as I was hurrying, that I was missing something. Because I've always enjoyed hanging up the clothes. Now it was just throwing them over my arm; I was missing all that enjoyment. I like shaking them before I hang them on the line. I like the wet swoosh of them against my cheek as I hang them up. I like, as I pull them out of the washer, I like figuring out whether they'll be too heavy on my arm and spoil my enjoyment, or whether I should come back and make two loads of them. As I throw each piece over my arm I like it not to be too heavy. And I missed all that.

My journal entry

We can't relate caringly to other people when we hurry. Specifically, we can pass right by others in distress without noticing them.

Scientists John Darley and Daniel Batson wanted to study to what extent being in a hurry would interfere with the helping impulse. They used forty volunteers from the Princeton Theological Seminary as subjects, thinking that they would be especially likely to help others who seemed to need it.

An assistant instructed each volunteer to prepare a three minute talk to be tape-recorded, telling half of them to prepare the talk on the Good Samaritan and the other half to prepare it on jobs seminary students might like. He then told each volunteer to leave for his recording appointment, directing him to take a shortcut through an alley to another building where a second assistant would meet him and record his talk.

To some of the volunteers (who came in one at a time and did not hear what he had said to others), he said, 'It'll be a few minutes before they're ready for you, but you might as well head on over.' To others he said, looking at his watch, 'Oh, you're late. They were expecting you a few minutes ago. The assistant will be waiting for you so you'd better hurry.' As he sent them off at fifteen-minute intervals, he alerted a confederate on a walkie-talkie. The confederate, another college student, was stationed inside a doorway opening into the alley. . .and at the alert he would come out, slump down in the doorway, head down and eyes closed, and, as the seminarian approached, cough twice and groan.

A total of forty volunteers walked down the alley on their way to their appointment and came upon the coughing and groaning student. Some went right by, some hesitated and then continued on, and some stopped and [tried to help].

Only sixteen of the forty seminarians offered any kind of help [and] those who were on their way to talk about the Good Samaritan parable weren't any more likely to stop and help than those who were on their way to talk about jobs. The hurry variable was extremely strong--it overcame any difference there might have been in what the students were supposed to be thinking about. In fact. . .we learned that some of those who had been in a hurry hadn't even NOTICED anyone in distress en route, although they had practically stepped over the victim. . . A person in a hurry is likely to keep going, even if he is hurrying to speak on the parable of the Good Samaritan."

Summarized from Morton Hunt, <u>The Compassionate Beast</u>,
pp. 80-82

We say that our natural agitation leads us astray, that no real relationship can be established with the world if we don't get peace of mind.

The Dalai Lama, <u>Violence and Compassion</u>, p. 124

<u>*We can't be creative or learn anything when we hurry.*</u> We're running on only one small, panicky part of the mind. We've dropped out of touch with the deeper part, the inner guidance system from which our power comes, so we're out of touch with our power, Samson without our hair. In the story about walking the dogs, the first dog would have been too anxious and preoccupied during the walk to learn anything; she ran heedlessly past everything, and nothing had a chance to sink in. Later, if she ever got lost in that area, she wouldn't remember the way home. But the second dog, if he ever got lost, would remember. "Oh, here's that bush I smelled, and the next thing that came was some grass I could roll in," and so on. He would have learned something during the walk.

People in a hurry are like the first dog. In their heedless rush onward and upward, they do what we might call "skimming"--that is, they scurry along on the surface of things without ever getting to the depths of them. And in the process, without even meaning to, they scorn things and people; they fling things about, and drop them; they rush past everything--they don't say hello to the mailman. They gulp their food instead of tasting it. They don't savor their gifts; they *miss out* on them. "Disorder is always in a hurry," said Gandhi, and I assert that the reverse also be true: "Hurry is always in disorder."

Finally, <u>we can't relate warmly to other people when we're hurried.</u> For the first dog, all the wonderful things on the walk were incidental; she didn't care about them; she didn't see them; for her they did not exist. That's the attitude the hurrier takes toward people who aren't likely to forward his specific project-- and those people sense very well that that's how he feels. As far as he's concerned, they don't count--and they're likely to reciprocate by scorning him back. They see him as a self-important, manipulative blow hard, and they dislike him.

A big wind blew into Winnetka.
A big wind blew right out again.

<u>Big Noise from Winnetka</u>, Bette Midler

Dalai Lama: In the west. . .it seems to me that you are living in a state of incessant tension, competition, and fear. Those who grow up in that atmosphere will always lack something, all their life.

Carriere: What will they lack?

Dalai Lama: Our most profound, most agreeable, and most fruitful dimension. They will remain on the troubled surface of the sea, without knowing the calm they're resting on.

Tenzin Gyatso, the Dalai Lama, and Jean-Claude Carriere,
<u>Violence and Compassion</u>, p. 61

It sometimes seems that third-world countries tend to think of such developed nations as the United States in this way.

Clearly, *our being in this hyped up, hurried state is harmful to the world*. To understand that, we need only ask ourselves, "If nations lived in this hectic, hurried way (and I believe some do), would there be more wars?"

And if there *were* more wars and you were one of the soldiers, whom would you rather have as your leader, the man who's always in a hurry, or the one who's calm and has things in hand?

> *The principle of non-violence is hurt by ... undue haste...*
>
> Gandhi, quoted in Ratan Das'
> Gandhi and Mao: In Quest of Analogy

Activists are especially vulnerable to the "hurry sickness" because they have always in mind that the victims they are trying to help are suffering *now*; this gives their work a special urgency. But if they work for their causes in this anxious, hurried way, share in the driven life style and goals of the West, then everything they do can only reinforce the same harassed life style we already follow, and they won't make any difference in the world. Things will just go on in the same old way. If we want a better world we will have to find some better, less hurried way of living.

*   *   *

What's all this hurry about? Why do we live in this frantic way?

We say we hurry because we're trying to catch up with everything we have to do; we have appointments, jobs, responsibilities, meetings, errands--on and on, and the need to get them all done on time is a pressure on us. And at first glance it does appear that the frantic pace of modern life is what pushes us to keep striving around the clock. We have to hustle just to keep up.

But this explanation doesn't ring quite true, because hurrying is not an efficient use of time; it *wastes* time. We're *less* effective when we hurry.

- *Haste makes waste.*

- *The hurrieder I go, the behinder I get!*

Folk sayings

We're certainly smart enough to have figured this out by now. So no, I don't think we're hurrying in order to be more efficient in meeting all our obligations. Nor is it the fast-paced society that's making us do it.

I observe time and again that we are pushing ourselves to go faster against something in us that doesn't want to go and is holding back. We've split into two parts, a grim, scared driver and a resistant donkey. As the driver, we push that donkey to "Hurry up!" with all our might. We threaten him with dire consequences (You'll be late!"); we scold him. We set up schedules and order him to follow them. We trick him by dangling carrots in front of him that we never let him reach. "If you can get to such and so (make it to that luncheon, meet that deadline, get that grade, get rid of that bulge)--then you may be happy." Of course, as soon as we reach the such and so, we tell ourselves the same thing again: "If you reach the *next* such and so in time--then you may be happy!"

But the donkey does not like being pushed and can't function properly under such pressure. The harder the driver pushes, the more stubbornly the donkey holds back. Sometimes the donkey won't go at all, no matter what punishment is threatened, and then we can't get anything done at all; we call that a "block."

Sometimes our driver lets up a little, and then things go a little better, but as long as he pushes at all, we can't go as fast or be as effective as we can when he gives the donkey his head and confines himself to taking the best possible care of him--when driver and donkey are one, and we are wholehearted.

Thorough understanding of the harm that comes from hurrying is all we need to dissolve our hurry habit if we want to.

*   *   *

I must be one of the world's experts on the use of hurry as a self-blocking mechanism, because I used it for nearly sixty years to keep myself from writing the books I very much wanted to write. I had plenty of ideas for books, so I would pick one of them, gather materials about it, and outline a book on the subject. All of this was fun and easy. Then I'd sit down to expand the outline into a book. But as soon as I picked up the pen to write the first sentence I would think, "*Hurry up* or you'll die before you get your books done!" and I would dutifully *hurry to write*, only to find I was so confused I couldn't think of a single line. And from then on, I used to "hurry to write" in this way for five or six hours a day, and it was a good day if I was able to complete one sentence, and a cause for celebration if I made it through a paragraph.

Then, as I pushed myself ponderously through the book in this way, the writing would gradually become even more and more difficult until I reached about the halfway point, when I could no longer write even a few words a day. I would then spend as long as *two years* struggling to finish that book, and give up only when I realized that at the rate I was going, it would take me several hundred years to finish it. At that thought, of course, I'd realize I had to hurry even more, and I'd put that book aside and start all over again with another idea, another set of materials and another outline, and the whole sequence would run off again.

Of course, I consulted many experts about my writer's block-- psychotherapists, writing coaches, hypnotists, even a brain wave expert. I joined writers' groups, signed up for writing classes. I did writing exercises. Nothing helped, and of course that fact only made me feel even more desperate.

But I wouldn't tell this story if it didn't have a happy ending. The writer's block did at last give way, and only someone who's spent a lifetime deprived of his or her heart's desire and then regained it would know how very good that feels.

Why are you banging your head against the wall?

Because it feels so good when I stop!

Now that the block is over, I can look back and perhaps learn something about how it worked from studying it. I see now that the block was a self-imposed impasse that boiled down to something like: if you write, you'll die--so which will you give up, your writing or your life? The basic issue was not hurry, not time, not saving time, not needing more of it to do my work. It seems to me now that the block dissolved when two things happened.

First, I took fifteen months of an intensive course in Tibetan Buddhism, during which I *allowed myself to believe* that its teachings—namely, that there were NO LIMITS--*might* be true.

Second, I read such books as Ian Stevenson's *Twenty Cases Suggestive of Reincarnation.* Before that I had not really thought about whether or not theories of reincarnation were true; I simply ignored them. However, Stevenson's evidence seemed to me to be incontrovertible proof that reincarnation *can* happen, so, again, I let a strange, new idea into my belief system.

I believe that my letting these ideas into my mind opened it in some way, because at some point during the period when these two things took place, I realized that my writer's block was gone, and writing had become easy and a joy and a treasure to me.

So what does all this have to do with why we hurry?

Through this I came to understand that we hurry in order to *distract ourselves from the Daring possibility of letting in new ideas.* We hurry in order to fill ourselves up so that there won't be room or time for new ideas to invade the structure of what we already know and shatter it; we foresee such a shattering as a kind of death. And in doing that we are Violent.

A thorough grasp of this is all we need to dissolve our hurry habit if we want to.

*   *   *

There *is* another way of doing things. We used it during those summer vacations when we were children. The job now is to get back to that way of being--peaceful, happy, and effective.

> *In its true nature, life is comfortable, easy, unforced and intuitively right.*
>
> Deepak Chopra, <u>Ageless Body</u>. p. 172

> *In particular the atmosphere of the monastery struck me as at once serious and smiling, with no hurry and no tension.*
>
> The Dalai Lama and Jean-Paul Carriere,
> <u>Violence and Compassion</u>, p. 1

We can do that, and we can use the hurry habit itself to get to that way of being. First, though, let's clarify one thing.

Notice Your Hurry to Find an Inner Peace

The antidote to the hurry sickness is *not* just to slow down; that is at best only an intermediary step toward changing the habit of hurrying. The antidote is to *heal the split* between the two parts of yourself, between driver and donkey, and since that split is based on the driver's fear, one way to do that is get him to stop fleeing (for hurrying is fleeing) long enough to look at what he's afraid of and decide whether it's as dangerous as he thought. To do that, yes, you must slow down--but remember that slowing down is not the final goal; it's the middle step that leads to healing the split and becoming more unified.

Once you're all in one piece, you won't be slowed down; you'll be able to go much faster than you ever could before, when you want to. You won't think about it or hold back or push forward; you'll just *go*, as this wildcat did.

> I once saw a film of the release of a wildcat into the wild. She had been captured wandering about in the city, where she didn't belong, and then transported in a small cage to a wild and hilly place in the country. The group that had organized the rescue wanted to record the proceedings, so the cage was set on the ground and a photographer stationed beside it with his camera focused on the wildcat, ready to film the release.
>
> When everything was ready, the president of the rescue group lifted the sliding door of the cage and the photographer pressed his start button--but it was already too late; no wildcat was in view. The photographer blinked and looked around for her; only when he raised his eyes to the nearest hillside was he able, by hastily swinging his view finder to the far horizon, to photograph a second of two of a dark spot already disappearing over the top of the hill, a quarter mile away. The cat was so fast that apparently no one present had even seen her emerge from the cage.

Such alertness, speed, and execution, such perfect attunement to the needs of a situation, such freedom from any block! Requiring no time to decide her direction, whether to go for it, or to change course: hard to believe as it may be, we can act with such perfect dispatch only if we learn not to hurry.

*   *   *

The *first step* in getting over the hurry habit is to *decide* whether you want what that habit is doing for you. It's protecting you from having a more peaceful, effective, Courageous life, and strange as it may seem, all of us are probably at least a little reluctant to give up that protection. We're afraid that if we stop pushing, we'll lose control and all sorts of strange, unknown things will come at us without our being able to protect ourselves. If that fear is stronger than your wish to live a fuller life, there's no shame in sticking to the hurry habit as long as you need to. Later, when you get to the point of wanting that Courageous life more than you're afraid of it, then you may be ready to do this Practice.

If you decide you've had enough of the rat race and do want a happier, more peaceful and effective life, then you're ready for this Practice. Move on to *the second step*, which is to *learn to catch the little impulses* that say to you, "Hurry up!" "You're late!" "It's already 11; in fact it's 11:10!" Bam bam bam; "This is taking too much time!" If you feel like Alice's rabbit, you're hurrying.

I'm late, I'm late, I'm late
For a very important date!

The rabbit, <u>Alice's Adventures in Wonderland</u>. Lewis Carroll

When you catch such an impulse, the *third step* is to *change its function*. In the old days, you used impulses like this to save yourself from falling to a more peaceful life. Now, instead, let it become a *signal* to tell you that you're at a choice point: you're about to fall to that fuller life and have invoked the hurry impulse just in time for it to save you if you want it to. Understanding this, you can now *choose* to go either way; you can move into the fuller life, or you can run away into hurry.

Step Four is to *follow through* on your choice of a fuller life. When you catch one of those little urges of panic, then (Hurry hurry hurry!)-- stop. Slow down. And, realizing that this choice point offers you a chance for freedom from the hurry habit, get back in touch with all of yourself.

One of the best ways of doing that is to undertake a formal meditation practice. Studies have consistently shown that meditators experience a lowering of all the indicators of stress, including increasing cardiac health, and feel more peaceful than they did before meditating.

There are also many less formal ways of meditating, maybe an infinity of them. You might want to use some of them besides or instead of a formal program. I think the best bet is to try a variety of ways and design your own Practice on the basis of how well they work for you.

Here are a few of them that have worked for other people. All of them assume that you've been identifying as the driver of your inner donkey, and ask you in some way or other to give up the attempt to *make* that donkey do anything. Doing any one of these exercises thoughtfully and seriously a few times can help you develop a wider perspective, heal the split between driver and donkey, and get back to peaceful, unstressed living for a few moments. Doing it regularly can help you maintain that peaceful living over time.

a. *Stop* whatever you're doing in such a hurry and spend a *full minute* (yes, that long!), *looking quietly at the details around you*, and *appreciating them*.

Think to yourself: "Here I am--sitting in this room, with the oak floor (really look at the oak floor, notice the grain, the various colors and tones, the joints--and appreciate it all); it's a cold day (appreciate the cold and the day); I see the trees blowing outside (appreciate the trees and the blowing wind). . .", etc.

Listen, too: "I can hear the refrigerator motor (appreciate it) and cars in the distance (appreciate them).

Touch, too: "I can feel the warmth between my hand and my pen as I'm holding it (appreciate the warmth)."

Be like the second dog, who enjoyed the details as he went along on his walk through life. Be like some natives who describe a journey not in terms of *how long* it took them to reach the end, but in terms of the adventures they had on the way.

> We crossed some bridges crowded with vacationers on foot also crossing, and we and they all laughed as they gave way to let us through, and then we came to some bumpy roads with rows of cotton plants on both sides. . .

You can't be anxious and push while you're appreciating, so this exercise can correct the hurry habit.

b. *Stop* whatever you're doing in such a hurry and *mentally take the reins out of the donkey driver's hands, and give them to the DONKEY,* who has now turned into your higher power in whatever guise you like to picture him, her, or it.

For this donkey is none other than the Lord, that high and joyous Being you should be serving. Say to this Being: "This situation is up to you; I give it to you. Here, I surrender it to you. *You* tell *me* what to do; I trust you to do the right thing about it. I trust you to run my life, and include this task in it if it seems right to you."

This exercise can develop an attitude in you so different from the push-the-donkey attitude that you will not be able to split and hurry as long as you hold it.

c. *Stop* whatever you're doing in such a hurry and *pretend you're standing waist deep in a wide, strongly flowing river, pushing it to try to make it go faster.*

Cup your hands and use them to throw handfuls of water farther downstream so it will go faster. Take a shovel or a board and try to push the water with it. You might even visualize a steam roller and run it through the water as fast as you can to speed up its flow. Stay with this project for a minute or so, long enough to realize how frustrating and essentially impossible it is. This is how I was trying to write--it cannot work! But it's so hard to give it up! Try even harder to make the water go faster!

Then let go. Imagine that you let yourself slide gently *into* the river, *become* the river, and let yourself be carried along to do or not do whatever you as the river feel is right to do. Let yourself be in what athletes call "the flow."

It's lovely to feel as quiet, strong, and sure as a majestic river in dealing with what you have to do.

d. *Stop* whatever you're doing in such a hurry and *pretend you're a cat.*

Have you ever seen a cat *hurry*? When she wants to get somewhere she can speed up all right, but notice how she comes when you open a door and call her inside: *at her own pace.* She may stop for a leisurely smell of the edge of the door; she may just sit down and gaze across the street--leisurely is the word. Sometimes she just stops and stands still, apparently doing nothing at all. I believe then she's waiting for her inner guidance to tell her what she wants to do next. She doesn't start out with a plan and then follow it. She certainly isn't hurried or driven. The job in this Practice is to be like that, to consult your inner guidance at every step. Don't push it; tenderly *consult* it.

Notice Your Hurry to Find an Inner Peace

If this exercise appeals to you, you can try it while imagining that you're the greatest spiritual master you know of. It's hard to think of Jesus hurrying, or the Buddha or--Mt. Kilimanjaro!

e. *Stop* whatever you're doing in such a hurry and: ask yourself, "What exactly is the hurry? What's the emergency?"

Really try to identify what you think would happen if you failed to accomplish, on time, what you were hurrying to do.

Once you do, you will find that it's rarely a true emergency. A true emergency will call us back to our true selves real fast, strip us of our pretentious splitting so that we do the needful with dispatch, just as the wildcat did. But whether it's a true emergency or not, asking these questions can free you to stay present and take care of it in an orderly way, without hurry.

f. *Stop* whatever you're doing in such a hurry and *ask this question of yourself*[2]:

How can I make what I'm doing right now lighter, looser, longer, and softer than it has been?

When you get an answer, do it!

In hurry, you're trying to work under pressure; it's heavy, tight, short, and hard. You can't get stuck in that hurry habit if you stay light, loose, long, and soft.

The Tibetan lama Tarthang Tulku was asked to say what Buddhism was in a single word.

"Lightness" was his response.

The *fifth and final step* of this Practice is to *go back to whatever activity you interrupted so you could unhurry yourself, and do it with your whole, relaxed self.* Decide what each next step is and then do it in an orderly, effective, quiet, and unhurried way.

Enjoy it!

An American technological expert was visiting a third-world country and saw a native farmer working leisurely on his land. The expert approached the farmer reassured him, "We're working on a way to do this faster." The farmer stopped, stood thoughtfully for a moment, and asked, "Why?"

---

[2] Part of the Trager treatment program -- see Trager, 2004

How to Think If You Want to Change the World

*   *   *

Quotes from great activists:

There is more to life than increasing its speed.

Mohandas Gandhi

It is up to you, the perceiver, to cut up the timeless any way you like; your awareness creates the time you experience. Someone who experiences time as a scarce commodity that is constantly slipping away is creating a completely different personal reality from someone who perceives that he has all the time in the world.

Deepak Chopra, <u>Ageless Body, Timeless Mind</u>, p. 30

[One of the main preparations to be made for receiving the vibrations of higher consciousness is] the cessation of hurry, especially of that restless, excitable hurry of the mind, which keeps the brain continually at work and flying from one subject to another...

Annie Besant, <u>Ancient Wisdom</u>, p. 251

I remember this great master, Tengokinso Rinpoche. He had been visiting the west, and I remember once asking him, "What is the thing that you really notice about the west, what is the thing, if you were to say one word. . ?" And he said that in the west, people waste time. And we waste our lives.

Because you see, in the west, and in the modern world in general, we fill our lives with so many activities. Even someone who's not working is still very busy. It's a form of laziness. . .a different type of laziness. I call it active laziness, because we fill our lives with so many activities so that there's no risk of really looking into the deeper issues. Because it's all filled up; the schedule is complete. And then what happens is that our lives get consumed in the mechanism of. work and doing things and projects. In the West it seems as though one is all the time doing, and achieving.

185

Notice Your Hurry to Find an Inner Peace

And at the end of the day, when you really look, we haven't really achieved very much. We've only been very busy.

Abbreviated from Sogyal Rinpoche,
<u>Tibetan Wisdom for Living and Dying</u>

I was notified that my time with the Dalai Lama would be cut that day; we would have only a very short together, and we needed to cover a great deal to have it ready for the book. I became anxious, and wanted to hurry with the interview material. His Holiness knew the time was very short, and he too wanted the book to be a success; yet he showed no signs of haste, but calmly and coolly went about the work, going into each point thoroughly before going on to the next one.

The Dalai Lama and Jean Paul Carriere,
<u>Violence and Compassion</u>

*   *   *

Exercise: The Exercise Of Describing

This is one of my very favorite exercises; I'm offering it to you here for two reasons: you may want to try it out yourself, and I'd like to take you on a little adventure and see whether it helps you become calmer and less hurried.

The exercise proper is to close your eyes and for fifteen minutes describe into a tape recorder what you *see* as you go on an imaginary journey that you make up as you go. You are to talk without stopping (talking and imaging at the same time is thought to engage both sides of the brain and to be helpful in integrating them). If you come to a point of not knowing what to say next, just repeat the last thing you said until something new occurs to you. Before you begin, ask a question that is important to you. Then decide where you want to start your journey from, dictate that place into the recorder, and begin the trip.

I am indebted to Win Wenger and Richard Poe for this exercise, which they describe as "Image Streaming" in their book, *The Einstein Factor*.

XVII

Identify as "Big You"

The Practice: *Learn to broaden your identity to the largest entity you can imagine, so that you feel you are Everything. Then alternate between being Everything and identifying with some version of your small self again, using smaller roles to accomplish your goals.*

This Practice is particularly powerful and basic because it strikes at the very root of what limits us and leads us to do Violence. That root is the sense each of us has of being an entity separate from everything else, the idea that there's an "I" and a "not-I". Each of us is born to one specific set of circumstances and we develop into that set, using only a very few of all our possibilities, and decide that these few, developed possibilities are what we *are*. Attributes may include being a man or a woman, an American or a Chinese or French person, a son or daughter, a parent, a Christian or Jew, Buddhist, Muslim or atheist, a teacher or plumber or doctor or farm laborer, etc.

Equating these attributes with ourselves *freezes* them; we are now stuck in them as "ego."

Many thinkers agree that this "ego" is the source of all our social problems. That's because, thinking that it is our very self, we constantly defend it against whatever is different from it. In our defensiveness we are selfish (thinking only to preserve our own identity), greedy (taking more, more, more in order to shore up this ego), and aggressive (attacking anyone whose differences from us seem to threaten the way *we* are).

Obviously the results are suffering, both for those who have dealings with us and for us ourselves too, as, without realizing it, we are cramped into a smaller and smaller identity by our own self-importance.

There is another way to go! Instead of identifying yourself as the tiny cluster of attributes you happen to be expressing right now, you can identify with the largest entity you can think of--bigger than your body and all the attributes you express in life; you can identify with the universe, with All and Everything, and from that base, holding in mind that you are All, develop smaller, temporary identities as merely *roles in a play*, deciding on them as if you were Director of the play. You now have two identities, one as Big You, Everything You, the Director, and another as little-you, the cluster of roles that you will act out in the play, and you alternate between these two identities.

> *It's as if you lived in a little town, and you go up to a mountaintop and looking down, you see how you move about in the course of an ordinary day. You see your route to work, how you go shopping, the main thoroughfares, your shortcuts, your daily routines--you're seeing all that from up there. Then you return to the village. But now, when you're moving around town thereafter, there's a part of you that always recalls the perspective from above. As you go through a day, you're still watching it all from up there.*
>
> Ram Dass, <u>How Can I Help?</u> p. 34

Notice that in this way of identifying yourself, an attribute is not something you *are*; an "ego" that limits you, but a power you can use. Your roles are not so heavy as they were, either. You take them seriously in that you do your best within each one, but at the same time you take them *lightly* because you know they are just roles, not your essential being.

Identifying as Big You is powered by love, in contrast to identifying as "ego," which is powered by fear. When you *are* everything, everything is part of You and You love it as Yourself. As Director You freely create the various roles and the differences between them; they are flexible and you play with them, change them around at will, and love them. You love them so much that You alternate between *admiring* them as something different from You, and *becoming* one of them. As Big You, you turn into little-you out of love, and as little-you, you turn into the Everything that is Big You out of love.

You are like a mother who alternately holds her baby away from her so she can gaze at it and then presses it to her to unite with it.

So you love everything.

Being able to identify in this way--now with Everything there is, now with the restricted little ego--is perhaps the greatest strength and blessing the serious activist can have.

This kind of great identification, as both Director and actor, is beneficial to you and to the world, so beneficial that Buddhists call the failure to recognize it as the only sin. They call that failure ignorance--ignorance of who you are, the belief that you are only your small and limited ego-self, ignorance of the fact that you are also All.

> *If then you do not make yourself equal to God, you cannot apprehend God; for like is known by like. Leap clear of all that is corporeal, and make yourself grow to a like expanse with that greatness which is beyond all measure; rise above all time, and become eternal; then you will apprehend God. ... But if you shut up your soul in your body, and abase yourself, and say: "I know nothing, I can do nothing; I am afraid of earth and sea, I cannot mount to heaven; I know not what I was, nor what I shall be"; then, what have you to do with God? Your thought can grasp nothing beautiful and good, if you cleave to the body, and are evil.*

Corpus Hemeticum, Quoted by Joseph Campbell in
<u>Great Rome</u>, pp. 366-7

*   *   *

Your identifying as Big You is helpful to the world because when you're in this attitude you are *benign, fair, wise* and *compassionate*, while *loyal to the roles you play in the world*--all enabling attributes in the project of changing it. Let us elaborate.

First, when you identify as Big You, you are *benign* toward all beings because you recognize in every other entity a fellow actor who is playing a role, just as you are, who is directed by the same Director Who directs you. In a word, you see that the two of you are One, and that One is the Director. In physics it has been found that when a particle of physical matter splits into two, even if the two parts immediately fly apart even to the ends of the universe, they retain a bond. If one of them changes so much as its angle of spin, the other changes its spin in a complementary way, across any distance. Like one of these particles, you were once One with every "other" entity you meet, and you bear a relationship to that other part of yourself forever after.

Identify as "Big You"

When you really feel this, everything becomes dear to you; you love everything, identify with everything. Every part, every role, every "thing"--*is* you; you respect, honor, love, hold sacred everything that is.

Second, you are *fair* and *wise* because as Big You, you can understand the viewpoints of all sides of a conflict rather than just the side that little-you happens to be playing on. When you feel angry and confused and in conflict you can know you've been caught in "ego" and are seeing the situation from only one position. This is not a good place from which to make decisions and change the world. But with the basic identification we're talking about, you can expand to Big You and from there see the whole picture, as a traveler lost in the jungle might climb a peak in order to see the whole landscape and direct himself. As Big You, you have perspective; you can see the broad implications of the situation. Then you can be fair. You can be wise.

And you can appreciate differences. A frozen "ego" dislikes differences and would erase them. As Big You, in contrast, you can see that without differences you would not be able to perceive anything at all; everything would be the same as You; there would be no "other"--and very lonely it would be, too. In a sense, you as Big You *make* the many different forms in order to be able to *relate* to them, to ease the aloneness of having everything be the same. Thus when you identify as Big You, you appreciate and honor the different roles we all play in the world. This doesn't mean you never change them; we all have a choice of roles we can take, but once you've accepted a role you put yourself into it and play it as well as you can, as any true and serious actor would do, and you honor the other person's acting of his or her role as well, and you see both roles from the perspective of Big You.

Third, and perhaps most important, you are *compassionate* as Big You; you *feel* what the other is feeling. When you identify with and love everything, suffering anywhere hurts you too, is your suffering, and--but still loving!--you act to ease it, as simply and naturally as you'd scratch an itch. To hurt any being is to hurt yourself; to let any being suffer is yourself to suffer.

*   *   *

The task, then, is to *learn to identify as Big You and from that viewpoint alternately first adjust your smaller roles and then give them reality by becoming them.*

The task is at once easy and difficult.

It's easy because we've all done it many times. Every larger-than-self identification is a form of this Practice. When you identify yourself as a member of a family, or a team, or as the citizen of a country, you're identifying with a larger-than-yourself entity--the family, the team, the nation--and then you come down from that identification to relate to others *within* one of these larger groups and play your smaller roles with them.

It's also very difficult, though, because the job in this Practice is to identify with far larger entities than most of us have ever consciously done. We must identify with larger and still larger and yet larger entities until we've gone all the way and identify with *All and Everything*, and exclude nobody and nothing. And every identification we have already made with a group that is smaller than the whole will resist us in doing this. When we identify with our family, our team, our school, we do become larger than our individual selves and in this we are Courageous-- but we go only part of the way because we also exclude *other* families, *other* teams, *other* schools. In this excluding we are still setting boundaries, limits, and so are Violent.

I may identify as an American, for example, but if this means *as opposed to* Japanese, German, or refugee, I haven't gone far enough. I will be able to think Courageously when units smaller than my country are involved, as the politicians in Kennedy's Profiles in Courage (Kennedy, 1955) did when they voted for the good of the nation rather than merely for the good of their individual states, but I can still be Violent toward things not-American. It would be even more Courageous of the politicians to vote for the good of the whole world rather than merely for the good of their country. And even if I do identify with something broader than my country, for example with the whole human race, and become benign, wise, compassionate toward all people, if I exclude the animal, plant, and mineral worlds from my identity, I can still be Violent toward animals and the environment. As long as I hold onto to any identity smaller than the Whole, I will still judge, make enemies, and cause suffering for myself and others. Hanging onto any identity *different from* something or someone else is the Violent attitude; it is the original sin. Only if I go all the way and identify with Everything That Is so that my attitude is totally benign can I avoid Violence.

That means I must drop "ego" entirely, a scary prospect for most of us, because we've bought the cultural instruction that letting

191

our small ego identities go is the same as death. Our fear is so great and our clinging to *being* our small roles so strong that giving them up can feel like giving up life itself.

Part of this Practice, then, is to understand that truly, we've had it backwards, to realize that in dropping ego, far from dying, we come to life. We don't lose our small, ego roles; we gain control over them. We don't fade away into the great nothingness; we become Director of far greater life than we had before.

I believe this is what Jesus meant when He said, "He who loses his life shall find it," and, "Give up all that thou hast and follow after Me." The "life" He would have us lose and the "all that we have" that He wants us to give up are the cramped-up ego, and the "life we shall find" is unlimited Wholeness.

Doing this Practice requires that you first develop a way of quickly expanding your identity to Big You. Here's one way to do that.

Whenever you are feeling less than perfectly happy, you can know you are identifying as small you and focusing on something as being *separate* from you. There is a duality; you are one part of the whole, focusing on another part which is not you. This is a good time to practice expanding your identity so that you become Everything. It can go something like this:

1. At first you're an individual focused on something other than yourself which is happening *to* you.

2. Then you mentally step *backward, out* of yourself, so that you can see yourself *and* the "other" situation at the same time. As soon as you realize you're angry at someone, for example, you can imagine that you're suddenly transported high, high up into space and from that vantage point can look down on the two of you, far below, going through some kind of conflict.

3. Then begin to notice the surroundings of these two tiny figures--the people, the buildings, the entire landscape around them.

4. Back up still further until you can see the entire planet on which these two are struggling, and further still until you can see the whole solar system, and then the galaxy.

5. Move back until the entire universe is in your view, all of it except the eye through which you are looking down at all this.

6. Let that eye get smaller and smaller, until you are looking at everything there is with one infinitesimally tiny eye, and then let that eye go as you realize that you *are* all this that you have been seeing.

Govinda describes this movement from individual to universal consciousness as a change in direction of "spiritual consciousness" which, he says, can be directed from the universal towards the individual (in which case it becomes a source of error) or from the individual towards the universal (in which case it becomes a source of highest knowledge).

> *The difference in the effect of these two directions may be compared to the vision of a man, who observes the manifold forms and colours of a landscape and feels himself different from it (as 'I' and 'here')--and the vision of another one who gazes into the depth of the firmament, which frees him of all object-perception and thus from the awareness of his own self as well, because he is only conscious of the infinity of space or of 'emptiness.' His 'I' here loses its position through lack of contrast or opposition, finding neither anything to grasp nor from which to differentiate itself"*

> Lama Anagarika Govinda,
> <u>Foundations of Tibetan Mysticism</u>, p. 75

My oldest son was doing something like this expansion of identity at age twelve when he signed a story he had written as, "David Bayard, 1221 Emblem Drive, Oak Manor, Pittsburgh, Pennsylvania, U.S.A., Planet Earth, The Solar System, The Milky Way, The Universe." I used to sign my name in this way too when I was a child, and so may you have done; doing it now may thus be a fairly easy thing to do.

Practice this expanding of identity to All until you can do it fairly quickly; then you'll be ready for the first part of this Practice, which is: *Whenever you experience any negative feeling (discouragement, sadness, anger, etc.), broaden your identity to Big You, so that you feel You ARE Everything.*

If you do it correctly you will find that *your mood, the way you look at the original problem situation,* and *the ease with which you bring about a good resolution of the problem* will improve with every switch.

This was the case with my oldest daughter, as it helps her deal with frustrating situations and advocacy. When she first read it, she had been embroiled in a controversy within her profession and couldn't understand what seemed to her to be unreasonable positions of others. But stepping back to see it as the Big You, she felt compassion, understanding and a sense of camaraderie with those she had been opposing, and an eagerness to work together for common goals. In another situation which seemed hopelessly discouraging because of competition among various components of her professional organization, seeing it as the Big You made the situation seem less important and much more tolerable.

Her situation is not unique--many organizations and advocacy efforts have controversy or competition among the members at one time or another, and energy that could be used to change the word is wasted dealing with these disagreements. Identifying as the Big You can improve morale and channel that energy to be more productive.

> *When you realize where you come from you naturally become tolerant, disinterested, amused, kind hearted as a grandmother, dignified as a king, immersed in the wonder of the Tao. You can deal with whatever life brings you, and when death comes, you are ready.*
>
> Lao-tzu, <u>Tao te Ching</u> (Mitchell's translation)

*   *   *

Quotes from great activists:

> *A human being is a part of the whole, called by us "universe," a part limited in time and space. He experiences himself, his thoughts and feelings, as something separate from the rest--a kind of optical delusion of his consciousness. This delusion is a kind of prison for us, restricting us to our personal decisions and to affection for a few persons nearest to us. Our task must be to free ourselves from this prison by widening our circle of compassion to embrace all living creatures and the whole of nature in its beauty. Nobody is able to achieve this*

*completely, but the striving for such achievement is in itself
a part of the liberation and a foundation for inner security.*

Albert Einstein, in <u>Mathematical Circles Adieu</u> by Howard
Eves

*When this vision is strong and durable--when it moves us,
when we truly love it--then we can take it with us wherever
we go. It becomes our practice. We remember the bottom
line: We're here to awaken from the illusion of
separateness. As we meet, as we plan, as we speak out, as
we march. . .a consciousness of unity is quietly there, at
the heart of our action. We call on it, in fact we look for it,
in whatever comes up. And we do so not because it's useful,
or generous, or conciliatory, but because it's true. Unity has
to be what's most real in consciousness if it's going to have
full power in action. Ultimately, it's got to be what we "are."*

Ram Dass, <u>How Can I Help?</u>

*That which fills the universe
I regard as my body
And that which directs the universe
I see as my own nature.*

Old Chinese poem by Zhang Zai,
quoted in Deepak Chopra's <u>Ageless Body</u>, p. 316-317

My Father and I are One.

Jesus

*Nobody is free just to act in his own interest; our human
freedom is to act within and for the sake of society.*

Lech Walesa, <u>A Way of Hope</u>, 1987

*When we stiffen under a shock we gather all our vital force
at a point, like a defense; abruptly an enormous current
passes through a minute orifice which turns red and gives
pain. If we could learn to enlarge our physical
consciousness and absorb the shock, instead of rejecting it,
we would not suffer--all suffering is a narrowness of
consciousness at every level."*

Sri Aurobindo, in Satprem's <u>Sri Aurobindo or the
Adventure of Consciousness</u>, p. 337

Identify as "Big You"

In 1927 I. . .committed all my productivity potentials toward dealing only with our whole planet Earth and all its resources and cumulative know-how, while undertaking to comprehensively protect, support, and advantage all humanity instead of committing my efforts to the exclusive advantages of my dependents, myself, my country, my team.

This decision was not taken on a recklessly altruistic do-gooder basis, but in response to the fact that my Chronofile clearly demonstrated that in my first thirty-two years of life I had been positively effective in producing life-advantage wealth--which realistically protected, nurtured, and accommodates X numbers of human lives for Y numbers of forward days--only when I was doing so entirely for others and not for myself.

Further Chronofile observation showed that the larger the number for whom I worked, the more positively effective I became.

Thus it became obvious that if I worked always and only for all humanity, I would be optimally effective.

Buckminster Fuller, <u>Critical Path</u>

And so what we have now discovered is that the world of many separate things, the ji bokkai, is not different from the ri bokkai. There is between the two no division. . . Though moving in the world the multiple, we realize also, "This is the One." We are experiencing as an actuality the unity of all--and not simply all of us human beings, but the light-bulbs up there on the ceiling as well, and the walls of the great old lecture hall, and the city outside, Manhattan, and yes! the gardens of Jersey too. We include equally the past--our numerous disparate pasts--and the future, which is already here, like an oak in the acorn. To walk about in knowledge and experience of all this is to live as in a wondrous dream.

Joseph Campbell, <u>Myths to Live By</u>, p. 147

The great German philosopher Schopenhauer... How is it, he asks, that an individual can so forget himself and his own safety that he will put himself and his life in jeopardy to save another from death or pain--as though that other's life were his own, that other's danger his own? Such a one is then acting, Schopenhauer answers, out of an instinctive recognition of the truth that he and that other in fact are one. He has been moved not from the lesser, secondary knowledge of himself as separate from others, but from an immediate experience of the greater, truer truth, that we are all one in the ground of our being.

Joseph Campbell, <u>Myths to Live By</u>, pp. 154-55

Once a skeptical disciple was visiting his guru. . ."Is there really any difference between you and me?" the disciple demanded. "I look at us and I just see two old men sitting in a room waiting for their lunch." The guru replied, "Your level of awareness forces you to see yourself as an old man sitting in a room. But to me, this room and everything in it occupy the smallest speck on the horizon of my awareness."

"Even if you have adopted that perspective, we still live in the same world," the disciple argued.

"No, your world is personal, private, and unshareable. No one else can enter it, because no one can hear or see things exactly as you do; no one else can have your memories, thoughts, and desires. And they are all you have. My world is consciousness itself, open to all, shared by all. In it there is community, insight, love. The individual contains the totality, which makes him real. You are unreal. This private reality you accept without question, bounded by these four walls, by your isolated body and your conditioned mind, is imaginary. It is nothing but a dream."

"Then why do you bother to be here?" the disciple grumbled.

"I don't have to be in your dream," the guru replied, "since I know the truth: I am infinite. But it gives me pleasure to visit your dream, because I may coax you to wake up."

Deepak Chopra, <u>Unconditional Life</u>, p. 255

*   *   *

Identify as "Big You"

Exercise 1:

Think about some situation in which you've been dealing with contention or struggling with adversaries. Close your eyes and view it from a distance, seeing not only yourself but everyone or everything in the situation. Imagine that all are struggling together, in their different ways. What needs and goals do they have in common with you? What struggles and strategies do they share with you?

Now pull back and view it from outer space. Think of the beings below, working and struggling, each in their own way, as they interact on our planet.

Now pull back so far that Earth is not even visible, and think about what is important from that perspective.

Exercise 2:

Schedule at least three times as you go through your day to stop and ask yourself, "What role am I playing right now?" and then name it. "The character who finds it hard to get out of bed." "The busy office worker." "The mad-at-my-spouse person." Naming your current role in this way helps you realize that it *is* just a role.

Exercise 3:

Notice that the Practice of alternating between Big You and little-you is similar to the Daring-thought/Counter-thought pattern. Counter thoughts maintain ego; Daring thoughts tend to break down ego and bring you closer to Big You. You can expand your identity simply by honoring Daring thoughts.

Go back to the exercises of Chapter 4: *Honor the Daring Thought* and do them now if you haven't already. Once you've identified the last Daring Thought from which you diverted yourself, what identity does it give you to have such a thought? What new role could you play by carrying it out? Once you answer this, decide if that role is right for you at the present time.

XVIII

Resolve Impasse by Welcoming Confusion

> *The Practice*: *Enjoy the state of confusion engendered by impasse, and allow solutions wiser than either side of the impasse to come to you.*

During the childhood compromise we described in Chapter One, we developed the basically self-contradictory belief that we must do things that destroy us if we are to survive. Once we've bought this basic contradiction, it continually recurs in our lives as insoluble dilemmas in which we feel forced to choose between two courses of action neither of which seems right or even bearable. It's as though we were stuck in one of those puzzles we probably all remember from childhood: Which came first, the chicken or the egg? But our real-life dilemmas involve much more important moral and strategic issues than this rather innocent example does.

- During the Vietnam War, United States forces were confronted by the dilemma: Should we kill everyone in the village or "lose" the whole village to Communism?

- Sophie, in the novel *Sophie's Choice*, was confronted by a terrible impasse when a Nazi officer told her that only one of her two children would be allowed to live, and asked her to choose which it should be.

- The Dalai Lama saw a chicken brutally slaughtered and decided not to eat meat any more. But one day, after contracting an infection causing jaundice, his doctor told him to try meat again to stay healthy. His impasse: to eat meat and forswear his principles or to abstain from meat and ruin his health.

- Vivisectionists present the public with this impasse: either support agonizing experiments on animals or let children die.

- Monkeys were eating the fruit that the members of Gandhi's ashram were growing to feed themselves. All attempts to shoo them away had failed. Gandhi was presented with this impasse: Should we do Violence by shooting the monkeys or starve because they're eating our food?

Here are some impasses activists sometimes run into.

- An activist feels he can't adequately serve his cause and also raise a family. Should he desert his cause or his family?

- Another activist wonders: should he show a legislator graphic materials about his cause that may shock and alienate her, or not show them and risk that she not be convinced of the urgency of his cause?

- A similar conundrum confronts another activist: Should he mount an extremely visible protest march so he can get media attention and thereby reach the public, or abstain because the march itself may put that public off because they see it as too extreme?

All of these impasse situations can be seen as derivatives of the conflict we failed to resolve in the childhood compromise: Should I kill the other in order that I myself may survive, or let him live, in which case I will die? There's not enough for both, so kill or die! On the one side, an ideal; on the other side your self interest; you can't satisfy them both, so Choose!

*   *   *

An impasse can't be solved head on, exactly because we ourselves have first set it up to be insoluble. An impasse *seems* to originate somewhere in the outer world, in the way things out there so stubbornly are, but in every case it is we, in fact, who have come upon some situation that calls for a Courageous decision and split it into two opposing parts in order to prevent that decision. Having set up this split, we then try to solve it and can't, because the person who set it up is exactly as smart as the person trying to solve it. Hence the impasse.

Thus, as long as we stay within the terms of our impasse, seeing the situation as a choice between two equally abhorrent alternatives, reasoning will not solve it for us, and we will feel safely helpless, merely done to, without real freedom to choose or make decisions.

But, safe as it makes us feel, the denial of power implicit in this whole operation hurts us and the world.

Both Gandhi with the monkeys and the Dalai Lama with the chicken created such impasses within themselves. They experienced their situations in terms of two hopelessly incompatible alternatives, and therein gave away their power.

*   *   *

So, taken seriously as an insoluble dilemma, impasse paralyzes us.

And yet if we only understand, it offers a great opportunity for effective work; we can use it to get where we want to go.

Creative thinking is the result of facing and going through impasses. It's the way new discoveries are made, and new ways invented.

> *If I had to state what was the most valuable notion that helped me to deal with the complex reality of Poland from August 1980 onwards, I would say that it was being able to point to a third way in those situations where everybody says there are only two. In life, it's sometimes essential to be able to think out different ways around a problem.*

Lech Walesa, <u>A Way of Hope</u>, p. 145

Because we ourselves create situations as impasses, we can also create them in some other way if we want to. Creators have choices.

Impasse is always about irrelevant issues, not the main point. That's why ordinary logic, which assumes it to be a block, doesn't work on it; the impasse is not *about* a block in thinking; it's about *protecting* us from the Courageous, creative thinking which is right behind it. We can see impasse then as *a chance to jump Courageously over it* to the more fundamental issue and solutions that lie behind it.

That's what Alexander the "Great" did when he was challenged to solve an "insoluble" problem, and untie a knot that no one else had ever been able to untie. He knew the real issue was not knots but whether he could claim his power. Alexander simply drew his sword and cut through it.

Resolve Impasse by Welcoming Confusion

So how can we get to the more fundamental issue that lies behind an impasse? Maybe Zen Buddhism can help us answer this.

An impasse is very like a Zen koan, which isn't "about" the literal terms in which it is expressed, such as "hands" or "clapping," any more than an impasse is. The koan is about whether you can let go your defenses against being fully present, which is much the same thing as claiming your power. And the way it can be resolved is very like the way in which an impasse can be resolved. In his recorded set, *The Science of Enlightenment*, Shinzen Young talks about one way to do this:

> You go to a Zen master, you have an interview, and the master says, "What is the sound of one hand clapping?" It's a very confusing question. You're confused about what the question means; you're confused about what the master wants you to do in response to it; you're totally disoriented and confused.

> If you look very carefully at the moment by moment thinking process, you'll see that the spectrum of "don't know," "have difficulty knowing," "can't know," "need to know"--that entire spectrum of experiences--is ...constantly goading the mind to think, to get answers, to be clear...

> The thing that we usually assiduously avoid in the mind is any state of chaos, confusion, etc. Paradoxically, if we're willing to not just avoid it but try to constantly find it present at some subtle level, and to relish every single experience of daily life that disorients us intellectually-- then we can start to develop clear contact with our sense of confusion, our fundamental confusion. . . And then we can begin to infuse equanimity into the confusion. We can . .say OK. Watch it get bigger, let it get smaller; I don't do anything in response to it.

> One is then starting to work through the directing that drives the mind to get answers, and this leads to two wonderful results. First. . . .the mind is less driven, so it becomes calmer. But more importantly, when the mind *needs* to have answers, it gets ordinary answers. When the mind thinks *without needing* to have an answer, it just flows spontaneously; it's part of nature. When the mind flows spontaneously as part of nature without a goal to have an answer, then it is participating in the nature of

nature, and the kinds of thoughts it starts to think are the wisdom insight thoughts that clarify the nature of nature.

If one were to condense that quotation into just a few words of advice, they might be, simply, "Don't try so hard! Welcome the confusion, let be and the answer will come."

This Practice is to work with an impasse in a similar way: *When faced by an impasse, lightly hold the two discrepant ideas in mind at the same time and notice the tension, confusion, this creates without doing anything about it. Let that tension be--and calmly wait for solutions to the whole, overall situation to come to you. They must solve both sides of the impasse better than going with either side alone would have done.*

The Dalai Lama wanted two things: he wanted to be humane, and he wanted to live and be healthy.

- He could have eaten meat and at the same time worked to change the methods of slaughter so that they were no longer brutal.

- He could have studied nutrition until he found proper vegetarian substitutes for meat to provide what he needed.

- He could have talked to vegetarians with similar medical conditions who had lived long and healthy lives and figured out how they did it.

Gandhi wanted two things; he wanted fruit to feed the members of the ashram, and he wanted to be nonviolent and spare the monkeys.

- He could have caught the monkeys and shipped them deep into the jungle.

- He could have designed monkey-proof fences.

- He could have sprayed the fruit with harmless but terrible tasting liquid until the monkeys realized they didn't want it any more and got out of the habit of raiding the orchard.

Notice that any one of these new solutions would have been better for the individual and the world than the choice of one side of the impasse. It would have been better for the individual thinker, because it would have empowered him. It's very exhilarating to have such insights; after a few experiences of this sort, solutions begin to come more quickly, one begins to enjoy the play of letting answers come, and finally one welcomes impasses because it's so much fun to solve them. All of this engenders feelings of joy and confidence, and a fullness of power.

And if Gandhi and the Dalai Lama had solved their impasses in this way, it would have helped the world, too. The new solutions would have brought new knowledge to the world, and a flavor of hope, too, rather than resignation. Above all, they would not have spread throughout the world the idea that we must compromise our ideals and thereby let the Violent side win.

Sophie also chose one side of her impasse. In doing so--in deciding which child should die--she was accepting the Nazi's terms and so agreeing that he had the right and the power to require this of her. Instead, she could have ignored his setting of the terms and announced her own terms. She could have insisted on saving *both* of her children. Then *he* would have had to take responsibility for the killing, not she--and the children, although they might still have been killed, would at least have died knowing they were both loved. They would have died within an atmosphere of family unity and loyalty to each other. By choosing one child over the other, at one stroke Sophie condemned one to die, the other to feel guilty all his life.

She could have refused to choose at all, and told the officer, "I want you to remember all your life that you did this to another human being. It's up to you to figure out whether this is the right thing to do, and ask yourself what you're going to do about it."

Alexander the "Great" fell for the impasse when he was asked whether he wanted a long or a glorious life. He chose glory, but to have answered, "Both" would be to transcend the impasse and claim his power.

*   *   *

Sometimes when you're confronted with an impasse you may not have time to wait even a few minutes for a good solution to come to you. For those times, you can achieve much the same positive, empowering, higher perspective results by *making the more Courageous of the two choices you have, picking the side of the impasse that more closely derives from the Daring thought.* There are several ways of doing that.

Choose the alternative that hurts *you*, not the other person.

An impasse derives from the conflict between the grown-up world and the beautiful childhood world, and at base that's a choice between killing and dying. If that's the choice---then it's more Courageous to die. Pick the side of the impasse that goes against your self interest and so hurts you.

The Courageous choice for the United States would have been to give the village up to Communism rather than kill the villagers.

Choose the more *creative* side.

In most impasses one side can be seen to be potentially more creative, the other side to be closer to being merely created.

Which comes first, the chicken or the egg? Choose the egg; it is more creative, more full of potential than the chicken, which is its product, or result. The chicken can be seen as just a vehicle for the egg.

Walk into the threat.

If there's any flavor of, "Do this or else!" about the impasse, you can choose the alternative which you're *not* being threatened--bribed or blackmailed--to take.

- The threat to the Dalai Lama was: "Eat meat or else you'll die." There was no threat that, "Become a vegetarian or else. . ."

- The threat to the United States was, "Kill the villagers or else they'll go Communist." There was no threat, "Let the villagers go Communist or else. . ."

Choose the side that's *scarier.*

Are we scared about what will happen if we kill the villagers? Not really. For one thing, we assume no one will ever know about it. Are we scared about what will happen if the villagers become Communist? Oh, yes! That, then, would have been the Courageous choice.

Choose the side that's more difficult.

Lastly, if you are still at an impasse, you can choose what seems harder.

Resolve Impasse by Welcoming Confusion

In the movie *Himalaya*, the "lama-in-training" decided to help his father in the yearly trek down the mountain rather than stay in the monastery and study his art as he would have liked to do-- because his master had told him, "When you have two choices, choose the one that's harder."

*   *   *

What if no answer comes to you and you *cannot* solve the impasse? That could very well happen under conditions of extreme stress, especially if you have not practiced Courageous thinking. Perhaps it would happen to any human being faced with an impasse like Sophie's, for example. Under such conditions it's best to break the impasse in any way you can and then move on. Impasse is the attempt of everything that's scared and Violent within you to make you deny your power and responsibility. Don't do that if you can possibly prevent it. If you can't think of any other way, then arbitrarily choose one side or the other--and *claim it as your own decision.*

The philosopher Jean-Paul Sartre asks what advice we should give a young man who has this impasse: his country is at war and badly needs him to go fight; his mother is very ill and badly needs him to stay home and take care of her. He is badly torn between these two choices. What should he do?

Sartre answers his own question: It doesn't matter which alternative he decides upon, says Sartre. What matters is only that *he decide*, that he take the initiative away from the outer world and make it his own. Decide!

Gandhi and the Dalai Lama may have done something like that in deciding to kill the monkeys and to eat meat. I don't think these were the best solutions, but at least both men *took responsibility* for their decisions; they openly told about them for the world to hear, thus reclaiming some of their power. I think that in some way *your* making *your own* decision is even more important than that it be the best decision. Don't let impasse pressure, scare, and hurry blackmail you into feeling stuck, helpless, and merely determined. If you would be effective in helping the world, insist upon making your own decisions rather than being forced into them.

It may be that *all* problems and questions that come up in our lives, even the smallest, are forms of impasse and could be resolved in the same way we solve impasse.

*   *   *

Quotes from great activists:

> *In the East. . .it has always been considered as essential for attaining enlightenment to go "beyond earthly opposites."*

Fritjof Capra, <u>The Tao of Physics</u>, p. 114

> *If I had to state what was the most valuable notion that helped me to deal with the complex reality of Poland from August 1980 onwards, I would say that it was being able to point to a third way in those situations where everybody says there are only two. In life, it's sometimes essential to be able to think out different ways around a problem, just as in some games--in billiards or tennis, for instance--the point cannot always be won by hitting the ball forcefully in a straight line. At times it is the ball that is skillfully or even cunningly played that will achieve its object; if you apply spin, the line the ball follows isn't necessarily the shortest but it can land in the right spot.*

Lech Wlesa, <u>A Way of Hope</u>, p. 145

> *Niels Bohr pointed out that the appearance of contradictions was a signal that the experiment was on the right track: "There is not much hope if we have only one difficulty, but when we have two, we can match them off against each other." Bohr called this "complementarity," meaning that the interplay of seemingly conflicting forces or opposites is the actual harmony of nature. Whitehead similarly observed, "In formal logic, a contradiction is the sign of a defeat, but in the evolution of real knowledge it marks the first step in progress towards a victory."*

Saul D. Alinsky, <u>Rules for Radicals</u>, pp. 15-16

*   *   *

Resolve Impasse by Welcoming Confusion

Exercise:

Apply this Practice to all the questions that come up in your life, from "Which shoes shall I put on today?" to, "How shall I vote in this election?"

Think of a decision you're wavering on now, such as:

"Shall I sit down or stand up?"

"What shall I do next?"

"Shall I take on this cause?" "Shall I support that one?"

"How can I help the world?"

When you encounter one today, go through the process from this chapter to solve the dilemma: hold the two choices lightly in mind, welcome the confusion and consider what is the more fundamental issue behind the dilemma, then calmly wait for solutions to the whole, overall situation to come to you until you've transcended it or made your choice and moved on.

If you really learn this Practice, you will discover that you can find just the answers to solve *any* problem.

XIX

Become Unshakably Happy

The Practice: Develop unshakable inner peace and joy by getting in touch with the core of happiness within you and changing the Violent rules that prevent you from feeling it.

It's important that the activist be a basically happy person, first of all for her own enjoyment of life but just as much because her work is with people and she's much better able to help them when she's happy than when she's not. Happy, she's more alive, has more energy, and cares more about others. People respond to all this; they're more attracted to her, more likely to listen to what she has to say. Together, she and they are much more likely to get something going. For happiness is a Courageous, Daring thought and lifts us all up; gloom is a Violent, Counter thought and a downer. One person's being happy spreads happiness--and Courage--throughout the world; being unhappy spreads gloom and Violence--so much so that you could say that as the activist it is your *job* to be happy.

We cannot afford to waste time being sad, emotional, or confused.

Tarthang Tulku, Gesture of Balance, p. 28

We must be able to radiate the joy of Christ, express it in our actions. If our actions are just useful actions that give no joy to the people, our poor people would never be able to rise up to the call which we want them to hear, the call to come closer to God. . .If we went to them with a sad face, we would only make them much more depressed.

Eifern and Egon Kasteen, editors, from Suffering into Joy, p. 38

Joy to the world!

Hymn written by Isaac Watts

Become Unshakably Happy

May all beings be happy.

Buddhist scripture

Yet activists may be uniquely prone to depression. More sensitive than most to the suffering in the world, they yet work in the midst of that suffering and so must see it every day. Their efforts to ease it are frequently met with hypocrisy, indifference, and downright hostility. And their struggles to change the systems that support suffering turn out to be futile again and again.

Thus activists are set up for chronic frustration, and sooner or later their happiness is likely to dim under it. Many become disillusioned, turn into grumpy, cynical, depressed people. I once polled the marchers at an animal rights protest, asking how they felt about their cause, and was surprised at the depth of feeling, the anger and despair in what they said and wrote.

Jane: The experimenters have no hearts.

Lucille: I'm so discouraged I could die. People are rotten.

Melinda: I wish human beings could be erased from the earth, and I wouldn't mind if I went with them.

I believe some activists have even died of despair about their causes, as if from broken hearts. The prominent sixties activist, Abbie Hoffman, for example, was depressed for a long time before his death and may have overdosed because of it. When I think of him I remember his desperate cry, "Don't you *care?*" at the college students he was lecturing about the state of the world, and I wonder whether their indifference was one cause of his suicide. And I know of at least one woman who I believe at last died of her depression:

There's a black X in my heart.

Realizing I couldn't save them and that other people don't care was a great blow to me. As if I'd discovered my country was Hitler. The pain was so intense and lasted so long I don't think I'll ever be happy again.

I'd just like to die and be out of it without feeling like a traitor.

*   *   *

I have no wish to live if India is to be submerged in a deluge
of violence as it is threatening to do. . . . I am in the midst
of flames. Is it the kindness of God or His irony that the
flames do not overcome me?

Mohandas Gandhi, The Infallible Remedy, p. 74

All this depression is understandable, for the suffering, the
injustice, the indifference are indeed overwhelming. To be
depressed about it may even be commendable, for it seems to me
that if you're unhappy because of the suffering in the world you're
still a large step up from being happy because you've ignored it.
You can at least congratulate yourself for having had the courage
to look at the suffering, for most of us maintain defenses that
enable us not to see it and we are to that extent unconscious--a
defense that like any unconsciousness limits our lives. You have
gone beyond that; you've dared to wake up and open your eyes to
the unbearable facts. In the long run that may lead you to a truer
happiness than *not* seeing would have done.

. . .one of the things that you're going to get caught in, that
I get caught in, is my reactivity to suffering. Because most
of us are living our lives in a way that we feel that in order
to be happy and fulfilled, and joyful at a moment, we must
look away from the pain. And it appears now, to me, that
the only true happiness is not built on denial. It's built on
embracing the universe into oneself, which includes the
suffering. And to open to embrace the shadow of the human
condition, or the world or the cosmic condition into oneself,
the earth as well, is heart breaking. It's beyond heart
breaking; it's unbearable.

Ram Dass, tape: Consciousness--Current Events

So if you're depressed about the suffering, that means that at
least you've awakened to it, and that's a plus. So far, so good.
However!--if it stops there, if you continue to suffer yourself
because there's so much suffering in the outer world, it's only a
half awakening, and becomes a Violence that hurts you and the
world. It hurts you because depression leaves you so vulnerable;
you're close to the suffering and taking it in with no protection,
and you sicken from it and grow more sad. It hurts the world
because when you're depressed your very presence broadcasts
suffering everywhere. And it deprives the world of your work,
because when you're unhappy you can't do it well. You need joy
to work effectively; it's your tool, and your power, as well as your

goal. Without it you're a gloomy robot and add to the suffering in the world.

It may be that you need happiness to not only work effectively, but to progress spiritually as well. Our suffering about the suffering in the world may be a stage on the spiritual journey. Perhaps we are meant to go through a crisis of despair and then regain our joy, which can then be deeper because it includes knowledge of suffering.

I used to feel a constant inner joy for most of my life. I was so happy that I thought nothing could be bad enough to make me lose it. And then, of course, I did, finally, lose it. And that experience of being happy and losing it makes me think that maybe that's part of the human journey on this earth; maybe we're meant to experience the happiness at first and then go through a crisis in which we lose it, our job then being to regain it now in a stronger way. Maybe joy that hasn't been tested is fragile, incomplete, and hasn't been forged. Maybe the truest happiness has been tested by adversity.

If you despair, then, you may be stuck on the path to true happiness. To help the world (and yourself), you must go the rest of the way and progress to a more mature joy, deeper and richer than you felt before going through this crisis. Doing so will help everyone else as well as yourself, for it turns out that only basically happy people can most powerfully change the world. And since the world very much needs changing, and you love the world (or you wouldn't have become depressed over what it's going through), why, then, if nothing else has motivated you to become happy, *let the urgency of the world's need for help do so!* Do it for the world and for your own spiritual progress. Wake up the rest of the way and achieve an inner peace and joy *independent* of the horrors you witness.

> *He who identifies himself with every living creature must feel for every kind of woe and yet remain unaffected by it. Action proceeding from such equableness is far-reaching, pervasive and quickest in its effect.*

Mohandas Gandhi, Ramanama, <u>The Infallible Remedy</u>, p. 16

*   *   *

We aren't used to thinking we can make ourselves happy, but spiritual teachers say we can. They say that we are already totally happy because at our very core we are all the joyous qualities.

Within the space of our deeper mind, everything is perfect. Despite the apparent difficulties common to our lives, here the essence of consciousness is seen to be peace.

Tarthang Tulku, <u>Hidden Mind of Freedom</u>, p. 46

At your very center is a being jumping for joy in the vastness of the universe.

Swami Rama, recording <u>Meditation for Intermediates</u>.

Spiritual teachers say that this peace and joy is at the very center of our being; it is basic, our natural state, and we ourselves create the unhappy moods which obscure it. And since we create them, we can of course dissolve them at will and get back to our happy core. It's a fairly simple thing to do, too.

- Mother Teresa would calmly tell a Sister who showed up for work with a sad face to go back to bed until she could be cheerful.

- As part of a longer meditation, Swami Satyananda Saraswati matter-of-factly tells his students to create their own pleasure.

"Pleasure; try to experience the feeling of pleasure, any pleasure. Concentrate and remember the feeling of pleasure. . .it may be according to your sense of touch, smell, taste, hearing or sight. . .any kind of mental pleasure. Recall that pleasure and try to develop it into an intense ecstatic experience."

Swami Satyananda Saraswati, <u>Yoga Nidra</u>, p. 131

[Train] yourself to. . .feel happy. In a manner everybody trains himself to do without things when he cannot get them. A follower of the Gita dharma [duty] trains himself to do without things with happiness. . .Prison life is a life of privilege if we learn to practise the Gita teaching. . .

Mohandas Gandhi, <u>The Infallible Remedy</u>, p. 274

Become Unshakably Happy

> *For example, every time you think you are not happy, say,*
> *"I am happy." Say it strongly to yourself, even if your*
> *feelings are contradictory. . .Just as fast as a fish can move*
> *in the water, you can instantly change to a happy, balanced*
> *attitude. Keep yourself there. Believe yourself. Be open to*
> *that positiveness. Your whole inner situation can change,*
> *even if the external conditions do not change right away.*

Tarthang Tulku, <u>The Self-Image</u> (18)

That "fairly simple thing" is the goal of this Practice: to become totally and unshakably peaceful and happy.

*　　　*　　　*

There are, of course, many different ways we can go in the pursuit of peace and happiness; we'll describe two of them here. One way is to go directly after our core of joy, stimulate it, work to contact it. Another is to tease out and change the Violent rules we are following which prevent us from being happy. Both ways can be useful in developing lasting happiness.

Let's start with the first way.

We seek out and learn to identify with our core of happiness by *deciding* that we want to, that we *will* be happy no matter what. We must make this decision against all the inertia of our own insistence that we can't and shouldn't and don't want to, and we do everything we can think of to strengthen our resolve. We get tired of gloom and depression, and we magnify that tiredness until these feelings become repugnant, disgusting, to us. We will tolerate them no more!

We remind ourselves that our unhappiness is Violent and adds to the suffering in the world, that regaining good cheer will not only feel better but help the whole suffering world as well. We recall what it felt like, perhaps long ago, to feel light and happy, and we *will* ourselves to feel that way again. We seize joy and run it through our body; we make our hands into fists and wave them high in the air in determination; we laugh jubilantly and look in the mirror so that we can *see* that we are happy. Maybe we hum a catchy tune, or put on some snappy music and make ourselves dance around to it and get our blood going. Take a walk and with every step say, "Wow! Wow! I'm the master here!" We *will* be happy; we *are* happy--and in that *being* happy we are identifying with our core, the true self, our Inner Being.

How to Think If You Want to Change the World

I set the fire of happiness ablaze!

Ananda Yoga affirmation

Once you have successfully done this a few times, every pang of *un*-happiness becomes a signal for you to look at what you're doing and start getting your mind back into control. It's as if you were driving a complicated car and wanted to get to the road called "Happy," but every once in a while the car, it seems of its own accord, runs off the road into un-happiness. Then you know you have been driving in some faulty way and your job becomes to take charge of the controls and get yourself back on the right road. Don't just put up with being driven to the wrong place. And remember that it takes time, and that if you keep at it, certainly at most within a day and usually much more quickly, often with a minute, you can get yourself happy again.

The Vietnamese activist monk, Thich Nhat Hanh, is very skillful in helping his students learn to feel peaceful and happy no matter what. Here is a variation of one of his exercises that works for me.

Close your eyes and take a few long, slow, deep breaths.

Then, as you breathe in, *Smile!* No matter how terrible you feel, how bad things are, actually curl your lips as you think: "Smile!"

As you breathe out, *think: "Let go."* When I do this I picture a wide blue sky cluttered with dark clouds--the heavy problems, the sad thoughts that are troubling me; then, as I think, "Let go," I see them become very light and float out the upper right corner of my sky, leaving only clear, open, beautiful blue.

During the next in and out breath, *think: "This is a wonderful moment!"* At this point I open my eyes and feel, see, and hear all sorts of things I hadn't noticed before--the roughness of the carpet under my toes, strange and beautiful gray and white shapes made by the markings of the cat's fur, a slight cramp in my leg, even the beat of my own heart in my ears. Always, as I look around, everything has a directness, an immediacy, it didn't have before; it is indeed a wonderful moment. Again and again I am surprised at the *impact* of these things I perceive; in their sharp clarity and aliveness they make up a rudimentary kind of haiku, and I suddenly understand that a haiku is meant to describe the direct experience of being in the present moment--which is also to be happy.

Toes on rough carpet.

Cat's fur of gray and white shapes.

A cramp in my leg.

This procedure by Thich Nhat Hanh is effective for seeking out and identifying with your core of happiness: to decide against all your own resistance that you *will* be happy, and then, whenever you notice the beginning of any depression, gloom, despair, unhappiness, or dire Counter thought, to repeat the following exercise:

Breathing in, Smile.

Breathing out, Let go.

Realize: This is a wonderful moment!

*   *   *

A second, more difficult but perhaps more thorough way of finding happiness is to investigate and revise the rules that decree you shall be *un*-happy. When we are depressed, if we think about it, we can usually point to something that we are depressed *about*--some cruel or unjust thing somewhere in the world, worry or regret about how it is turning out, our own lack of money, time, energy, power to do anything about it. What we cannot so readily identify is the rules we are following that tell us we are to feel unhappy when such things happen. When we as children made the Violent compromise from the first chapter, we also bought a sizable bundle of rules about when we might be happy and when not, rules that we are no longer consciously aware of but which dictate our feelings nonetheless. The basic ones go something like this:

There is some thing you need before you can be happy--to have some situation turn out better, to get higher status, a better income, better health, better parents or children, a new car or a new trinket; better living quarters, or better weather--and on and on.

The way you feel is to depend on whether you obtain that something. If you don't get it, or if you had it but lose it, you are to feel bad. If you get it you may feel (temporarily!) happy. You're

216

a yoyo thrown up or down by whether or not you get what you want.

As soon as you get what you want, you are to want something more and not be able to be happy until you get it. Therefore you will never be able to be happy for very long.

You may promise yourself happiness in the future, though, if and when what you currently want shows up.

But you'll never be able to pay off on that promise, because after all, you will always want still another thing, and the whole series of wantings and fulfillments ends in death. So you'll never reach happiness.

Could it be that you are following these rules in your unhappiness? Are you wanting something--victory, a better world, a kinder race of human beings--and feeling bad because you don't have it? Do you see how unconscious and habitual these rules have become and how they make it impossible for you to be happy?

Our materialistic society lays rules like this upon almost all of us, but then we individuals make sure we follow them by adding our own supporting rules about how happy we may be and when. As children we could be wholeheartedly happy, shout and laugh and play without reserve, but we soon learned to button it down. Remember that old children's game in which the winner was the one who *didn't* laugh?

No laughing, no talking, no showing your teeth!

By the time we grow up we have learned to follow that rule in earnest, to laugh and show our teeth only when society says it's appropriate, to feel by the numbers so to speak, and we have definite rules against being totally happy.

Would you like to know what your rules are? Just tell yourself, "I can be totally happy, all the time!" and then listen to the Counter thoughts that follow.

No, that's not possible!

You can't be happy all the time!

If I get too much of what I want I won't be happy; I'll be punished!

Become Unshakably Happy

I don't deserve it.

That would be wonderful!. . .But. . .

Even, as one man told me in all seriousness,

"It's all right for other people to be happy, but I can't."

Do you see how such rules bind us, limit us, keep us from that boundless freedom which is also boundless peace and happiness?

Of course happiness can't be legislated, by society or anyone else, any more than gravity can, or the wind. It's always just there at the base of things, that center jumping for joy going right on jumping regardless of what happens in our lives or what society tells us to feel about it. However, we--mixed beings that we are-- cannot help listening to the rules, and we get into the habit of obeying them, feeling joy or sadness as we're expected to. And in the end, we get so used to legislated feelings that we *forget* about our ever-present inner happiness. We get out of touch with it. The rules have, in effect, outlawed it.

If we are to be happy we must *look at the rules we're following* and *decide whether they make sense*. Write out your responses to the idea that you could be happy all the time and *ask whether it's reasonable for you to live by those rules*.

"It's only natural to feel bad when things go wrong!"

"No, you can't be happy all the time!"

Do these rules result in a benefit to you or the world? What about the rule, "Feel bad when things go wrong?" Does your feeling bad improve the situations you feel bad about? Or does it in fact make them worse? Does it help anyone? Is it reasonable? Wouldn't it be just as reasonable to make a rule: "Stand on your head when things go wrong?" That at least might improve your circulation, while feeling bad is not good for your health, and spreads gloom in the world as well.

If you have rules by which you're limiting yourself, here is a new one you might consider: "I am allowed to be happy no matter what the world situation is, no matter what I am or have right now, with whatever status, health, family, security, money, car, living arrangements I have right now, *regardless of what they are.*"

In other words, if we are to be happy, *we must disconnect our feelings from the rules of society and take charge of them ourselves.* Do you see how in being unhappy we set ourselves up as poor things, victims who've given up? We must become masters of our own moods; that is our right, and I think when we take it we will decide, always, to be happy!

> *A human being is like a television set with millions of channels. . .If we turn sorrow on, we are sorrow. If we turn a smile on, we really are the smile. We can't let just one channel dominate us. We have the seeds of everything in us, and we have to take the situation in hand to recover our own sovereignty.*

> Thich Nhat Hanh, <u>Being Peace</u>, between pp. 3 and 9

I am *not* saying that we should rebel against any society's rules of proper behavior. As activists, we are fully committed to playing out our roles in each society, and to do that we must understand and be able to use feelings as society has decreed. But we must not do so as slaves, automatically. Let us make a new rule about happiness: that when we think it would be good for the world, we will *decide* to feel and act appropriately to social conventions, and we will do such feeling and acting with awareness, knowing that we do it. And--*we will stay in firm touch with our core of inner joy throughout.* Then we will be able to laugh at parties and cry at funerals, on purpose, in charge of our feelings, and still be totally and unshakably happy, because in the back of our minds we are tending always the blazing core of our joy. This will help us, too, to be more powerful and effective activists.

*   *   *

Quotes from great activists:

> *I must admit that sometimes I get so overwhelmed by the odds against us that I break down and cry. I see our children dying of hunger, and the ones that live have no jobs, no education, no future. I see the military getting more and more repressive. I see us being persecuted, jailed, tortured. I get exhausted by all the internal problems between the campesino organizations. And I see all of Central America going up in flames.*

> *I start to wonder if it's worth it. I start to think maybe I should just stay home making tortillas.*

But whenever I have these doubts, whenever I start to cry, I put my hands into fists and say to myself, "Make your tears turn into anger, make your tears turn into strength." As soon as I stop crying, I feel a sense of power go through my body. And I get back to work with even more enthusiasm, with more conviction than ever.

When I see some of my other companeros get depressed, I say to them, "Snap out of it. Get back to work. We have too much to do to waste our time getting depressed." And they do the same to me.

Elvia Alvarado, Don't Be Afraid, Gringo!

In letting go our belief that suffering is a necessary part of human life, we can take a few steps forward, easing pain in our time and creating the potential for eliminating it completely in the future.

Tarthang Tulku, Knowledge of Freedom, p. 160

If in our daily life we can smile, if we can be peaceful and happy, not only we, but everyone will profit from it. This is the most basic kind of peace work.

Thich Nhat Hanh, Being Peace, p. 3

A lover of truth feels undiminished joy till the end of his life.

Mohandas Gandhi, in Martin Green's
Gandhi in India in His Own Words

Release others; release yourself; be gay, be reborn, be refreshed.

Mary Strong, Letters of the Scattered Brotherhood, p. 4

How to Think If You Want to Change the World

If you can remember your true identity in the throes of suffering and become that original self in the face of limitation, you have become happiness itself and attained to yoga.

Deva Das, <u>Basic Yoga Class</u>

If you're not having fun, you're not doing it right.

John F. Kennedy, quoted in Jon Pearson's
<u>Drawing on the Inventive Mind</u>,

Happiness radiates like the fragrance of a flower and draws all good things toward you.

Maharishi Mahesh Yogi

As human beings, we all want to be happy.

Dalai Lama

We talked about personal suffering. "When someone does something that hurts you, let it pass through." She pointed with her index finger to her left ear, and then to her right ear, as though the hurt were leaving, not remaining.

Never let it stay here," she said, placing her hand over her heart. "When you do that you can go on happily. You do not lose joy.

Mother Teresa

The crucial point is that bliss is not our goal but our starting point. Unless it is present, one has no foundation for climbing to any of the higher spiritual states.

Deepak Chopra, <u>Unconditional Life</u>, p. 146

Become Unshakably Happy

*   *   *

Exercise 1:

Ask yourself, "Would I have been upset about (whatever you're unhappy about) if I were a two-month-old baby?" If the answer is, "No," then the only reason you are upset is that you have *learned* that the thing you're upset about is a tragedy and that you *should* be unhappy about it, and you are automatically obeying society's rules. Get back in touch with your inner core of joy and hold to it while you make a plan for how you will handle whatever the problem is!

Exercise 2:

Every once in a while during your day, ask yourself,

> *"Am I totally happy?"*

If the answer is anything but an unqualified, "Yes!" then ask:

> *"In what way am I not totally happy? What prevents me from being totally happy?"*

When you get an answer, ask yourself,

> *"Does my being down about this thing benefit me or the world in any sway?"*

If you can't think of any way in which your gloom is a good thing, realize you made a faulty choice back there when you decided to follow some unconscious rule about being unhappy, decide what feeling you would *like* to have, and seize it instanter!

Bibliography

Alinsky, Saul D. (1972). <u>Rules for Radicals.</u> Vintage Books

Alvarado, Elvia (1987). <u>Don't be Afraid, Gringo: The Story of Elvia Alvarado</u> (translated and edited by Medea Benjamin). Harper & Row Publishers

Besant, Anne (1939). <u>Ancient Wisdom</u>. Theosophical Publishing House

Besant, Annie (1979). <u>Thought Power</u>. Theosophical Publishing House

Campbell, Joseph (1969). <u>Occidental Mythology</u>. The Penguin Group

Campbell, Joseph (1973). <u>Myths to Live By</u>. Bantam Books

Capra, Fritjoff (1975). <u>Tao of Physics</u>. Shambala

Carroll, Lewis (1993). <u>Alice's Adventures in Wonderland</u>. Various editions

Chopra, Deepak (1993). <u>Ageless Body, Timeless Mind</u>. Harmony Books

Chopra, Deepak (1989, 1990). <u>Quantum Healing</u>. Bantam Books

Chopra, Deepak (1991, 1992). <u>Unconditional Life</u>. Bantam Books

Clemens, Samuel (1986). <u>Huckleberry Finn</u>. Penguin Classics

Conrad, Joseph (1899). <u>Heart of Darkness</u>. Various editions.

Darley, J.M., and Batson, C.D. (1973). From Jerusalem to Jericho: A Study of Situational and Dispositional Variables in Helping Behavior. <u>Journal of Personality and Social Psychology</u> Vol. 27, No. 1, pp. 100-108

Das, Deva (Instructor) and Laswell, Bill (Music). <u>Basic Yoga Class</u>. Audio Cassette, Jivamukti Yoga Center, New York

Dass, Ram, and Bush, Mirabei (1992). <u>Compassion in Action</u>. Audio Cassette, Publishing Mills

Dass, Ram (1985) <u>How Can I Help?</u> Knopf

Davis CM (1939). Results of the Self-Selection of Diets by Young Children. <u>Canadian Medical Association Journal</u>; 41:257-61. Retrieved July 2017 from Dharma Publishing Staff (1993). <u>Ways of Enlightenment</u>. Dharma Publishing

Dvorak, Robert Regis (1991). <u>Experiential Drawing</u>. Crisp Publishers

Egan, Eileen and Egan, Kathleen (1994). <u>Suffering into Joy: What Mother Theresa Teaches About True Joy</u>. Servant Publications

Eves, Howard (1977). <u>Mathematical Circles Adieu</u>. Prindle, Weber & Schmidt, Inc.

Ferguson, Marilyn (1987). The Aquarian Conspiracy. Jeremy P. Tarcher

Freire, Paulo (1968, translated 1970). Pedagogy of the Oppressed. Retrieved July 2017 from https://selforganizedseminar.files. wordpress.com/2011/08/freire_pedagogy_oppresed1.pdf

Fuller, Buckminster (1982). Critical Path. St. Martins Griffin

Gandhi, Mohandas, Ramanama (1947). The Infallible Remedy. In Hingorani, Anand T. Karachi "Gandhi series" Brochure No. 4. Rupa & Co., Calcutta

Goldberg, Natalie (1986). Writing Down the Bones. Shambala

Goswami, Amit (1993). Self Aware Universe. Jeremy P. Tarcher

Govinda, Lama Anagarika (1976). Creative Meditation and Multi-Dimensional Consciousness. Theosophical Publishing House

Govinda, Lama Anagarika (1960). Foundations of Tibetan Mysticism. Weiser, Inc.

Green, Elmer and Alyce (1977). Beyond Biofeedback. Dell Publishing Co. Inc.

Green, Martin, editor (1987). Gandhi in India In His Own Words. University Press of New England

Gregg, Richard (1966). The Power of Nonviolence. Schocken Books

Gyaltsab, Zhechen and Namgyal, Padma Gyurmed (1995). Path of Heroes: Birth of Enlightenment, Volume I and II. Dharma Publishing

Hanh, Thich Nhat (1987, 1996). Being Peace. Parallax Press

Hawkins, David (2002). Power vs Force. Hay House

Heath, Ralph (2009). Celebrating Failure: The Power of Taking Risks, Making Mistakes, and Thinking Big, The Career Press, Inc.

Holmes, Ernest (1996). The Science of Mind. Dodd, Mead and Co.

Hunt, Morton (1990). Compassionate Beast. William Morrow and Co.

James, William (1890). Principles of Psychology. Holt, New York

Jesus of Nazareth, The Holy Bible, various editions

Kane, Professor Robert Hilary, Quest for Meaning. Audio Tape Set, Teaching Company

Kasteen, Eifern and Egon, editors (1986). Suffering into Joy. Servant Publications

Kennedy, John F. (1955). Profiles in Courage. Harper & Brothers

King, Jr., Martin Luther (1986). A Testament of Hope. Harper San Francisco

Lama, The Dalai, and Carriere, Jean-Claude (1994). Violence and Compassion. Doubleday Image Books

Lama, The Dalai, and Cutler, Howard D. (1998). The Art of Happiness, Riverhead Hardcover

Lama, The Dalai, (1990). Freedom in Exile. Harper Collins

Lama, The Dalai, (1997). Sleeping, Dreaming, and Dying, edited by Varela, Francisco J. Wisdom Publications

Langer, Ellen J. (1989). Mindfulness. Perseus Books

Lao-tzu (1988 translation by Stephen Mitchell). Tao Te Ching (Book of the Way). HarperCollins

Macy, Joanna (1983). Despair and Personal Power in the Nuclear Age. Society Publishers

Merton, Thomas (1964, 1965). Gandhi on Non-Violence. New Directions Publishing Corporation

Meyerding, Jane (1981). We Are All Part of One Another: A Barbara Deming Reader. New Society Publishers

Moore, Frances Lappe (1971). Diet for a Small Planet. Ballantine Books

Parker, Jonathan, Pathways to Mastery. Audio Tape Set, Quantum Quests International

Parker, Jonathan. Quest 4. Audio Tape Set, Quantum Quest International

Pearson, Jon (1995). Drawing on the Inventive Mind. Jon Pearson

Puzo, Mario (1978). The Godfather. Signet, an imprint of Dutton NAL

Rama, Swami. Meditation for Intermediates. Audio Tape Set, Himalayan International Institute

Rinpoche, Sogyal. Tibetan Wisdom for Living and Dying. Audio Tape Set

Saraswati, Swami Satyananda (1993). Yoga Nidra. Bihar School of Yoga, Munger, Fifth edition

Satprem (1964). Sri Aurobindo or the Adventure of Consciousness. Mira Aditi, Mysore, & The Mother's Institute of Research, New Delhi

Solzhenitsyn, Aleksander (1973). The Gulag Archipelago. Harper and Row, Inc.

Spirit Rock Meditation Center Newsletter, Woodacre, California

Stevenson, Ian (1966, 1973, 1992). Twenty Cases Suggestive of Reincarnation. University Press of Virginia

Strong, Mary (1948). Letters of the Scattered Brotherhood. Harper and Row

Swearer, Donald (1971). Secrets of the Lotus. MacMillan Publishing Co.

Thoreau, Henry David (1999). "Walden: or, Life in the Woods" and "On the Duty of Civil Disobedience." Signet Classic, Penguin-Putnam Inc.

Thurman, Robert, Buddhism. Video Tape Set, Mystic Fire Video

Thurman, Robert (1998). Inner Revolution. Riverhead Books

Tolle, Eckhart (2004). The Flowering of Human Consciousness: Everyone's Life Purpose. Sounds True, The Power of Now DVD Teaching Series

Tolstoy, Leo (1892). Help for the Starving (translated by Nathan Haskell Dole) retrieved July 2017 from https://en.wikisource.org/wiki/Help_for_the_Starving

Trager, Milton (2004). Movement as a Way to Agelessness: A Guide to Trager Metastics. Barrytown Limited

Tulku, Tarthang (1977). Gesture of Balance. Dharma Publishing

Tulku, Tarthang (1981). Hidden Mind of Freedom. Dharma Publishing

Tulku, Tarthang (1984). Knowledge of Freedom. Dharma Publishing

Tulku, Tarthang (1978). Openness Mind. Dharma Publishing

Vyasa, Bhagavad Gita II

Walesa, Lech (1990). A Way of Hope. Henry Holt and Co.

Wenger, Win, and Poe, Richard (1996). The Einstein Factor. Prima Publishing

Williamson, Marianne (1992).A Return to Love: Reflections on the Principles of "A Course in Miracles". Harper Collins Publishers

Yogananda, Paramahansa (1973). Autobiography of a Yogi. Self-Realization Fellowship

Young, Shinzen, Science of Enlightenment. Audio Tape Set, Sounds True

Zukav, Gary (1980). The Dancing Wu'Li Masters: An Overview of the New Physics. Bantam Books

Zukav, Gary (1989). The Seat of the Soul. A Fireside Book

Afterword

It is with special honor that we commit this seminal work of Jean Bayard's for publication to the world on behalf of the Jean Bayard Legacy Foundation.

I further extend grateful acknowledgment to Dona Sauerburger and David Bayard for additional proofreading and the rest of the Bayard family for moral support.

You may direct comments, stories and inquiries regarding this book series, the author, or your personal journey through the Practices to:

Magissa Foundation of Jean Bayard
1606 Huntcliff Way
Gambrills, MD 21054

info@magissa.org

She meant for the wisdom in this book to fall into the correct hands, and would desire that you use it toward the betterment of the best cause. Please choose yours with utmost wisdom, take in one exercise at a time, develop yourself, take responsibility for your thoughts and feelings, and be the one to step up to change the world for the better.

Stephan Sauerburger, Editor
July 24, 2017
editor@jeanbayard.org